A CULTURAL HISTORY OF MONEY

VOLUME 1

A Cultural History of Money
General Editor: Bill Maurer

Volume 1
A Cultural History of Money in Antiquity
Edited by Stefan Krmnicek

Volume 2
A Cultural History of Money in the Medieval Age
Edited by Rory Naismith

Volume 3
A Cultural History of Money in the Renaissance
Edited by Stephen Deng

Volume 4
A Cultural History of Money in the Age of Enlightenment
Edited by Christine Desan

Volume 5
A Cultural History of Money in the Age of Empire
Edited by Federico Neiburg and Nigel Dodd

Volume 6
A Cultural History of Money in the Modern Age
Edited by Taylor C. Nelms and David Pedersen

A CULTURAL HISTORY OF MONEY

IN ANTIQUITY

Edited by Stefan Krmnicek

BLOOMSBURY ACADEMIC
LONDON • NEW YORK • OXFORD • NEW DELHI • SYDNEY

BLOOMSBURY ACADEMIC
Bloomsbury Publishing Plc
50 Bedford Square, London, WC1B 3DP, UK
1385 Broadway, New York, NY 10018, USA
29 Earlsfort Terrace, Dublin 2, Ireland

BLOOMSBURY, BLOOMSBURY ACADEMIC and the Diana logo are trademarks of
Bloomsbury Publishing Plc

First published in Great Britain 2019
Paperback edition published in 2023

Copyright © Bloomsbury Publishing, 2019

Stefan Krmnicek has asserted his right under the Copyright, Designs and Patents Act, 1988, to be identified as Author of this work.

For legal purposes the Acknowledgments on pp. 61, 84, 103 constitute an extension of this copyright page.

Series design: Raven Design
Cover image: Tax payment by settler of Roman occupied Germanic provinces. Relief in Neumagen near Trier, Germany. Third Century AD (© Bettmann/Getty Images)

All rights reserved. No part of this publication may be reproduced or transmitted in any form or by any means, electronic or mechanical, including photocopying, recording, or any information storage or retrieval system, without prior permission in writing from the publishers.

Bloomsbury Publishing Plc does not have any control over, or responsibility for, any third-party websites referred to or in this book. All internet addresses given in this book were correct at the time of going to press. The author and publisher regret any inconvenience caused if addresses have changed or sites have ceased to exist, but can accept no responsibility for any such changes.

A catalogue record for this book is available from the British Library.

A catalog record for this book is available from the Library of Congress.

ISBN:	PB Set:	978-1-3503-6718-0
	HB:	978-1-4742-3702-4
	PB:	978-1-3503-6381-6
	ePDF:	978-1-3502-5338-4
	eBook:	978-1-3502-5346-9

Series: The Cultural Histories Series

Typeset by RefineCatch Limited, Bungay, Suffolk
Printed and bound in Great Britain

To find out more about our authors and books visit www.bloomsbury.com and sign up for our newsletters.

CONTENTS

LIST OF ILLUSTRATIONS vii
NOTES ON CONTRIBUTORS x
SERIES PREFACE xii

Introduction: Money Made the Ancient World Go Around 1
Stefan Krmnicek

1 Money and its Technologies: Production, Distribution, and Impact 21
Andrea Casoli and Marc Philipp Wahl

2 Money and its Ideas: State Control and Military Expenses 43
François de Callataÿ

3 Money, Ritual, and Religion: Noneconomic Qualities of Coinage 63
Stefan Krmnicek

4 Money and the Everyday: Multiple Moneys for Multiple Users 85
Stéphane Martin

5 Money, Art, and Representation: A Look at the Roman World 105
Nathan T. Elkins

6 Money and its Interpretation: Archaeological and Anthropological Perspectives 123
Alicia Jiménez

| 7 | Money and the Issues of the Age: Power, Contact, and Identity
Clare Rowan | 141 |

| BIBLIOGRAPHY | 161 |
| INDEX | 191 |

LIST OF ILLUSTRATIONS

INTRODUCTION

0.1	Metal cast of an *aes signatum* struck in Rome around 280–250 BCE.	4
0.2	*Sestertius* of Gaius (Caligula) struck in Rome, 37–8 CE.	5
0.3	Electrum coin struck in Cyzicus around 500 BCE.	6
0.4	*Stater* of "Siris and Pyxus type" struck in southern Italy.	8
0.5	Electrum *stater* struck in Miletus, *c.* sixth century BCE.	10
0.6	*Tetradrachm* of Alexander III struck in Amphipolis around 336–323 BCE.	10
0.7	Celtic imitation of a *tetradrachm* of Thasos, *c.* first century BCE.	11
0.8	*Radiate* of Tetricus II struck in Cologne, 270–4 CE.	18

CHAPTER 1

1.1	Mining process, simplified scheme after Conophagos 1980: 129.	25
1.2	*Tessera* struck at Rome(?), *c.* first half of the fourth century CE.	30
1.3	Striking coinage.	31
1.4	*Solidus* of Constantius II struck at Antiochia, *c.* 347–55 CE.	33
1.5	*Tetradrachm* of Messana, *c.* 478–476 CE.	40

1.6	*As* of the Emperor Nero, struck at Rome, *c.* 64 CE.	41
1.7	*Double maiorina* of Julian, struck at Sirmium, *c.* 361–3 CE.	42

CHAPTER 2

2.1	Recorded numbers of coins and dies for the dated *tetradrachms* of Mithradates of Pontus.	47
2.2	Precious metals deposits for the years 238–59 CE.	48
2.3	Map showing the nature and the purpose of the heavy strikes of Alexanders in some harbors in 325–323 BCE.	50
2.4	Percentages of coins recovered at Athens, Susa, Seleucia-on-the-Tigris, and Delos (fourth to first century BCE).	54

CHAPTER 3

3.1	Excavation plan of Artemision (Naos 2) with findspot of pot hoard.	68
3.2	Coin finds in the basis of the temple of Artemis at Sardis.	70
3.3	Coin finds around spring tappings at the temple of Neuenstadt.	72
3.4	Bronze coin (*dupondius*) of Trajan from the thermal spring "Großer Heißer Stein" fused with pebbles.	74
3.5	Deliberately deposited coins grouped according to their archaeological context.	78
3.6a	Site finds ("accidental loss") in %.	83
3.6b	Deliberately deposited coins in %.	83

CHAPTER 4

4.1	Graffito from the sanctuary of Châteauneuf (France).	87
4.2	Weighed money from Egypt.	90
4.3	Plan from the second-century BCE mint of Karnak (Egypt).	93
4.4	A Roman bronze arm-purse from Mook (the Netherlands).	95
4.5	Distribution map of coins found in the excavations of the Anglo–American Pompei Project.	96

CHAPTER 5

5.1	Silver *tetradrachm* of Cyrene, *c.* 435–375 BCE.	106
5.2	Silver *denarius* of Brutus, struck in Greece, 43–42 BCE.	108
5.3	Billon bronze coin of Julian II, struck at Antioch, 361–3 CE.	109
5.4	Framed brass *sestertius* of Caligula, struck at Rome, 37–41 CE.	109
5.5	Brass *dupondius* of Tiberius, struck at Rome, 16–22 CE.	113
5.6	Silver *denarius* of Septimius Severus, struck at Rome, 202–10 CE.	115
5.7	Brass *sestertius* of Nero, struck at Rome, 64–8 CE.	117
5.8	Silver *denarius* of Hadrian, struck at Rome, 134–8 CE.	118

CHAPTER 7

7.1	Copper coin of the Indo-Greek Bactrian king Menander, *c.* 160–145 BCE.	144
7.2	Athenian silver *tetradrachm*, fifth century BCE.	145
7.3	*Ban Liang Qian*, 400–100 BCE.	148
7.4	Silver *denarius* of the second Jewish revolt, 134–5 CE.	150
7.5	Silver *stater* of Kroton, Southern Italy, 500–480 BCE.	154
7.6	Argentiferous bronze *nummus* of Julian II, 361–3 CE.	158

TABLES

INTRODUCTION

0.1	Coins for the female members of the imperial household among single finds	18

CHAPTER 2

2.1	Coins registered by the Portable Antiquities Scheme for Britain.	53
2.2	Coins registered by the Numis database for the Netherlands.	53
2.3	Per capita equivalent silver as coin at different times and places.	55

NOTES ON CONTRIBUTORS

François de Callataÿ is Head of Department at the Royal Library of Belgium, Professor at the Free University of Brussels and Directeur d'études at the École Pratique des Hautes Études (Paris-Sorbonne). He has published extensively on Greek numismatics, the ancient economy, and history of research. His latest books include *Quantifying the Greco-Roman Economy and Beyond* (2014) and *Cléopâtre, usages et mésusages de son image* (2015).

Andrea Casoli is Research Associate at the State Collection of Coins and Medals of the Canton of Ticino (Switzerland) and researches primarily Roman numismatics and Ancient to Medieval coin finds. He is currently writing a monograph on the Imperial coinage of Emperor Nero.

Nathan T. Elkins is Associate Professor of Art History at Baylor University. His research areas and expertise include Roman art and archaeology, coinage and coin iconography, topography, and architecture. His publications include *Monuments in Miniature: Architecture on Roman Coinage* (2015) and *The Image of Political Power in the Reign of Nerva, A.D. 96–98* (2017).

Alicia Jiménez is Assistant Professor at Duke University. Her research focuses on the study of Roman expansion in the western Mediterranean, Roman colonialism, cultural change, and monetization in Hispania. She is author of *Imagines Hibridae. Una aproximación postcolonialista al estudio de las necrópolis de la Bética* (2008) and editor (with M. P. García-Bellido *et al.*) of *Barter, Money and Coinage in the Ancient Mediterranean* (2011).

Stefan Krmnicek is Junior Professor of Ancient Numismatics at the University of Tübingen. He has published on many aspects of Roman archaeology, with a special interest in questions of ancient coin use, economic history, and coin iconography. His publications include (with C. Haselgrove) *The Archaeology of Money* (2016) and (with M. Flecker *et al.*) *Augustus ist tot—Lang lebe der Kaiser!* (2017).

Stéphane Martin is Postdoctoral Associate Researcher at HeRMA, EA 3811 of the University of Poitiers. His research interests lie in the intersection of Roman archaeology, the ancient economy, and Celtic and Roman numismatics. He is author of *Du statère au sesterce. Monnaie et romanisation en Gaule du Nord et de l'Est* (2015).

Clare Rowan is Associate Professor in Classics and Ancient History at the University of Warwick and primarily researches on how ancient coinage was used as a medium for the negotiation of power and the expression of identity. She is author of *Under Divine Auspices: Divine Ideology and the Visualisation of Imperial Power in the Severan Period* (2014) and (with A. Bokern) *Embodying Value: The Transformation of Objects in and from the Ancient World* (2014).

Marc Philipp Wahl is Assistant Curator at the Martin von Wagner Museum of the University of Würzburg. He completed his Ph.D. in Numismatics at the University of Vienna in 2017. His latest project is concerned with the iconography of Greek coins in Classical times and the digitization of the coin collection of the Martin von Wagner Museum.

SERIES PREFACE

When the British Museum decided in 2012 to redesign Room 68, the hall containing objects from its Department of Coins and Medals, its curators made a bold departure from how numismatic material had conventionally been displayed. Rather than cases filled with row upon row of gold, silver, and bronze coins of European antiquity, the new gallery design featured all manner of objects, not limited to coin or paper currency, capturing the history of transactional artifacts and infrastructures from shells to mobile phones. Each case had a theme: cases on one side of the gallery spotlighted money's institutional supports and issuing authorities, while cases on the other underscored all the myriad ways people use money, not just for exchange or payment but for ritual or religious observance, political contestation, adornment, and storytelling.

The intention in preparing these six volumes was to provide readers with a similar experience, inviting them into the wonder-cabinets of money in all its variegation, multiplicity, and complexity. What emerges is money's irreducible plurality, the multiple stories it tells. Money opens windows into plural economic and moral worlds, too, worlds of value and evaluation, wealth and worth. Never merely coin, cash, or credit rendered in strictly economic terms, money is so much more than the old couplet would have it: "Money is a matter of functions four: a medium, a measure, a standard, a store." Instead, money is always also a medium of communication, a set of instruments with which people exchange messages with one another—about price, to be sure, but also about political conviction and authority, fealty, desire, or disdain. And money is a method of memorializing the past so that relations established among people, institutions, the gods, and the ancestors can be carried forward through the present and into near, distant, and imaginary futures.

Money is in this sense both irredeemably "cultural" and "historical," and so it is apt that this six-volume Cultural History of Money should spotlight money's relation to religion, technology, the arts and literature, everyday life, metaphysical interpretation, and a wide variety of issues of the age. While many contributors to the first several volumes are numismatists and archaeologists, trucking in the material evidence of coin and bullion, the volumes also contain contributions from scholars of digital infrastructures, literary and legal historians and science fiction scholars, sociologists and anthropologists, economists and artists.

Archaeologists have long bemoaned the fact that the great majority of ancient coins in museums and private collections today were unearthed without any data having been collected on their surrounding context, rendering much of the ancient and even more recent past a mystery. Even where the context for a particular find is present, its interpretation is always ambiguous. In the contemporary period, money is surrounded by context—cables and wireless signals, data protocols and computer servers, lobbying groups' and legislators' voluminous writings, television soap operas and online social media. Yet just as with ancient hoards, we have difficult escaping our own assumptions about what money is, what people do with it, and the style with which they do so.

Take a basic plastic credit card transaction at a physical till. How many users of this everyday payment device would be able to explain how it works? How would a museum curate this technological assemblage? Moving from the simple act of paying to more involved interactions with money, how might an archaeologist of the future deduce, for example, the practice in some Central Asian Muslim immigrant communities known as the "Imam Zamin," which consists of wrapping a coin in a piece of cloth tied about the upper arm to protect a traveler? Or the practice from around 2005–9 of what people called "doing tuning"(튜닝하다) to a transit card in Seoul, Korea—dissolving the plastic payment card with acetone so as to remove the radio-frequency identification (RFID) antenna and chip, and creatively stitching it into one's pocketbook, bracelet, or the elbow patches of one's blazer, so you can breeze through the turnstile with style?

Trapped in our own "coin consciousness," we assume money has to be, or that its value should be found in, a tangible thing, despite the fact that our own interactions with it are increasingly dematerialized in digital networks. We hold on to bullionist conceptions of money's worth, despite our bearing continuous witness to its fluctuations based on prevailing political whims. We think of money as abstract, even as we use it in the most concrete and interpersonal relations. We believe money equilibrates values, rendering goods and services commensurable with one another measured on one scale of value, even as we use money to demarcate difference—national difference, religious difference, intergenerational difference, differences in class, race, and gender.

The periodization of these volumes is somewhat arbitrary but still Eurocentric. The selection of authors and themes is intended to help disturb this Western-oriented history by globalizing it and insisting on bringing into the frame its political, imperial, and often racial dynamics.

The chapters in these volumes capture money's complexities in both substance and form. In substance, in so far as they attempt a cross-cultural, transhistorical survey of money technologies and cultures that will illuminate its variability and complexity. In form, in that each volume takes up the same thematic areas; but in reading across the volumes one will discover that these themes are themselves complicated by having different eras' understandings of said theme juxtaposed with other eras' often incompatible understandings. Like a ledger book, then—one of the most basic manifestations of money's recordkeeping devices—the series can be read "down," reading the chapters within one historical period, and "across," reading the affiliated thematic chapters from volume to volume. What emerges is an affirmation that money itself is a cultural history.

Bill Maurer
University of California—Irvine

Introduction

Money Made the Ancient World Go Around

STEFAN KRMNICEK

The time span covered by this volume ranges from the introduction of coinage in the seventh century BCE to the fall of the Western Roman Empire in the fifth century CE. In addition, some contributions explore the topic of currency before the introduction of coinage, as far back as the twelfth century BCE, while other chapters deal with specific concerns up to the early Middle Ages in Europe. Geographically, the focus of our deliberations is the ancient world. This is owed in part to our contributors' particular expertise and research interests in the Greco-Roman world and, in part, to the importance of ancient Mediterranean coinage in itself. In terms of conception, use, and socio-cultural integration, the origins of our modern, Western concept of money can be traced back to the earliest electrum coins that emerged in the seventh century BCE in Asia Minor (Scheidel 2008).

Today most people could not imagine a world without money. In our modern world, our dealings with the physical medium of money in its many manifestations (coinage, paper money, electronic transactions, etc.) are quite different from those of the ancient world. In antiquity the principle was that coins were just one specific form of money, if especially well-developed for that purpose (see Jimenez in this volume). As for forms of currency pre-dating coinage among communities without written records, identifying the possible proto-monetary use of certain objects remains a challenge (see Hensler 2014). Only archaeological investigations are able to demonstrate monetary use or give an estimation of value between the Neolithic/Copper Age and the invention of coinage proper in Late Iron Age western Anatolia. In the Neolithic, objects such as shells or stone implements were best suited for use beyond their primary purpose, to serve as means of exchange in various instances. The relationship between value and mass had not yet been established and it seems that value only became standardized in the Bronze Age with the invention of weights and scales. From then on, metals became the common denominators of value and the new means of meeting social obligations (Rahmstorf 2016). The invention of weight metrology in the third millennium BCE paved the way for the introduction of seals which enabled individuals and institutions to certify the weight of the metal and guarantee its authenticity (Thompson 2003). It was then only a small step to move over to a system of money-to-money exchange and of coinage under authoritative control. Silver was the dominant metal in economic life before coinage in the early Greek and Near Eastern worlds. Finds of so-called hacksilver (i.e. cut or chopped up pieces of silver such as silver currency bars, jewellery, wire, vessels, fragments of foil, silver plate, ingots, etc., which served as currency in economies that preceded or lacked coinage, were weighed each time a transaction was carried out and, if necessary, cut to reach the required weight (Kroll 2013)) indicate that weighed metal played a well-established role as currency in society before the introduction of coinage (Kim 2001). Taking a long view, there is much in favor of John Kroll's argument, that "coinage did not do anything that other forms of money had not always done; it only did them better" (Kroll 2012: 40). The following pages will outline the most significant achievements of ancient coinage.

It is worth noting how far the notion of money in the form of coins had developed in the two Mediterranean (Greek and Near Eastern) civilizations between the fifth century BCE and the fifth century CE, and in how many respects it corresponds to those of our current times: it encompasses technically highly sophisticated manufacturing processes that could deliver objects to the nearest fraction of a gram, produce coins in their thousands (de Callataÿ 2011a), and reproduce them in series (Grüner 2014); the conditions necessary for conducting long-distance trade and banking (Andreau 1999), wealth creation through credit, and social differentiation; and the perspectives of the users of money in philosophical considerations (Seaford 2004), in religious practice, and superstition (Maué and Veit 1982). Aspects of our recent past, such as inflation, monetary instability, and the breakup of monetary unions were already of serious concern in antiquity, as were questions relating to their causes and how to counter them (Meadows and Shipton 2001; Scheidel et al. 2007).

The relationship between money and power is an aspect that is particularly prominent and ever-present when considering the evolution of coinage in the ancient world (see Conzett 2005). It is already evident when the medium of coinage emerged and was adopted by the (royal, urban) elites of a given society. Coinage plays a leading role in the financing of military and political power and consequently becomes a driving force in social change. For example, the growth in the use of mercenaries in the Greek world in the fourth century BCE is closely connected to the existence of coinage (Trundle 2013; see de Callataÿ in this volume). When Greek city-states were able to raise the necessary financial resources, recruiting mercenaries for military enterprises became the preferred option. This led to profound changes in the way warfare was conducted and military strategies applied. The ideal Greek army consisted of a majority of land-owning citizens, who supplied their own military equipment and usually acted as reservists to protect their *poleis* and estates from attack. These military duties corresponded to the ideal of a citizen and attendant political rights. The introduction of the use of mercenaries challenged this system because the primary driving force was no longer based on membership of, and loyalty to, a particular *polis* but the expectation of lucrative gain in a career that was considered respectable. Mercenary activities also became one of the most important factors linking the Mediterranean world to the Iron Age Celtic world north of the Alps, through the medium of coinage (Creighton 2000).

In Republican Rome the influence of money in an emerging regional power can be outlined reasonably well in macro-historical terms. While the political and social institutions of the city-state that were important for internal cohesion had been in place for several generations, the transition to a monetary economy in Rome only took place in the context of military expansion into Italy in the third century BCE. It was a necessary step, enabling the city of Rome to build ships, produce war materiel, and meet other military expenses without having to raise funds from private individuals, making it possible to conduct wars outside the borders of Italy (Bringmann 2011: 183–4). The monetary landscape of the Roman state grew out of various traditions and looked quite diverse in the third century BCE (Burnett 2012). Cast currency bars of standard weight made of an alloy of lead-tin bronze came out of the Italic tradition of metal bars and became current in Rome; they are known as *aes signatum* because of the symbolic images that appear on their obverse and reverse (see Figure 0.1). Changes in imagery (thunderbolts and Pegasus, thunderbolts and trident, elephant and boar, etc.) are generally linked to military events such as the Pyrrhic War (280–275 BCE) and First Punic War (264–241 BCE). Cast bronze coins, the so-called *aes grave*, were also circulating. The application of value symbols denoting subdivisions of the Roman pound has its roots in this Italic tradition. Greek influences are responsible for the striking of bronze and silver coins on the Greek drachm system. The former were also struck outside Rome in Cosa and Naples. During the Second Punic War, when power over the Mediterranean was shifting, Rome's reform of its monetary system led to a radical change: the newly introduced silver *denarius* replaced the older debased Roman silver drachms and a new bronze denomination replaced various older bronze currencies. The earliest coin series from the destruction level associated

FIGURE 0.1: Metal cast of an *aes signatum* (currency bar) (British Museum, no. 1867,0212.2) struck in Rome around 280–250 BCE. Obverse: elephant right. Reverse: sow left (Tübingen University inv. I 94a/f) (photograph: Thomas Zachmann, University of Tübingen, Numismatic Department).

with the conquest of Morgantina in 211 BCE give us a *terminus ante quem* for the introduction of the *denarius* (Buttrey *et al.* 1989). The extent of the circulation of this new silver currency is probably also related to obtaining access to the resources of the cities of Syracuse and Capua after their conquest. Such an evolution follows in the tradition of earlier events, which document a causal relationship between access to resources and the issuing of new coins, for example the link between Athens and the exploitation of the mines in the Laurion region or between Philip II of Macedon and the takeover of the mines in the Pangaion mountains or, again, between Alexander the Great and the capture of the legendary royal treasure of the Achaemenids after his victory over the Persian king Darius III (de Callataÿ 2012: 176–8).

We should not forget, in all our synchronous and diachronic perspectives on the cultural history of money in antiquity and its appearance as the prime mover of cultural development, that coinage is by no means the only indicator of a social, economic, political, or military supremacy. For example, Sparta, which was a leading regional power throughout the fifth century BCE and had become a supra-regional hegemony since its victory in the Peloponnesian War (431–404 BCE) at the latest, did not issue any coins until the third century BCE. The city-state, organized on military lines, and its social order, were perfectly able to function without coinage; it only started to issue coins—and this in small quantities—after it lost its supremacy and the regal coinage of the Hellenistic kings had come to dominate the Greek world. Pharaonic Egypt also followed a path that did not require its own coinage. Although tetradrachms of Athens were widely imitated in late fifth-century BCE Egypt (van Alfen 2005), it was only under the Ptolemies, toward the end of the fourth century BCE, that the first mints began to issue regular, official coins, when a new (Greek) system of government was being instituted (von Reden 2010: 41–7).

Finally, we should also not forget that coinage in antiquity was produced, circulated, and distributed at a rate that was completely different from that of

FIGURE 0.2: *Sestertius* of Gaius (Caligula) struck in Rome, 37–8 CE. Obverse: laureate head left, C CAESAR AVG GERMANICVS PON M TR POT. Reverse: Gaius's three sisters standing facing, AGRIPPINA DRVSILLA IVLIA (Yale University Art Gallery 2004.11.1).

the constantly circulating money of our own times (see Casoli and Wahl in this volume). This is shown by hoards assembled in the second half of the sixth century BCE, which in many cases still contain a mixture of coins and pieces of precious metal as well as chopped up chunks of ingots (Kroll 2008). It illustrates that the medium of coinage had not been fully adopted in the many parts of the Greek world that were using forms of currency older than coinage. In Classical, Hellenistic, and Roman times we encounter instances where old coins (sometimes over 200 years of age) were circulating alongside freshly minted coins. The late Republican *denarii* of Mark Antony of 32–31 BCE, which still turn up in hoards of the second and third centuries AD (Butcher and Ponting 2014: 161), provide the best example of such a practice. The fact that the state in antiquity did not have the mechanisms for an instant and complete recall of old coinage could lead to some quite absurd situations. A series issued by Gaius (Caligula) bearing the images of his three sisters, Agrippina, Drusilla, and Julia standing side-by-side, illustrates this (see Figure 0.2). The coins, intended to portray harmonious family relations, started to circulate widely over the Empire at a time when two of the sisters had been sent into exile by the emperor for taking part in a conspiracy against him (Wolters 2003a: 198). The coins remained in circulation—as attested by archaeological finds—and the outdated message they conveyed must have had a counterproductive effect.

THE GREEK WORLD

When considering fixed points in the cultural history of money in antiquity we must not overlook the fact that the various stage of its development took place within political and socio-cultural theaters. The earliest step in this process—the introduction of standardized pieces of metal struck with an official stamp by an issuer guaranteeing their weight and alloy, and its further evolution into a bi-metallic currency system based on gold and silver (see Wartenberg 2016)—took place within centralized kingdoms (those of the Lydians and the Achaemenids). This new and evidently very workable idea was adopted soon afterwards by the Greek *poleis* (city-states) in the form of struck coins. The production and use of coined money became widespread from the sixth century BCE up to the Persian Wars. The rapid spread of silver coinage at this time appears to have been closely linked to three interconnected factors: (1) the political and social development of the Greek *poleis* and the high degree of connectivity among the settlements of the Greek world; (2) the exploitation of sources of metal; and (3) the formation of supra-regional economic centers such as Aegina. The latter is documented by the dominance of its coins with turtle motif throughout the Aegean from the late sixth century to the early fifth century BCE (the same circumstances were to apply some two generations later when the coinage of Athens assumed an internationally dominant position; see Rowan in this volume). In the early phase of coinage in the sixth century BCE, similar symbolic designs are found among royal Lydian coins (in contrast to the explicit representations of power shown on Achaemenid coins) and the early coinage struck by city states: this imagery suggests that the coins were badges or emblems and, to modern eyes, they give the impression of being primarily local and only secondarily mythological or religious in intent. These motifs include animals and local products or other features attributable to a specific city, or even designs which make a pun of the name of the issuing authority (Carradice and Price 1988: 57–8; see Figure 0.3).

FIGURE 0.3: Electrum coin struck in Cyzicus around 500 BCE. Obverse: ram kneeling left, head turned back, beneath tuna fish. Reverse: incuse square of mill-sail pattern (Tübingen University SNG 2213) (photograph: Thomas Zachmann, University of Tübingen, Numismatic Department).

From the fifth century BCE onwards, the political entities that made up the urban communities of citizens developed new designs for their own issues, which mirrored those of the *polis* and its political constellation. Here, portraits of deities on the obverse of the coins became more frequent, and they became the hallmark of specific city-states. The naming of the civic authority in the legend of the coin followed. Naming the citizenry of a given city, the so called *ethnikon* (i.e., only the free male citizens who had full legal and political rights), generally abbreviated in the genitive plural form, notionally indicates that "this is a coin or a certified form of currency of the [Athenians, for example]" and refers to the civic authority of the issuer.

In this respect it is worth pointing out that the images figuring on the coins issued by Greek colonies are highly significant because they are the only direct surviving evidence of the identity of a settlement and its population, represented symbolically as an image (see Elkins in this volume). But the imagery on Greek coinage only ever illustrated local identity as perceived by the upper echelons of society and its ruling classes and never represented the perceptions of the wider population, as illustrated, for example, by the coins from Zancle/Messana (Fischer-Bossert 2012: 149–50). The ancient city of Zancle, present-day Messina in the northeastern corner of Sicily, struck silver coins bearing the image of a dolphin and sickle from the end of the sixth century BCE onward. In 494/493 BCE refugees from Samos in Asia Minor took control of the city by force and produced a new series of coins featuring designs that were adapted from the motifs of their original city. The obverse bears Samos's typical lion's scalp and the reverse a Samian warship. Only a few years later Anaxilas, tyrant of Rhegium (Reggio di Calabria across the Straits of Messina), conquered the city and renamed it Messana, allegedly in memory of his family's Peloponnesian origins, thus commemorating the arrival of Messenians from the Peloponnese. The new coins struck by Anaxilas were joint issues of the two cities of Rhegium and Zancle, with shared imagery: a full-face lion's head recalling the earlier Samian lion's scalp on the obverse, and a calf's head looking left on the reverse. This example clearly illustrates how perceptions of identity and self-representation were determined in a "top-down" manner and only had a superficial validity—it is difficult to imagine that local people adjusted their self-identity every time power changed hands (for a similar phenomenon with Greek coinage under Roman rule, see Martin 2013). Coins and money were a product of the elite in the Greek world; this is evidenced also by the subdivision into denominations of high value and purchasing power among silver coins (see Scheidel 2010).

The choice of imagery and symbols on Greek coins to represent a city's identity not only took no account of the perceptions of the wider population of Greek city-states, the indigenous populations' existence was also left unacknowledged on the coins struck in colonial settings, i.e. the *apoikiai* (Greek "colonies" that were established during the eighth, seventh, and sixth centuries BCE) where an indigenous presence is archaeologically attested. In southern Italy, where Greek settlements had been striking coins since the sixth century BCE, we come across small coins that have the typically southern Italic incuse production technique, the weight, and bull motif of the earliest coins struck by the Greek city of Sybaris on the Gulf of Taranto but which have their own legends (SIRINOS-PYXOES, AMI, SO in Archaic Greek script) (see Figure 0.4). This must be the only case where we encounter indigenous communities through the Greek medium of coinage, and yet we know nothing further about the location or context in which these coins were struck (Horsnaes 2011). From a stylistic viewpoint, the coins give the impression that the dies were made by the same craftsmen as those responsible for making the Sybaris coins. A recent analysis of the techniques used to produce these coins supports such an interpretation (Sheedy 2015). The small quantities of coins recovered suggest that such productions were an episodic affair. The few archaeologically provenanced coins come from southern Italian fifth-century BCE hoards, which indicates that these coins circulated regionally alongside other regular Greek issues.

In the Greek world the Bactrian coinage provides us with an instance of a trend going exactly in the opposite direction (see Rowan in this volume). Around the middle of the third century BCE Bactria split from the Seleucid Empire under the rule of its governor Diodotos and for almost two centuries enjoyed the status of being the easternmost independent Greek state. The coinage of the Greek kings of Bactria is our best source of information for the history of the Bactrian dynasties and state ideology: many names of rulers are

FIGURE 0.4: *Stater* of "Siris and Pyxus type" struck in southern Italy. Obverse: bull standing left, head turned back, ΣΙΡΙΝΟΣ. Reverse: same as obverse, incuse and reversed, ΠΥΧ (Copenhagen National Museum inv. KP 2090, SNG Cop. Suppl. no. 53) (photograph: Helle W. Horsnaes, CC-BY-SA, Copenhagen National Museum).

only known to us from the coinage. The Bactrian coins struck in the area of present-day Afghanistan and Pakistan represent, in terms of style, production, weight, denomination, and imagery—the latter depicting the king as a diademed portrait wearing the *kausia* (a traditional Macedonian flat hat) on the obverse and traditional Greek representations of gods on the reverse—are representative of Greco-Mediterranean money. With the expansion of the Bactrian kingdom into India, the dual character of the Greco-Indian state is reflected in the form of bilingual legends (Greek on the obverse, Kharosthi on the reverse) and the minting of currency on an Indian weight standard, the coins' square shape, Buddhist symbolism, and representations of Hindu deities (Hoover 2013). The nature of the relationship between the indigenous and Greek–Bactrian population in this ethnically hybrid state is difficult to establish, but at the very least the elite product that is coinage conveys the idea of a fusion of Greek and Indian culture combining bilingual legends and Indian practice. Unfortunately, the context of most coins is not sufficiently well recorded archaeologically, making it impossible to distinguish potentially different spheres of use of Greek money in local traditions. Nevertheless, a comparison with better-documented coin assemblages in other instances of coexistence in cultural settings and transition periods in the Old World suggests that such a scenario is plausible (see Luley 2008; Krmnicek 2010).

Two further significant turning points need to be taken into account in an overview of the history of money in Greek antiquity at a macro scale. Both had consequences that still resonate in our modern Western world. The first is the round shape as the standard configuration of the medium of coinage. The early electrum coins were more or less nugget-shaped or irregularly ovoid (see Figure 0.5). The early Lydian and Achaemenid currency was also quite oblong. The Archaic Greek coinage was based on generally irregular, round or oval flans. In southern Italy, where coinage was adopted in the Greek *apoikiai* in the sixth century BCE, the general physical appearance of the early series differed quite substantially from that of contemporary coins in the eastern Mediterranean. The coins were produced using the incuse technique (i.e. the image on the obverse was struck in deep relief on the reverse). This unusual technique required great skill and effort (see Casoli and Wahl in this volume). It is still a matter of debate among numismatists why this technique was adopted by Greek settlements in southern Italy. We can nevertheless deduce that there was no consensus about what early Archaic coins should look like. With the widespread introduction of portraits of gods on the obverse of Greek coins in the fifth century BCE—when in southern Italy, too, coins were no longer struck in the incuse technique but in the "normal" way (i.e., struck in high relief on both sides)—well-shaped circular flans became the norm. This raises questions as to whether there is a causal relationship between the round shape and the proportions of the portrait represented on the surface of the coin.

FIGURE 0.5: Electrum *stater* struck in Miletus, *c*. sixth century BCE. Obverse: lion recumbent right, head turned back, the whole within a frame. Reverse: three incuse sunk images with stag's head, fox running and cross (Tübingen University inv. ZWVerz. 16044) (photograph: Stefan Krmnicek, University of Tübingen, Numismatic Department).

The second aspect to mention is closely linked to the representation of portraits. While only portraits of gods or mythological heroes (but never living individuals) appeared on Greek coins, this rule changed in Hellenistic times (Dahmen 2007; Lichtenberger *et al*. 2014). Alexander the Great used a portrait of Heracles—which to a contemporary observer looked like the young ruler because of the resemblance of their youthful facial traits (see Figure 0.6)—on the obverse of his silver tetradrachms. An actual portrait of Alexander only appeared after his death, among the coins issued by his successors. Perhaps the tradition of the newly conquered regions of the Persian Empire of representing

FIGURE 0.6: *Tetradrachm* of Alexander III struck in Amphipolis around 336–323 BCE. Obverse: head of young Heracles right, wearing lion's skin. Reverse: Zeus, wearing *himation* over knees, seated left on throne without back, resting with left hand on sceptre, in field left monogram, ΒΑΣΙΛΕΩΣ ΑΛΕΞΑΝΔΡΟΥ (Tübingen University SNG 1091) (photograph: Thomas Zachmann, University of Tübingen, Numismatic Department).

INTRODUCTION

in a few rare cases living rulers on coins (Persian satraps and Lycian dynasts in Asia Minor) had an influence on the choice of such an ambivalent portrait. In the new coin series issued by the Diadochi, Alexander is depicted in the Greek tradition as a god with the ram's horns of the god Zeus Ammon, Alexander being acknowledged as his son at the Oracle of Siwa. In the wake of this gradual unraveling, the hitherto strict rule not to show a living ruler on Greek coins was broken by the Hellenistic cult of royalty under the successors of Alexander, when the Diadochi began, in the early third century BCE, to show portraits on their coinage executed in the style of the depiction of Alexander. The introduction of realistic portraits of rulers constitutes one of the most enduring iconographic innovations in the medium of coinage; consider the portraits of Roman emperors, the sequence of portraits of rulers on Western Early Modern coins, and the portraits of monarchs and heads of state on modern coins and banknotes from Queen Elizabeth to Mobutu Sese Seko.

THE CELTIC WORLD

The coinage of Iron Age societies stands, so to speak, on the threshold of the Greek and Roman civilizations. As mentioned earlier, mercenaries from temperate Europe encountered the Mediterranean world through military service and brought these coins and the idea of coinage back home (see Čižmár *et al*. 2008). The ensuing striking of coins was essentially imitative, adopting types current in the Mediterranean sphere and further developing them (see Figure 0.7). Nearly all types derived from coinages struck by known employers of "Celtic" mercenaries. The coinage can be divided into broad

FIGURE 0.7: Celtic imitation of a *tetradrachm* of Thasos, *c*. first century BCE. Obverse: imitation of head of Dionysus right, wearing crown of ivy leaves and grapes. Reverse: imitation of Heracles standing left, with legends of dots (Tübingen University SNG 207) (photograph: Thomas Zachmann, University of Tübingen, Numismatic Department).

geographical zones, where specific prototypes or kinds of metal were dominant (Kos and Wigg 2002). Unlike the Greek and Roman world, the *Keltike* (or Iron Age Celtic cultural sphere) did not immediately evolve into a developed monetary economy. Coins circulated primarily among the elites, serving as objects of value in the exchange of gifts, in ceremonial, and in religious practice. It is only in the last phase of the European Iron Age, in the second and first centuries BCE when contacts with the expanding Roman world were becoming more intensive, that the archaeological record shows a rapid increase in the use of Iron Age coinage in the economic sphere of exchange (Howgego 2013; see Martin's and Krmnicek's chapters in this volume).

Lattes (ancient Lattara), near modern Montpellier in southern France, provides an excellent framework for the investigation of the latest developments that entangled Celts with Romans (Py 2006; Luley 2008). The triangular settlement of around 3.5 hectares, with its characteristic single-width house blocks, was founded in the late sixth century BCE and was fortified from the outset. It rapidly became a major port for the exchange of goods between the Mediterranean and the hinterland. The inhabitants were a mixture of local Celtic speakers with Etruscans and Greeks. Excavations yielded some 7,000 coins as well as an abundance of local and imported artefacts from the sixth century BCE to around 200 CE, when the settlement was abandoned. Most of the coins were found in the center of the town, apart from four large hoards found on its fringes, close to the ramparts. Interestingly, although apparently a thriving commercial hub, Lattara never minted its own coinage and the vast majority of coins used throughout the life of the settlement come from nearby Massalia. In Michel Py's model of the spheres of exchange operating in pre-Roman Lattes (Py 2006: 1160–2), foreign merchants did not trade directly with the indigenous population but through locally based middlemen. These "brokers," perhaps from the upper echelons of society, were probably the only residents making large-scale monetary transactions, albeit only occasionally (perhaps seasonally?), and were thus able to accumulate large sums in silver coins. Although the site was founded in the sixth century BCE, there is no sign of coinage at Lattes until the later fourth century BCE; this was a large hoard with Massalian silver obols and a handful of other finds found elsewhere on the site. After 250 BCE, coin loss increased appreciably but remained on a fairly modest scale.

Roman intervention, followed by conquest in 121 BCE, was certainly the main factor in the rapidly increasing coin losses after 150 BCE; the Roman presence promoted monetization through taxation, land reallocation, and commercial development. Roman coins, however, remained rare at Lattara during the first century BCE, but there was a rapid expansion of crafts and specialization, indicated by the establishment of metal and pottery workshops along the settlement's main roads. The best evidence for the increased monetization of society under Roman rule, however, comes from the changing proportions of silver and bronze among the site's finds. Very soon after their introduction, Massalian bronze coins appeared in Lattes and quickly accounted for a significant proportion of the losses, at the expense of silver coins. After 125 BCE, the proportion of silver dropped sharply, and never recovered. It was only the introduction of bronze that made it possible to conduct small-scale transactions with ease. This allowed a wider spectrum of society to participate in monetary transactions, although the evidence indicates that this shift was very gradual.

Several decades of excavations provide excellent data for comparing the archaeological contexts in which the coins occur. Most date to after the Roman conquest. Interestingly, as Benjamin Luley's study shows (2008: 182 fig. 7), pre-Roman finds overwhelmingly come from domestic contexts. Only later are coins found in association with industrial or craft activity. To see whether these foreign monetary objects were used differently in non-economic spheres, it is worth briefly examining the coins recovered in ritual contexts. At Lattara domestic ritual practices take various forms: infant burials in a pit beside the wall of a house, dog burials, and urns deposited upside down in houses or courtyards. Five such deposits yielded coins. A Massalian obol is the only find from the pre-Roman phase (225–200 BCE) and the only silver coin deposited in a ritual context. The other four were deposited in the first century BCE. Three are Massalian bronzes; the final coin is a "potin au long cou," made either in the lower Rhône valley or central Gaul and quite rare at Lattara (there are only twenty of these among the Lattes finds). We can say little based on this tiny sample, but the increase in the use of coins for ritual acts does mirror the overall trend toward monetization. It is probably no coincidence that local people started to incorporate these "imported" but by now familiar objects into their offerings at a time when their traditions and beliefs were coming under the powerful influence of Rome. However, as the only finds classified as "ritual" in Lattes were coins associated with clearly ritual deposits, it remains to be seen whether more examples can be identified by applying different criteria. For example, coins from foundation trenches might repay attention; many British archaeologists would point to the liminal location of the four hoards near the settlement boundary (see Haselgrove and Webley 2016).

THE ROMAN WORLD

Its different political, social, and demographic circumstances make the Roman imperial period and the coinage of that time fundamentally different from the Archaic, Classical, and Hellenistic coinage of the Greek world. There are also substantial differences in research. The study of Roman coinage occupies a favorable position compared to Celtic and Greek numismatics. Roman numismatics is far better represented worldwide in universities, museums, and other academic institutions than its Greek counterpart. The greater number of researchers and research projects dedicated to Roman coinage is reflected in the larger number of publications dealing with that topic than those devoted to Greek numismatics. Research in other disciplines associated with the Roman world also has a multiplying effect (e.g., 46,091 followers of "Roman Archaeology" vs 12,431 followers of "Greek Archaeology" and 33,491 followers of "Roman History" vs 19,488 followers of "Ancient Greek History" at www.academia.edu/, accessed July 11, 2016). Two further factors, which give the study of Roman money a methodological advantage, will be briefly discussed here.

First, Roman culture is geographically imbedded in the western Mediterranean sphere and in northwestern Europe. It is in these regions that Roman archaeology is strongly represented in universities and heritage agencies. In northwestern Europe, a number of long-term national projects have made great efforts since the middle of the twentieth century to assemble systematic corpora of finds containing information on coins found over an entire country's territory, thus making it possible to compare finds at a supra-regional level. The project "Fundmünzen der römischen Zeit in Deutschland" (Coin Finds of the Roman Period in Germany), whose goal it was to "document scientifically all ancient coins found in the territory of the Federal Republic of Germany," provides an example. By making this material available it has become possible to subject a reliable and manageable set of data to the scrutiny of numismatists, archaeologists, historians, and scholars of economic history. The success of the project found international resonance and soon led to the adoption of its aims and methodology in neighboring countries. In recent years, most national finds inventories and data have been transferred to an electronic format. Today the most important database of numismatic finds is the database of the Portable Antiquities Scheme, which has recorded approximately 221,000 Roman coins from England and Wales (see http://finds.org.uk/database, accessed July 11, 2016). As there are hardly any established inventories of finds in the eastern and southern Mediterranean area, and because a centralized record of single finds is less well developed there than in western Europe, hoard finds remain the most important source of information for a large-scale or diachronic study of coinage in these regions. Inevitably, this has had an influence on the theories and methods applied in researching the medium of coinage (de Callataÿ forthcoming).

Second, innovative approaches to the material constitute the other decisive factor that gives an advantage to Roman numismatics as compared to the study of Greek coinage. The thorough examination of the archaeological evidence from recent investigations of Roman sites has shown that it is only through the study of coins in their archaeological context that questions relating to the reasons why a particular find ended up in that context and to its original function can be answered (see Martin in this volume). The studies carried out on material from the Roman settlements of Augst (Peter 1996b) and the Magdalensberg (Krmnicek 2010), the sanctuary on the Martbeg (Nüsse 2103), the Roman legionary fortress of Nijmegen (Kemmers 2006), the analysis of the coins from the forts and settlements on the Upper German-Raetian *limes* (Krmnicek and Kortüm 2016), and the volume about coins and context edited by von Kaenel and Kemmers (2009) which presents the topic from different perspectives (for Greek numismatics see Frey-Kupper 2013), represent significant steps along this path.

It is also essential to closely link research in the field with the study of coins in Roman inhumation burials. For the area between the Moselle, Rhine, and Somme an exhaustive study of the practice highlights the great diversity of the archaeological evidence (Gorecki 1975). This analysis revealed that the so-called "obol of Charon" (payment to the ferryman whose task it was to convey the dead to the Underworld; Alföldy-Gazdac and Gazdac 2013) was not universally adopted in Roman burial practice, nor is it necessarily verifiable. The analysis, however, indicates that coins were occasionally deliberately selected for the message they contained and hence given to the dead. Such coins have expressive legends, including AETERNITAS ("eternity"), FELICITAS PERPETVA ("perpetual felicity"), or MEMORIAE AETERNAE ("for eternal memory") (see Elkins in this volume).

The deposition of coins in religious or ritual contexts is a further example of a phenomenon that can only be apprehended by recording its archaeological context (see Krmnicek in this volume). This includes offertory containers (i.e. containers in which coins were deposited); such repositories, made of stone, have been found in both Greek and Roman sanctuaries (Kaminski 1991). The typology of these containers includes block-shaped, conical, cylindrical, and pillar-shaped objects, the latter only known on Roman cult sites. Inscriptions and ancient texts inform us that these repositories were known as *thesauri* in Roman times and that the offerings of money were called *stips* (Crawford 2003). The origin of these containers does not, therefore, lie in Roman cults; presumably it was only in the second century BCE that the containers took on the role of repositories for ritual deposits from the Greek world where they are known from the fourth century BCE onwards. Offerings of coins that ended up in a *thesaurus* are in many cases distinct from other deliberate ritual depositions: the offering was reversible, and in most cases the money was intended to go back into circulation. The income paid for such items as statues, repairs to temples, or cult festivals, financed *ex stipe*. Inscriptions tell us that these repositories were emptied usually once a year, in a few cases every other year, and sometimes even twice a year. Only rarely were they not emptied; here, they would be open to the ground so that the offerings would go straight to the gods without funds being spent on their wellbeing. Most offertory containers and their contents were discovered in the eighteenth and nineteenth centuries and hence their publication is insufficient by today's standards. More recent discoveries show the great potential of such finds, provided their contents are still in position. When subjected to a spatial micro-analysis of the choice of offerings and the sequence of deposition of coins in circulation, they provide valuable insights into the significance of the *thesaurus* in the context of cultic practices (Ranucci 2010). Similarly, the micro-stratigraphic excavation of coins in vessels containing hoards under controlled laboratory conditions can illuminate the original use of the objects and their circumstances of deposition. The best examples of such investigations are those found in a Roman villa at Neftenbach in Switzerland (von Kaenel *et al.* 1993) and the massive hoard discovered in Frome (Somerset, UK), which weighed 160 kg (350 lb) and contained over 52,000 coins; the Frome find is thought to represent a communal votive offering (Moorhead *et al.* 2010).

As the hoards mentioned here show, Roman coinage characterizes a highly monetized society. This monetization and a complete redesign of coinage went hand-in-hand with the development of a new form of government in the Principate of the last three decades BCE. Gaius Julius Caesar had already broken the mold and struck coins bearing his portrait as head of state during his lifetime. From a cultural perspective, it is worth noting that his contemporaries were not pleased about this, even though in the Greek world, a world whose customs Rome had absorbed, rulers had already been represented on coins for some 250 years. The tradition was adopted under Augustus, the first Roman emperor, and the custom of representing the emperor in portrait developed, and remained the norm right up to the end of the third century CE. In addition to the by now omnipresent images of emperors on every coin, all other elements and writing on coins became subordinated to the imperial ideology (see Elkins in this volume). Coins dating to the reign of Augustus indicate that, from an administrative perspective, Roman coinage was by all appearances primarily destined to pay the wages of the military and only secondarily used to meet the economic needs of the civil population (Wolters 2015). The best evidence for this is the temporary transfer of the early imperial mint from Rome to Nemausus (Nîmes) and Lugdunum (Lyon), logistically close to the troops stationed on the Rhine, and the fact that archaeological finds of newly struck coins have only ever been recovered in military camps there. In parallel with the territorial expansion of the Roman Empire in the first two centuries CE, the Roman administration managed to impose the empire-wide (i.e. in the whole Mediterranean sphere and beyond, from present-day Morocco to Iraq and from Egypt to northern England) validity of Roman coinage and legal protection of monetary transactions. From the fourth century CE onward the political reforms of the administration meant that an even more strictly organized monetary system came into existence, determining that coins had a consistent imagery and exact indications about the production of the coins (identifying even each workshop unit of the mint responsible for each series of issues) in the decentralized mints spread over the Empire (see Casoli and Wahl in this volume).

A predecessor, so to speak, of the decentralized mints of Late Antiquity was Antioch (present-day Antakya in Turkey), which began to strike Roman imperial coins outside Rome from the third century CE onward, regularly issuing Roman silver *denarii*. In the course of that century some other strategically important locations in the Empire, such as Mediolanum (Milan), Treveri (Trier), Siscia (Sisak in Croatia), also took on the role of official mints of Roman imperial coinage. Interestingly the third century CE is noted for being the period in which there were many cases of usurpation of power with respect to the minting of coins by individuals. Once again, this demonstrates the close connection between money and power, as illustrated by the coins issued by the usurper Regalianus and his wife Dryantilla (Dembski *et al.* 2007). Regalianus was governor of Upper Pannonia and appears to have seized power in 260 CE for a few months at Carnuntum (Austria), the military and administrative center of the province of Upper Pannonia. Finds of silver *radiates* struck in his name and that of his wife Dryantilla have been recorded from the brief period he governed as rival emperor. The crude style of the imagery and the execution of the writing on the coins suggest that these coins were made locally in Carnuntum by unskilled craftsmen. Many pieces also show that they were not manufactured in the approved manner, but re-struck, using older coins—perhaps available from stocks held by the province or the military at Carnuntum. Nevertheless, despite the shortage of coins and the seemingly improvised way these coins were produced, the imagery and legends depict the issuer of the coins as the *de facto* Roman emperor with the same conviction as the contemporary coins of the legitimate ruler in Rome. This is particularly evident at the time of the split of the so-called Gallic Empire (a separate state including the territories of Gaul, the German provinces, Britain, and for a time the Iberian Peninsula) from the central government in Rome in 260–74 CE. During this phase coins with a similar iconographic repertoire were minted both in the Gallic Empire and the actual *Imperium Romanum*; the issuers of these coins each sought to legitimize their claim to being the emperor through the right to mint coins, their representation in portrait, and the full identification of their title (Imperator, Augustus) on the coins (see Figure 0.8). The issues of the Gallic Empire go hand-in-hand with the growth of an autonomous state infrastructure on its territory and represent an extremely valuable source of information about regional identity in the north-western provinces in the 260s and 270s CE (Fischer 2012).

From a gender-oriented perspective that sees Roman society as a patriarchal social system it may seem surprising that there is a multiplicity of representations of women and female imagery on Roman coins. Among the coins of the second

FIGURE 0.8: *Radiate* of Tetricus II struck in Cologne, 270–74 CE. Obverse: radiate bust of Tetricus II right, IMP C TETRICVS PF AVG. Reverse: Virtus standing left holding shield and spear, VIRTVS AVGG (Tübingen University inv. V 235/25a) (photograph: Thomas Zachmann, University of Tübingen, Numismatic Department).

century CE there is a particularly high proportion of coins depicting empresses and princesses which were struck in the name of these women. This can be documented on the basis of a representative sample of over 3,000 single finds (excluding hoards and burial finds, and counting only bronze coins) from the northwestern provinces struck by Hadrian (for Sabina), Antoninus Pius (for Faustina I and II), and Marcus Aurelius (for Faustina II and Lucilla): almost 40 percent of bronze coins issued under Marcus Aurelius are coins for female members of the imperial household (see Table 0.1). The reasons for such a strong female presence on the coins of the later second century CE must be sought in the political situation, namely who was next to accede to the throne. The period is marked by adoptions and marriages of the future rulers into the imperial household, which is why the princesses came to play a prominent role, ensuring the dynasty's future. Consequently, specifically female attributes, and

TABLE 0.1: Coins for female members of the imperial household among single finds (no hoards, no burial finds, only bronze coins) from the northwestern provinces (Cologne, Mainz, Baden-Württemberg, Trier, and Wetterau *limes*) (FMRD II 1-4, FMRD IV 1N, FMRD IV 3/1, FMRD V 1/1, FMRD VI 1/1) (n = 3085).

Emperor	Coins for ♂	Coins for ♀	Total
Hadrian	94% (n = 89)	6% (n = 50)	100% (n = 948)
Antoninus Pius	68% (n = 765)	32% (n = 352)	100% (n = 1117)
Marcus Aurelius	62% (n = 636)	38% (n = 384)	100% (n = 1020)

aspects relating to preserving the dynasty, were celebrated as allegorical motifs on coins of princesses and empresses: *Fecunditas* (fertility), *Pudicitia* (modesty), *Venus* (femininity), the birth of a prince, or marriage to an adopted son. In addition, some imagery of power (e.g., representations of the goddess Juno [Jupiter's wife], peacocks, or moon crescents in the case of coins issued posthumously after an *apotheosis* [deification]) was exclusively shown on women's coins.

CONCLUSION

The invention of coinage in seventh-century BCE Lydia built on an earlier system that had used other objects as money. The introduction of weights and scales in the Bronze Age marked a significant step in an evolution toward an objectively measurable valuation of objects by weight. The next major stage occurred in the Near Eastern Iron Age (before *c.* 600 BCE) when seals affixed to bags containing precious metals (hacksilver hoards) guaranteeing their weights according to set standards as well as controlled composition (Thompson 2003) qualify them, in a numismatic sense, as proto-currency. From this it was but a small step for ancient people to invent actual coins—a pre-weighed piece of metal guaranteed by a stamp—but a giant leap for humankind.

All these milestones in the evolution of money within the broader history of humankind, all too briefly sketched and only partly outlined in this introduction, are comprehensively examined, presenting the most recent advances in research, in the following chapters. Andrea Casoli and Marc Wahl's contribution deals with the political and technical basis for coinage in antiquity and its cultural context. François de Callataÿ considers the economic foundations of ancient money, concentrating on the Greek world. In his chapter on "Money and Religion" Stefan Krmnicek uses case studies from Greek and Roman times to illuminate the multiple uses of coinage in cult and ritual beyond the economic spheres of exchange, while Stéphane Martin presents the sources pertaining to the daily use of money and its social impact on society. In the chapter on "Art and Representation" Nathan T. Elkins scrutinizes the iconography on ancient coins in a context of tension between producers and recipients. Alicia Jimenez's contribution is a discussion of the theoretical background to the interpretation of coinage in antiquity. Clare Rowan's concluding chapter examines the agency of money in cultural contact, in the development of social systems, and in the creation of identities.

Finally, readers should note that, although we have tried to make our chapters as consistent as possible, we have left it to each author to cite the titles of ancient sources in Latin or English. Abbreviations of modern source collections used in the chapters are listed in the reference lists.

CHAPTER ONE

Money and its Technologies

Production, Distribution, and Impact

ANDREA CASOLI AND MARC PHILIPP WAHL

Coinage is a particularly successful form of money, already in widespread use in antiquity. It goes without saying that the appearance of the coins, as well as the expectations on coinage, changed over the centuries. Our understanding of the evolution of coinage and appreciation of its far-reaching implications can greatly benefit from examining the processes governing its production.

Questions regarding the methods, reasons, and means of coin production, the organization of coinage in antiquity, and the interaction between the users of the coins and the mints that issued them will be addressed in this chapter. A number of different sources are available; in addition to the coins themselves—which have survived in large quantities and almost unchanged since antiquity—archaeological contexts and artefacts can also provide valuable information. Furthermore, a wide range of written sources, be they literary works, inscriptions, or documents on papyrus, inform and enrich this topic.

The fundamental questions relating to coin production are closely intertwined with socio-cultural, economic, and technological issues, and their repercussions; pursuing such aspects therefore enhances any study of money.

GENERAL CONSIDERATIONS: WHY PRODUCE COINS?

> Coinage did not do anything that other forms of money had not always done; it only did them better.
>
> —Kroll 2012: 40

The first question to consider concerns the reasons why coins were produced in antiquity or, as Christopher Howgego put it: "Why did ancient states strike coins?" Here, we are not so much concerned with how the idea of issuing coins first came about around the middle of the seventh century BCE or how it rapidly spread over the Mediterranean sphere during the seventh and sixth centuries BCE than with why coinage became a particularly successful form of currency in antiquity (Howgego 1990; Melville-Jones 2006).

Valuable information can be gleaned from Plato and Aristotle. Aristotle highlights the usefulness of coinage as a means of facilitating trade, of measuring and storing valuables, and standardizing values (Melville-Jones 1993: nos. 2 [= Plato, *Res publica* 371b], 11 [= Aristotle, *Ethica Nicomachea* 1133a–b], 12 [= Aristotle, *Magna moralia* 1194a], 13 [=Aristotle, *Politica* 1257a–b]). From an anthropological perspective, the types of coinage circulating in antiquity can be defined as *general purpose money*. How the value of coinage was perceived in antiquity fluctuated between metallism (i.e., the metal content of a coin gives it its value) and nominalism (i.e., a coin represents credit). The pseudo-Platonic dialog *Eryxias* (399e–400c = Melville-Jones 1993: no. 8) emphasizes that the value of money does not have to correspond to its intrinsic metal content, but that it rests on social convention. It was accepted from early on that objects without significant intrinsic value could and were put into play in lieu of precious metals (Lo Cascio 1996; Wolters 1999). The element of expediency which we can glean from the discussions of the ancient philosophers is, however, insufficient when we consider real-life conditions. It would be a mistake to attribute the issuing of coinage to a single cause. So, what other factors came into play?

There is no doubt that the striking of coins related to state expenditure in antiquity; in fact, the consensus among researchers is that this aspect ranks highest (Crawford 1970; Howgego 1990; Bresson 2005). The cost of conducting wars accounts for a significant part of state expenditure and is reflected in the close relationship between the issuing of coins and military enterprises. This refers not only to military armament and the payment of soldiers and mercenaries but also to the direct benefits of warfare such as loot, payments in compensation, and tribute. In addition to military costs there were further items of expenditure, including construction works or, especially in Roman times, public games. Finally, we should bear in mind that by no means all payments were made with freshly minted coins and that, in addition to old and new coinage, ingots or goods could be used. Coins were not just struck to cover expenditure but were capable of generating income for the state. Their role in generating profit is clearly documented by an inscription of the late second century BCE in honor of the benefactor (*euergetes*) Menas in Sestos which refers to a wish to gain from the minting of bronze coins (Melville-Jones 1993: no. 377 = OGIS 339: "the city might receive the profit which would accrue from a revenue of such a kind"). The restriking of coins may also have served such a purpose. As recently demonstrated by John Kroll (2011), coins were recalled on a massive scale in Athens in the middle of the fourth century BCE, restruck and then reissued with an *agio*. The Sestos inscription throws light on a further aspect often encountered in connection with the minting of coins. The text states that the newly commissioned bronze coins were to circulate as the coins issued by the *polis* of Sestos. It is thus hardly surprising that the designs on the coins were significant. The role of coinage as a medium of communication and identity was already well understood and exploited in antiquity; a Late Roman instruction to the senior fiscal official (*comes sacrarum largitionum*) speaks for itself: "imprint the shape of our face on metals in use and issue coin to inform future ages [. . .] so that the image of the emperors, whose counsels never cease to have regard for the safety of all, may be seen to nourish their subjects through the medium of commerce" (Cassiodorus, *Variae* 6.7 = MGH AA, XII 180–1). We shall return in greater detail to the motifs on the coins and the role they played in communication.

Whether it was possible for a private individual in antiquity to strike their own wealth in metal in the form of coinage (i.e., free coinage) is a matter of debate. References to such a practice are few, but it is fairly certain that it was possible to do so in late antiquity (*Codex Theodosianus* 9.21.7–8; 10). There is also an inscription from Olbia, dated to the second half of the third century BCE (Melville-Jones 1993: no. 900 = SIG^3 495 = IOSPE I^2 32), which refers to such a practice; perhaps the evidence from the highly interesting papyrus Cairo Zenon 59021 (Melville-Jones 1993: no. 496), dated to 286 BCE and concerning the administration of a mint striking coins for private individuals, points in the same direction (Crawford 1985; Howgego 1990; Wolters 1999: 349; Foraboschi 2006). That the state at least tolerated base metal coins struck by others is possibly attested by coins of the Greek cities in the east of the Roman Empire (the so-called Roman provincial coins) which were issued well into the third century CE.

TECHNICAL ASPECTS

In antiquity coins were almost exclusively struck (i.e., manufactured) by hammering a die. The few known exceptions are cast coins—for example early Roman bronze coins (*aes grave*) or the so-called *limes falsa* (i.e., the emergency currency of the frontier provinces on the Danube). In the following, our attention will mainly focus on the struck coinage.

Mani, the Persian founder of Manicheism who was active in the third century CE, especially in the Arsacid and Sasanian empires, provides us with a rare insight into the production processes that took place in a mint. One of his texts compares metaphorically the origin of "the Word" in the human body with the minting of coins. Mani described in simplified manner the operation of a mint, most probably the mint of Seleucia-Ctesiphon, the capital of the Sasanian Empire. He states that five craftsmen (*technites*) were present in the workshop (Hommel 1965; 1966; Göbl 1967):

1. one who casts the coin (i.e., casts the metal strip, the blank metal piece);
2. another who hammers the coin (i.e., hammers the metal strip to achieve the correct degree of strength);
3. another who cuts the coin by turning it (i.e., cuts out the flan or the blank);
4. another who "seals" the coin (i.e., strikes it with a die); and
5. another who cleans the coin with a sieve (?) (i.e., cleanses the coin, perhaps in an acid bath).

Raw Material Acquisition

To produce coins metal must obviously be available. Gold, silver, and base metals (*aes*), generally copper, bronze (an alloy of tin and copper), and *orichalcum* (brass, an alloy of zinc and copper) could be obtained in a variety of ways for minting. The metal could have been available in the form of old coins or it had to be freshly acquired (e.g., by mining). It was possible to take older or foreign coins out of circulation to obtain the raw material for coinage and either melt it down or restrike it. Before turning our attention to a few well-known mines exploited in Roman times we shall first present a case study which is highly significant for Athens's acquisition of silver in late Archaic and Classical times.

The Laurion mines in the mountainous landscape of southern Attica were the source of silver for Athens. Both the rise of Athens in the sixth century BCE and its temporary decline at the end of the Peloponnesian War against Sparta in 404 BCE had major repercussions on the exploitation of the silver mines. Apparently, this exploitation contributed some 3,500 tons of fine silver from its beginnings (as early as the third millennium BCE) to Roman times. Slaves brought the metal to the surface in a complex (and still visible) system of shafts and galleries, and the processing of the ore took place in the immediate vicinity (Conophagos 1980: 151–2, 167–212). After the silver-bearing ore had been extracted through shafts and tunnels—there may have been some 2,000 of these—the ore needed to go through a series of stages to prepare the resulting silver for trade and especially for the minting of coins (see Figure 1.1). The first stage in this process consisted of crushing the ore into minute grains, which separated the lead-silver from the rest of the ore. The raw material extracted from the mines was crushed to grains the size of a pea in mortars or on large marble slabs with home-made iron pestles. The workers then brought the crushed ore to special mills where trachyte millstones reduced the material to grains about 1 mm in size. The so-called "concentration process" was designed to separate the lighter grains with a low silver content from the heavier lead-silver grains and hence to concentrate the raw material. This was achieved by washing the finely ground material with water. This process took place in dozens of "washing installations" that still survive to this day and which are archaeologically attested. Slightly inclined undulating wooden planks were laid into these washing establishments, letting the water run over them. Being heavier, the "pure" grains rich in silver and lead sank, whereas the lighter "impure" grains were washed away. The slaves then collected the silver-rich grains which had "concentrated" at the beginning of the

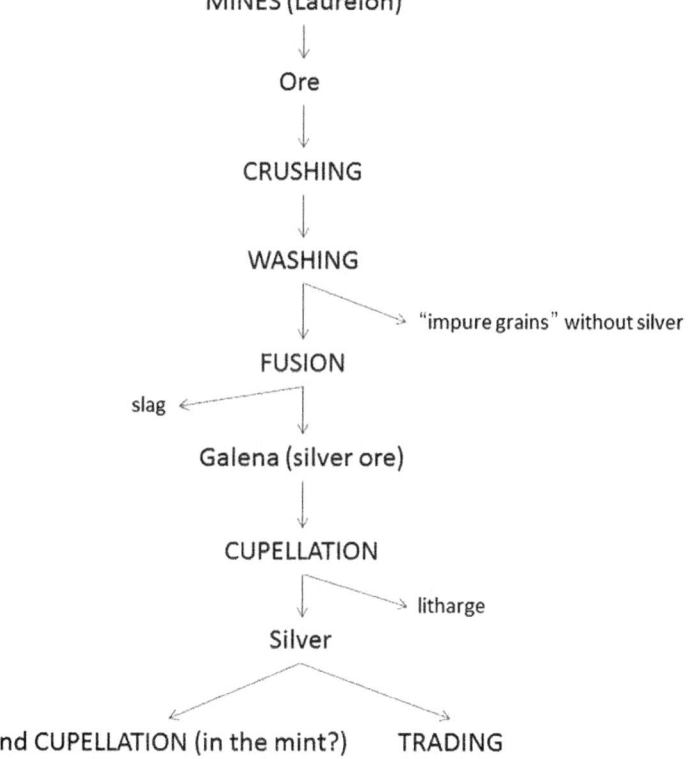

FIGURE 1.1: Mining process, simplified scheme after Conophagos 1980: 129. Marc Philipp Wahl.

stepped basin and brought them to the smelting furnaces (Conophagos 1980: 213–47, figs. 10–19).

Two further stages now came into play: fusion and cupellation. Fusion served to separate the galena (lead sulphide, PbS) from the ore. The ground and washed grains of ore were heated in large cylindrical ovens up to 4 meters high. These ovens could reach a temperature of around 950–1200°C. Galena and slag dripped from smelting furnaces provided with an opening that could be closed. When open, the metal flowed into a container positioned below. Given their different specific weights, lead and slag formed two layers which were easy to separate mechanically once they had set (Conophagos 1980: 274–8). After the galena—λίθος τοῦ ἀργύρου (silver stone, silver ore)—had been extracted, the next stage was cupellation, the process that separates silver from lead (Conophagos 1980: 305–30). The principle is simple, even though it was hard to achieve in practice. Lead, which is not a noble metal, oxidizes very quickly on contact with air. To achieve this separation a roofed furnace with openings was necessary to achieve and retain the required high temperature inside the domed structure. The furnace's construction ensured that lead reacted quickly with oxygen—it oxidized into lead oxide (litharge, PbO). This "burnt" layer, as it were, can easily be separated from the liquid metal with an iron rod because the lead oxide attaches to the colder iron pole. If this process is repeated several times, the amount of lead oxide gradually diminishes in the oven, leaving almost pure silver (Moesta and Franke 1995: 64–7; Ramage and Craddock 2000: 208–9).

This is but the first stage of cupellation. In a second stage, known as "refining," the metal that was previously extracted was put into a so-called cupel. This cupel had to be made of porous and heat-resistant material (e.g., ceramic with medium-sized pores). It absorbed the remaining lead in the heating process, leaving behind pure silver. When it cooled down, the thin and already-solid skin on the surface exploded, liberating gases within the still-liquid inside (rather like air bubbles in boiling water). This created small blisters or pustules on the surface (Moesta and Franke 1995: 67), which is why such pure silver was called *pustulatum* or *pusulatum* and why its abbreviation PS appeared on Late Roman coins. If refining of the silver is carried out correctly in the first place it is possible to skip the next stage, namely the casting of blanks. Presumably, this last stage took place in another workshop—perhaps at the mint itself.

The Laurion case documents all the stages in the production of silver in antiquity. It also documents a particularly interesting reaction on Athens's part when it lost its silver mines in the Peloponnesian War with Sparta (431–404 BCE). This loss took place in 413 BCE during the so-called Decelean War, when some 20,000 slaves, some specialized, deserted and joined the Spartan side (Thucydides 7.27.5). The exploitation of silver must have stopped almost completely (against this view cf. Treister 1996: 182–3). This was a blow of such magnitude that the Athenians eventually lost the war in 404 BCE. Indeed, the city was in such dire straits that it had to melt down several gold Nike statues from the Parthenon in 407/406 BCE (Philochorus, FGrH 328, F141a) to strike an emergency issue of gold coins; a few examples of these exceptional coins have survived. By 406/405 BCE the situation in Athens had not improved and the lack of silver forced the city to produce token money in silver-plated bronze coins. Several thousand such plated *drachms* and *tetradrachms* were found at the beginning of the twentieth century in the so-called Piraeus hoard; these coins were most probably struck with regular (official) dies (Aristophanes, *Ranae* 718–26; Flament 2007: 119–20). These plated coins, struck by Athens in an emergency, continued to be used up to about 394/393 BCE (Aristophanes, *Ecclesiazusae* 815–22).

Silver played a significant role in the Greek and Roman world. In the early days, however, coinage consisted of a valuable artificial alloy of naturally occurring gold and silver called "white gold" or, more commonly, electrum. Herodotus reports that in the reign of the Lydian king Croesus (561–547 BCE) gold and silver coins were struck separately for the first time (Herodotus 1.94.1) and the archaeological evidence appears to support the statement of the Greek historian (see Ramage and Craddock 2000). The Spanish mines yielded much gold and silver during the Roman Republic and Empire but also other base metals (Diodorus Siculus 5.36; Pliny, *Naturalis historia* 33.6.96; Polybius 3.57.3; further indications in Gozalbes and Ripollès 2002: 11). Ancient authors also mention the gold mines of Dalmatia; these produced enormous quantities of gold on a yearly basis from the time of Nero onwards (Pliny, *Naturalis historia* 33.67). Copper and brass were also of great importance for Roman coinage, at the latest since Augustan times. The relevant metals were exploited in mines located in Italy, Germany, Cyprus, and Gaul (Pliny, *Naturalis historia* 34.2; further indications in Szaivert and Wolters 2005: 213–15).

The Production of Blanks or Flans

There are at least six possible ways of producing flans (i.e., the coins' "blanks" Gozalbes and Ripollès 2002: 13–14). First, a coin that had already been struck could be recalled, hammered flat, heated, and then simply restruck. Because such a procedure was often executed fairly roughly, it is sometimes possible to recognize traces of such restriking. A group of Athenian *tetradrachms* exhibits a form of restriking; these so-called "folded flans" were first hammered flat and then folded (Kroll 2011; most recently, see Fischer-Bossert 2015 for Cyzicus). Second, a thin sheet of precious metal could be cut up into blanks with a metal-cutting tool, as was current among the Sasanians. Third, cylindrical blanks could be "sliced" from rod-shaped ingots.

Casting blanks was a more common method. Once again there are mainly three ways to do it. The first consist of using coin-molds or "pellet trays." The surface of the mold, usually made of clay, has rows of small depressions which received the exact amount of metal (in the form of small fragments or powder) which had previously been weighed out. Heating the precious metal melted it into a small ball. Such a procedure was used by the Celts, with excavations frequently yielding examples of such multiple molds (Militký 2015: 681–95). Small flans could be cast just by pouring the liquid metal onto a flat surface. The surface tension of the metal caused it to form into a small pellet, which could then be coined directly or hammered flat before being struck. With a little practice it was apparently possible to achieve the required weight. A third possibility was to fill a two-part mold, which had previously been provided with the depressions for the blanks, with liquid metal. After casting, this was split to remove the blanks; these formed a "tree" with hanging branches. The flans then had to be separated from their branches. The latter method was only used to produce blanks of non-precious metal.

The Production of Dies

We are fortunate that a few dies have survived from antiquity. William Malkmus (2007, based on Vermeule 1954) has published an extensive catalog of known dies accompanied by a discussion of their authenticity. The few genuine dies, mostly made of bronze, as well as details observable on the ancient coins themselves, provide some insights into the production of dies. Two different techniques can be reconstructed. Preliminary drawings on the die can be recognized on some of the resulting coins; the purpose of these drawings was to distribute the elements of the design as well as possible, given the constraints on space. Furthermore, there is no longer any doubt that positive models (male molds) were used in the manufacture of dies—in other words, a positive of the coin was created whose imprint onto the die was then reengraved. This is the only plausible explanation for the similarities, sometimes of minute details, exhibited by some dies (Göbl 1978: 52–3; Fischer-Bossert 1999: 405–7; Berthold 2013: 64–5). While there is evidence for such a technique among Greek coins, such clear evidence for the production of Roman coins seems to be missing so far.

It has long been known that the die-makers of antiquity modified their dies for a variety of reasons. This refers to the secondary modification of a die that had already been used in the manufacture of coins. Modifying a die saved time and materials. All phenomena observed in die production in antiquity can, in fact, be boiled down to three categories: modification, repair, and correction.

By *modification* we mean the intervention into a design and the resulting reworking of the die (see e.g. Hill 1922: 24–5). Gela, a *polis* on the coast of southern Sicily, provides a good example of a simple modification from Greek antiquity. At Gela the addition of letters to an already used die is documented in several instances; in one case the addition consists of the letters phi and iota (dated to the beginning of the fifth century BCE; Jenkins 1970: 121). Such modifications require little and make sense if the die is still in good condition. An equivalent light modification of a die exists for the time of Nero in the middle of the first century CE at the mint in Lyon. In this case the modification consists of deleting one element, not adding to it. An obverse die showing the busts of Nero and his mother Agrippina was first used to strike a very rare type of *aureus*, which also has an additional symbol on the obverse (e.g., RIC I^2 no. 3). Later, these dies were recut and reused to strike *denarii*; the latter exhibit a slight rise on the area which corresponds to where the additional symbol was erased (e.g., Robertson 1962, pl. 19, no. 2). However, if large parts of a die were cut out, then we are dealing with heavy modification of the image that it produced. This is the case of a die from the city of Sinope dated to the fourth century BCE (Robinson 1930: 9): large parts of the die were reworked, apparently by first hammering it flat and then carving it anew. Some oddities have also come to light in the coinage of the Roman provinces. A drachm from Alexandria dating to the time of Hadrian even shows a secondary manipulation, suspected to have been applied not on the die but on the hub, which must have been used to make the modified die. It was thus possible to recycle a tool, which could produce several new dies, with just a little work on the positive element (Milne 1922: 43–6).

The die eventually wore out through use, with smaller or larger breakages, and would require repairs. Another possible reason for repair may have been the presence of metal residues left on the die after striking and ultimately clogging it up. The late Archaic coins from Gela provide once again an example of such a practice: a die, dated to the early fifth century BCE, was recut (Jenkins 1970: 121), as attested by the thicker parts of the design on an otherwise unmodified die.

Small mistakes can also happen when making a die. If noticed at the mint itself, this would have led to *correction*. This usually affected the legend on a die, involving single words or letters that had been omitted. Good examples exist when coins were minted in great quantities, as in the Roman Republic. Crawford (1974: 458, no. 4b) refers to the case of a coin where the mention of the consulship (COS) had been forgotten and was only engraved later on the die, when some coins with the missing legend had already left the mint.

Coin Production and Minting Techniques

Following this overview of how blanks and dies were made and adapted, let us turn to the processes involved when minting coins. Few written sources shed light on how this was carried out in antiquity. An inscription dating to the reign of Trajan distinguishes between three groups of workers at the mint of

Rome: *suppostores* who laid the flans onto the lower die; *malliatores* who struck the coin; and *signatores* who were responsible for the die. Some figurative representations give us further information on the minting process, but they must be treated with the utmost caution because they simplify the procedure considerably. In the Coin Cabinet at the Kunsthistorisches Museum in Vienna there is a Late Roman (*c.* first half of the fourth century CE) *tessera* (token) on whose reverse a splendid representation of the minting process is depicted, complete with *malliator*, *suppostor*, and *signator* (see Figure 1.2). Another staged minting scene is also visible on a contorniate (medallion) featuring the name of Nero and dated to the late fourth century CE (Woytek 2013).

Dies are basically either upper or lower. While the latter were set into a fixed anvil, the upper dies were loose (see Figure 1.3). The upper die was thus subjected to stronger force and usually wore out more quickly than its lower counterpart. When large and heavy coins had to be struck, a single strike was often insufficient; the coin had to be struck several times. While it is attested that coins were struck cold in the Roman Empire it is not always clear whether the blanks were heated before striking or whether this was done cold in Greek times. A slight doubling-up of the contours of a coin can reveal that the flan had shifted slightly between strikes (this is called a double strike). It has been shown that when coins were continually produced en masse, the dies were in use for only a few months (in a few exceptional cases somewhat longer). In fact, during the Roman Empire, a die generally lasted just a few days (see von Kaenel 1986: 259–61). Its lifespan obviously depended on a variety of factors, including how

FIGURE 1.2: *Tessera* (token) struck at Rome(?), *c.* first half of the fourth century CE. Obverse: frontal view of a tetrastyle temple; between the columns the *tres monetae* with scale and cornucopias and small piles of coins at their feet; Reverse: representation of the minting process with three workers, the *malliator*, the *suppostor*, and the *signator*. (Vienna, Kunsthistorisches Museum inv. RÖ 032652).

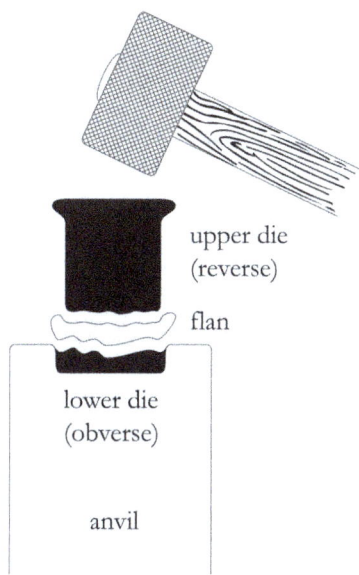

FIGURE 1.3: Striking coinage. Scheme of the minting process with lower die fixed in the immobile anvil (obverse), mobile upper die receiving the strike with the hammer (reverse) and flan in between. Marc Philipp Wahl.

hard the metal was, how large the flan was, and how pronounced the relief was. From this we can deduce that it was only the larger mints that could afford to produce coins on a permanent basis and that the smaller mints may have used their dies over several years (Mørkholm 1983).

Apart from the double striking of coins, further errors or peculiarities are worth noting. If the flan is not exactly centered between the die, it is described as "off center." In this case the image struck onto the flan shifts outwards. A so-called "blind spot" occurs quite often when thin flans are struck because the amount of relief on the obverse and reverse is greater than the thickness of the flan. This results in an incomplete image on the coin. An incuse striking (brockage) refers to a situation when a coin remains stuck on upper die. When the next coin is struck, the coin that remains on the die creates a negative image on the new coin. As for die axis, numismatists commonly use the term to describe the orientation of the upper and lower die; it is generally described like the face of a clock, for example 12 o'clock for a vertical position on the axis. Given that the two dies were not always fixed, it is often possible to identify local or regional patterns in the striking of coins (de Callataÿ 1997).

Another kind of mistake occurred when coins were struck on a lower (anvil) die, which bore two or more obverse types engraved next to each other. Sometimes the blanks were not well centered, thus the coins show on their obverses traces of a second obverse die. There only are few examples but the phenomenon is well known throughout Classical, Hellenistic, and Roman republican times. Two of those "multiple obverse dies" were found in two Celtic hoards in Germany (Woytek 2006).

THE ADMINISTRATION OF COINAGE

The choice of motif is a particularly complex topic in ancient numismatics involving a whole series of factors influencing the designs that appear on the obverse and reverse of the coins. The coins of Classical Greece featuring "simple designs" are frequently described by researchers as emblem-like—and in fact such a concept is often reflected in reality. Indeed, a surprisingly abundant body of written sources contains references to the types of coinage of a given *polis* and attempts at explaining them. The legend of Taras riding a dolphin recounted by Aristotle (Melville-Jones 1993: no. 656 = Pollux, *Onomasticon* 9.80 = Aristotle, *Fragment* 590, Rose) can be seen on designs on the coins of Tarent or, for the Lion of Miletus, in an epigram inscribed on a statue of a lion at Miletus and featuring on the coinage of this city (Melville-Jones 1993: no. 346 = SEG I 425). When cities minted coinage in substantial quantities the types of motifs often act as metaphors. So, for example, the *staters* of Corinth were known as *poloi* ("foals," because of the Pegasus motif on the obverse) and the *tetradrachms* of Athens as *glaukes* ("owls"). The so-called punning types go one step further, translating a city's name into a motif, as for example at Selinunt whose coins feature a leaf of parsley (*selinon* in Greek). While the examples given above represent motifs that have become fossilized on coins, there were many other *poleis* that strived to depict a variety of motifs; in fact, some may have preferred it, as at Cyzicus which constantly and frequently changed its designs. At Syracuse, during the fifth century BCE, the motifs on its *tetradrachms* remained a quadriga on the obverse and Arethusa on the reverse, but the arrangement of these motifs varied greatly, especially in the constantly changing hairstyle of the local nymph Arethusa. The examples of many Greek *poleis* in Roman times are impressive too: at a local and regional level they produced a very large number of different coin types depicting a multitude of different motifs (Howgego, Heuchert, and Burnett 2005).

Interplay with the economy is an important aspect determining the choice of motif. Currency zones oriented on a "leading currency" developed as early as in antiquity. The Athenian *tetradrachms* were particularly influential, as were the coins of Alexander the Great and the Late Roman *solidi* and *tremisses*, of which the Germanic tribes in the frontier zones repeatedly took account. The imitation of motifs on coins was not only dictated by economic concerns; surely their artistic value also played a part. Motifs that belong to the political sphere are especially eloquent—and researchers have mined this field with great determination even though they have far from exhausted its possibilities. At the core of these designs lie political events and representations of power, which—following Hellenistic models—became particularly important in the Roman Empire. Given the increasingly unchallenged supremacy of its coinage built up since Republican times, the Empire could afford to dispense with an image-based legitimation of its currency directed to the outside and instead emphasize the communicative components of representation and the propagation of Roman ideals on its coins (Hill 1906; Howgego 1995; Wolters 2003b; Noreña 2011a).

The Management of Mints

When a large quantity of coins was being struck at a given mint, several workshops (*officinae*) were used rather than one single anvil. Such an organizational structure is documented when coins were mass-produced in the Classical and Hellenistic period (e.g., in Syracuse under the Deinomenids in the first half of the fifth century BCE) but it is also highly relevant for the Imperial Roman and Late Roman periods. A multiple workshop system becomes visible from the middle of the third century CE onwards, because from then on marks and numbers on the coins themselves indicate which of the many mints in the Empire and which *officina*, in this particular mint, produced the coins. A *solidus* of the emperor Constantius II (reigned 337–61 CE) illustrates the model that underpins the marks and symbols that figure on it (see Figure 1.4). On the

FIGURE 1.4: *Solidus* of Constantius II (337–61 CE), struck at Antiochia, c. 347–55 CE. Obverse: draped and cuirassed bust of the Emperor right with pearl-diadem, FL IVL CONSTAN-TIVS PERP AVG; Reverse: Roma with spear head facing and Constantinopolis with scepter and foot on prow turned left both enthroned, supporting a shield, therein VOT/XX/MVLT/XXX, GLORIA-REI-PVBLICAE, in exergue SMANΔ. (RIC VIII, p. 518, 83; Vienna, Kunsthistorisches Museum inv. RÖ 27832).

reverse, in exergue we find the letters S M AN Δ which stand for *sacra moneta Antiochensis (officina) quarta* (i.e., the fourth workshop of the Antioch mint). Such indications—originally intended for quality control—give us an insight into the organization of the mints. In addition, the *Notitia dignitatum* provides an overview of the administration of the Empire in late antiquity: each of the many mints operating in the Empire was overseen by a *procurator monetarum* who answered to the *comes sacrarum largitionum*. A central administration was responsible for the production of the coinage emanating from each mint (van Heesch 2012). In Republican times the management of the mints was in the hands of the *tresviri monetales* or, more precisely, of the *tresviri aere argento auro flando feriundo*. This three-member college was an established state office in the Roman Republic and its tenure was limited to a year. During the second half of the second century BCE these mint-masters acquired more influence over the images featuring on the coins and began to inscribe them not only with their names but also with motifs that referred to their ancestors.

With their multiplicity of cities and rulers minting coins, conditions in Classical and Hellenistic Greece are similar only at first glance. Here, too, the coins often bear the names of individuals, but it is rarely clear in what capacity these people appeared on the coins. Scholars have favored four interpretations, listed here: people commissioned with the task of issuing coins, eponymous magistrates, liturgies, and engravers. By consciously or unconsciously drawing an analogy with the Roman Republic, current research often interprets the personal names on coins as referring to the individuals who were contracted to strike coins, the so-called "mint officials." But this is problematic since we have no evidence that the Archaic and Classical *poleis* had well-established administrative roles such as those of the *tresviri monetales*. We must assume that, at the mints that did not produce large quantities of coins, contractors were commissioned on an *ad hoc* basis. There is often convincing evidence for eponymous magistrates like *strateges* or *archontes* on coins struck by a league such as the Thessalian or Boeotian leagues, where the eponymous *strategos* appears in the genitive form and the contractor in the nominative. The liturgies of antiquity refer to financial contributions to the common good by private individuals (e.g., the funding and upkeep of a trireme in Athens). Was the minting of coins financed by private individuals so that their name could figure on these coins? This hypothesis has, surely rightly, been met with skepticism on the part of researchers since it rests on an erroneous interpretation of the inscription of Menas in Setos (see above). As for the die-makers, they proudly signed their work in a few exceptional cases. These artists are known mainly from the end of the fifth century BCE and appear in abbreviated form (such as Ai in Lirisa and Trikka, or Simo in Larisa) and more rarely in full (e.g., Kimon or Euainetos in Sicily or Pythodoros in Crete) (Furtwängler 1982; de Callataÿ 2012a).

A set of dedicatory inscriptions on statues provides a snapshot of the management of a mint in Rome. Three statue bases were discovered in 1556 in front of the church of San Clemente on the Caelian Hill in Rome, where the Roman mint was located after the fire of Rome in 64 CE (Coarelli 1994: 47–50; Burnett 2001: 41). There were three separate dedications: one to Apollo (CIL VI 42), one to Fortuna Augusta (CIL VI 43), and one to Hercules Augustus (CIL VI 44). All three inscriptions name workers at the Roman mint, with CIL VI 44 being the most informative. It dates to the reign of Trajan and the dedication took place on 28 January, 115 CE (a most meticulous study can be found in Woytek 2013; see also R.-Alföldi 1958/9; Wolters 1999: 85–99; Woytek 2010: 45–55; Woytek 2012a: 100–17).

An *optio et exactor auri argenti (et) aeris* was responsible for running the mint in Trajanic times. His duties were most probably rather technical-administrative and served to control the mint's output. In the hierarchy he stood below the *procurator monetae*, a mint official from the *ordo equester* who himself answered to the *a rationibus* (Woytek 2013: 255–6). The latter was the finance administrator from the private household of the emperor and was in close contact with him (Wolters 1999: 87; Herz 2003). The *tresviri monetales* mentioned earlier may have played a role in the administration of the mint given that they are known from inscriptions up to the third century CE (Sutherland 1976: 9, 13). How the responsibilities were shared out between the *procurator monetae* and the young *tresviri monetales* is unclear.

Felix, a former slave freed by the emperor, is mentioned in the Trajanic inscriptions as an *optio et exactor auri argenti (et) aeris* of the mint; in the CIL VI 43 inscription he stands next to Albanus, another *optio*, and presumably his deputy; sixteen freed slaves called *officinatores monetae aurariae argentariae Caesaris nostri* and a further nine slaves are listed. The CIL VI 44 provides indirect but significant insights into the workings of the mint (see illustration in Instinsky 1962: pls. 5–6). Felix figures on the front of the statue base; on one side sixty-three names of freed slaves and slaves are listed in four columns, probably in hierarchical order. The *signatores* are listed first (seventeen, including two slaves), then the *suppostores* (eleven, including four slaves) and finally the *malliatores* (thirty-two, including twenty-one slaves) close the list of dedicators (three men are listed without a function; for a table giving an overview see Woytek 2012a: 102). While the terms for the *malliatores* ("hammerers") and *suppostores* ("setters" of the blanks onto the lower die) are easy to grasp from a philological viewpoint, the exact meaning of the *signatores* has long been debated (see Woytek 2013: 261–4 and Instinsky 1962: 44–50). These workers were originally, and often since, taken to be the die-makers. But, since these die-makers had already been designated *sculptores*, it is likely that the *signatores* of the inscription are workers that were responsible for the die and operated the movable upper die after the *suppostores* had placed the flan over the lower die; thereupon the *malliatores* could strike. This apparently fine division of labor in the Trajanic inscription could no doubt be fleshed out further. For example, we know that blowers also operated in mints in Athens in the fifth century BCE (SEG X 394–5 = Melville-Jones 1993: no. 516). All this leads to the conclusion that there was a high degree of specialization in the mints of antiquity.

Transport

There was no specialized system for distributing money in antiquity as exists today, with banks or private firms acting on behalf of central banks. The state had to rely on other means. Here, we shall focus mainly on conditions in Roman Republican and Imperial times. Money—whether in the form of ingots or coins—moved in different ways and for a variety of reasons. Yet we observe time and again that the physical transport of money was avoided. Not only was it expensive and logistically challenging but it was also dangerous (Wolters 2006: 33–4; 49). Of course, it could not be avoided altogether.

At the end of the Second Punic War in 201 BCE, Carthage was bound for fifty years to send at its own expense 10,000 talents of silver to Rome (Polybius 15.18.7, and Livy 30.37.5). The way this payment was to be made, however, remained open. There was a similar situation in Athens at the time of the Delian League in the fifth century BCE. Because the treasury of the league had been in Athens since 454 BCE, the tributes of the members of the league were sent there in large containers (de Callataÿ 2006b). In Roman Republican and Imperial times, the end of a successful military campaign was marked by a triumph where the booty was paraded in the open. This booty—which included precious metal in coinage and in other forms—was brought to the state treasury, the *aerarium*, in the temple of Saturn on the Forum (references in Szaivert and Wolters 2005: 141–9). In Republican times it was also the custom to bring the taxes and revenue from the provinces to the *aerarium*. But even then, the practice was used not only to nominally record surpluses in Rome but also to let a neighboring province benefit if it was in urgent need of funds (Wolters 2006: 44–6). The physical transport of money to Rome could thus be avoided.

The supply of newly minted money to the market was one of the core functions of the Roman administration. While larger and valuable coins of gold and silver could be put into circulation as *donativa* for the troops and *congiaria* for the urban population of Rome, to pay the city's officials or to honor contracts for public building works, smaller denominations that had a comparatively smaller purchasing power (but were all the more important for day-to-day transactions) were probably distributed to the population in the form of *sportulae* (small donations) (van Heesch 2009). Private retailers and *publicani* may have played a role not only in terms of financial cooperation but also in the distribution of small change (Wolters 2006: 41–4; van Heesch 2009). Trade was very active in the legionary camps and especially around them, in the *canabae*. Indeed, the degree of monetarization in the regions where the military was stationed grew markedly. Small denominations made of non-precious metal were particularly needed for such transactions. Sometimes, although not always, the state took its responsibilities and supplied military camps with small change apparently *en bloc*; this is the case of Nijmegen in the Netherlands where *quadrantes* of Domitian were sent to this Roman legionary camp (Kemmers 2003; 2006: 147–65).

Today, it is common practice that the production of one country's currency is contracted to the mint of another country. Some African nations but also European states have recourse to this (e.g., in the nineteenth century the first Swiss coins were minted in Paris and Brussels). Therefore, it is not surprising that the Rome mint also followed this procedure at various times. An example in the first century CE sees Rome producing coinage for circulation in Syria and transporting it there; it consists of *tetradrachms* of Attic standard (i.e., not Roman nominals). A similar case is recorded in the third century CE under Philip I (244–9 CE) (Butcher 2004: 248–9, pls. 20–1; Baldus 1969: 27–9).

Quantification

Even though every single ancient coin is a hand-made artefact it is nevertheless a mass-produced item, as has been made clear above. It is, therefore, not surprising that numismatic research has focused for some time on questions of quantification. While most early attempts were methodologically flawed, so never became established, some new methodological approaches offer a better basis for quantification; one such approach will be briefly presented here.

The method that consists of estimating the volume of coins issued based on the dies used is widely accepted today. Studies focusing on the dies are of particular importance in this respect: it is often apparent that two (or more) different coins had been struck by the same die. When compiling a corpus of dies, the coins manufactured by a given mint are collected as exhaustively as possible and evaluated as to whether some have been produced from the same dies. This painstaking, but rewarding, examination makes it possible to obtain a good overview of the work of a mint; because of the immense effort involved, such studies tend to focus on less widespread coins. It is particularly in Greek numismatics that the method of critically evaluating the dies is widely applied. For quantification this means that a robust number of dies can be exploited from such corpora. The so-called Carter formula (Carter 1983; Esty 1986; most recently Moens 2014) posits that the number of surviving coins, and hence the dies detectable through them, allow us to calculate approximately the total number of dies. But the question of roughly how many coins a given die could have produced until it went out of use is a subject of lively debate in numismatic research (Buttrey and Buttrey 1997; de Callataÿ 2005, 2006a). The oft-quoted range of around 10,000 to 40,000 exemplars per obverse die rests on shaky foundations and is far from proven. The only robust evidence comes from Delphi, where an inscription mentions the quantity of silver to be struck. Thus, research should account for a degree of fluctuation—owed to numismatic as well as epigraphic issues—ranging between *c*. 14,350 (Marchetti 1999) or 23,333 and 47,250 coins per die (Kinns 1983).

METALLURGY, COUNTERFEITS, AND RECEPTION

A basic distinction must be made between contemporary counterfeits (i.e., fraudulent issues made at the time the coins were issued) and modern forgeries. Here we shall focus exclusively on counterfeiting (i.e., attempts at deceit in antiquity). What kinds of counterfeits are known from antiquity and how was this counterfeiting done? According to Isidore of Seville (Isidorus, *Etymologiae* 16.18.12 = Melville-Jones 1993: no. 1) a coin's significance is judged under three headings: metal, appearance, and weight ("In coinage three things are sought: metal, design and weight. If one of these is missing, it is not a coin"). Peter van Alfen (2005) thus developed a fine-grained typology resting on these three elementary categories and based on examples from Classical and Hellenistic times. Not all cases that fit into one of his categories are counterfeits. But let us see what these basic cases are.

Imitation is a process whereby mint B adopts a design based on a model issued by mint A. Such imitations vary widely in terms of diversity and intensity, ranging from simple inspiration to total takeover, including the smallest detail. Studying the few literary sources available and observing the practice of coin circulation allows us to conclude that there was no objection to such imitation as long as the metal and the weight corresponded to a "good coin." But if the metal content or the weight of a coin were modified, it was a different matter.

Such so-called "debased" coins do not contain the full amount of metal required but have been mixed with another metal of lesser value. A mint can thus profit significantly from such a modification in metal content. This procedure was frequently employed in Roman Imperial times (see Butcher and Ponting 2014 on the development of silver *denarii* in the first century CE). By the end of the second and in the third century CE the quantity of silver contained in *denarii* and *antoniniani* (i.e., double *denarii*) had sunk to a very low proportion (as little as 2.5 percent)—but coins retained their silver appearance thanks to a blanching treatment. This process—known as "depletion silvering" whereby the copper on the surface was first oxidized and then removed in an acid bath (e.g., vinegar)—produced an enrichment of the silver on the surface. When struck, the surface became compact, closing the pores left by the oxidized copper and the coin thus exhibited a shiny silver "coat."

Achieving the appearance of a full-value coin was also behind the practice of plating; plated coins have an iron or, more frequently, a copper core (*anima*), which is then coated with a layer of precious metal. Whether the state issued plated coins is a subject of much debate (e.g., Crawford 1968 classified all Republican plated coins in the category of private counterfeits). An "official" emission is without any doubt a whole series of subaerate coins found among the Samnite tribes in and around Campania like the Hyriani and Fenserni in the fourth century BCE. As they are closely linked to full-value coins and were clearly issued by the mint of Neapolis, they are official in character (Rutter 1979).

Private counterfeiting was punishable in antiquity, sometimes severely. It was not just the issuing of false money (*adulterare*) that was punished, but the modification of officially struck money: writing in the third century CE, the Roman lawyer Paulus (*Sententiae* 5.25.1) refers to the "washing" (*lavare*) of money—meaning that the coins were dipped in a solution to dissolve some of the metal—melting it down (*conflare*), filing it down (*radere*), corrupting it (*corrumpere*) and generally making it defective (*vitiare*). The words chosen by Paulus depend largely on the *lex Cornelia de falsis* of Republican times which has not survived. The few Greek sources that describe the practice from Archaic to Hellenistic times (e.g., the well-known anecdote that the father of the philosopher Diogenes the Cynic was exiled from Sinope because of counterfeiting) refer to punishment as either exile or execution (Melville-Jones 1993: nos. 523–4, 529–30, 534). We are better informed for the Roman Empire and late antiquity. Three important traits are apparent: the modification of coins attracted higher penalties than their imitation; it seems that only gold and silver coinage was protected by law, there being no mention of bronze coinage; for a long time counterfeiting was not included among the five offences that warranted capital punishment (*quinque crimina quae capite vindicantur*), a change that was only implemented under Theodosius II (Grierson 1956; Wolters 1999: 361–71). A look at the sources further indicates that it was the workers in the mints that were mainly suspected, illustrated for example by the important coinage contract between Phocaea and Mytilene (Melville-Jones 1993: no. 348 = IG XII 2.1; see Bodenstedt 1981: 29–33) or the passage in *De rebus bellicis* 3 containing an unusual yet amusing suggestion to transfer a mint and its workers in whole to an island.

Private counterfeiting can be identified in a few instances, but it was of a quasi-official nature because coinage was badly needed for small transactions. The so-called *limes falsa*, which were issued in the frontier zone of the Germanic and Norican kingdoms to preserve the currency needed for local transactions, are an example of such a practice. A workshop dedicated to the production of counterfeits and dated to between 195 and 210 CE was excavated in the center of the ancient *colonia* of Augusta Raurica on the Rhine (Peter 1990; Foraboschi 2006; Pfisterer 2007).

The Users' Response

> ... ancient authors often succeed in hopelessly confusing matters to do with monetary history.
>
> —Rutter 1993: 188

For the Classical period, the coinage issued by the tyrant Anaxilas, who ruled over Rhegion and Messana (Reggio Calabria and Messina in southern Italy and Sicily) in the fifth century BCE, constitutes a particularly impressive example, providing us with an insight into how ancient authors reacted to the images on coins. During his rule over the two towns, Anaxilas minted *tetradrachms* featuring a leaping hare on the obverse and a mule biga on the reverse (see Figure 1.5). We have at our disposal a series of works penned by Aristotle and his pupils concerned with the constitution of various Greek city-states—but unfortunately these *Constitutions* survive mostly only as fragments; nevertheless, they indicate that the designs on the coins and their origin attracted particular attention. This was the case for Rhegion, where we are told: "Anaxilas of Rhegium, since Sicily was barren of hares until that time, imported and bred them. And because at that time he won an Olympic victory with a chariot drawn by mules, he placed as a type on the coinage of Rhegium a mule-cart and a hare" (Melville-Jones 1993: no. 652 = Pollux, *Onomasticon* 5.75 = Aristotle, *Fragment* 568, Rose). While the interpretation of the team of mules is early evidence that coins were clearly used as means of representing power, the explanation offered for the hares is hardly convincing. Indeed, it is highly

FIGURE 1.5: *Tetradrachm* of Messana (Messina, Sicily), *c.* 478–476 BCE. Obverse: biga of mules right, in exergue olive(?) leaf; Reverse: Hare springing right, MESSEN—ION (S and N retrograde). (SNG ANS IV, 314–320; Vienna, Kunsthistorisches Museum inv. GR 6590).

unlikely that Anaxilas introduced hares to Sicily. Aristotle probably misinterpreted his source, his text having been written a good century-and-a-half after the introduction of this type of coin.

There are *asses* of Emperor Nero (reigned 54–68 CE) showing on their reverse an image of Apollo Citharoedus singing and accompanying himself with his *cithara* (see Figure 1.6). The biographer Suetonius reports that this representation of Apollo was understood to represent Nero: "he suspended the sacred crowns in his chamber, about his beds, and caused statues of himself to be erected in the attire of a harper, and had his likeness stamped upon the coin in the same dress" (Suetonius, *Nero* 25.2). Nero is highly unlikely to have chosen this motif, which is unusual for a ruler; rather, some other official must have done so. We can assume that Nero approved this choice, since many different dies showing this design have survived from the mints of Rome and Lyon, suggesting that the coins were minted in considerable quantities. The fact that this motif was chosen specifically for one of the small denominations, the *as*, is significant. We can thus conclude that it was taken for granted at the beginning of the second century CE—when Suetonius was writing—that the image of Apollo Citharoedus (*cithara*-strumming) represented Nero.

A type of coin issued by the Late Roman emperor Julian (known as Julian the Apostate) was also much noticed by his contemporaries. After his comprehensive reform of coinage in early 363 CE the emperor surprised his subjects with a double *maiorina*. A standing bull with two stars above features on the reverse of these large bronze coins (see Figure 1.7); the legend SECVRITAS REI PVB(licae), which refers to the ruler's care for the good of the state, accompanies

FIGURE 1.6: *As* of the Emperor Nero (54–68 CE), struck at Rome, *c.* 64 CE. Obverse: laureate bust of the Emperor right, NERO CLAVDIVS CAESAR AVG GERMANICVS; Reverse: *Apollo Citharoedus* advancing right with *cithara* and plectrum, PONTIF MAX—TR POT IMP PP. (RIC I², p. 160, 122, Copenhagen: Royal Coll. of Coins and Medals, The National Museum of Denmark inv. Nero 356).

FIGURE 1.7: Double *maiorina* of Julian (360–3 CE), struck at Sirmium (Sremska Mitrovica, Serbia), *c.* 361–3 CE. Obverse: draped and cuirassed bust of the Emperor with pearl-diadem right, DN FL CL IVLI–ANVS PR AVG; Reverse: Bull standing right, above two stars, SECVRITAS REI PVB, in exergue BSIRM. (RIC VIII, p. 392, 107; Vienna, Institut für Numismatik und Geldgeschichte inv. 4271).

the design. Julian's political program was focused on reversing the so-called Constantinian shift, a reversal of policy that was widely rejected among Christians. The Christians issued numerous pamphlets against the emperor— even the new type of coin with its unusual representation of the bearded emperor was criticized and subjected to cruel mockery. Ephrem the Syrian, who lived at the time of Julian, sought to equate the bull with the Golden Calf (*Hymns* I *contra Iulianum* 16–9) and the church historian Socrates of Constantinople claimed that the bull was a symbol of the many pagan bull sacrifices the emperor made (Socrates, *Historia ecclesiastica* 3.17). Julian explicitly countered such propaganda, and things came to a head at Antioch (Julian, *Misopogon* 355 D). There is still no consensus in modern numismatic research about the interpretation of the bull (Gilliard 1964; Szidat 1981; Ehling 2005/6). The coins of Julian with bull design illustrate that imagery was open to debate already in antiquity and that the intended message was either not understood or willfully misunderstood.

CHAPTER TWO

Money and its Ideas

State Control and Military Expenses

FRANÇOIS DE CALLATAŸ

Coinage, *stricto sensu*, appeared in Western Asia Minor in the last third of the seventh century BCE when the area was under the domination of the Lydian kingdom. In many respects, it was a further step in an already long tradition. For millennia, precious metals had been treated in Mesopotamia or in Egypt as advantageous commodities for any kind of exchange. Coinage, however, was a revolution since coins (i.e., standardized lumps struck with an official stamp guaranteeing the weight and the alloy) no longer needed to be weighed but could instead be counted. For this change to take place, an issuing authority powerful enough to create trust in instruments accepted as having a fixed and known value was required.

This chapter will focus on the fortune of this great invention, one of the few ancient ones which still shape our world, with a special emphasis on the peculiarities of the Greco-Roman world—especially the period characterized by high-level economic performance (*c*. 250 BCE–*c*. 200 CE). This chapter constantly tries to keep with the main scheme or pure type Idealtypus). As such, it cannot avoid reducing reality, which was much more subtle and diverse. It leaves aside many aspects (mostly concerning coin circulation and economic integration: on this see first Howgego 1994) to concentrate on what is deliberately assumed as a Weberian *Ideal-Type*.

WHO? A HIGHLY STATE-CONTROLLED PROCESS

In comparison with Medieval or Modern times, coinages struck during Greco-Roman times appear to have been highly controlled by strong issuing powers leaving little place, if any, for individuals, families or the socio-economic groups responsible for producing them. Minds have symptomatically changed: we no longer believe that the so-called *Wappenmünzen* display the badges of prominent Athenian families (second half of the sixth century BCE) and few will still support the idea that the first electrum coinage (last third of the seventh century BCE) was invented by merchants trying to maximize their profits.

In the Greek world, there was *no free minting* allowing private individuals to convert their precious metals at a state mint for a fee, as was the practice in Venice for example (Stahl 2000). However, we will discuss some exceptional cases such as the rare mine districts (Athens [Laurion] and Southern Thrace [Pangean mines]).

Out of the *c*. 1,000 classical cities recorded in the Greek classical world by the *Polis* project (Copenhagen), about one-half never struck coins; of those who did, only a tiny percentage did it on any kind of regular scale. Most of them issued in a very sporadic way, often only once or twice over many centuries. Such a pattern is clear with respect to Roman provincial issues, which are precisely dated. For Roman Imperial issues, monetary production was so centralized that it left no opportunity for the average citizen of the Empire to go to a mint to convert precious metals into coins. In addition, monetary production is likely to have been systematically performed by public issuers and not, as a rule, delegated to private contractors, at least for gold and silver. There are a couple of major exceptions for bronze: when economic markets grew in central Italy from about 150 BCE to the time of Augustus, it sparked a growing and unmet demand for small change. This led to the issue of imitative coinages, such as the Pompeian pseudo-mint, and many non-state informal bronze issues, as well as the use and even importation of foreign change, sometimes displaying what looks like unofficial iconography (*fornicator*, strigils) (Stannard 2005; Stannard and Frey-Kupper 2008; Frey-Kupper and Stannard forthcoming).

Another common feature of the Greco-Roman world in great contrast with Medieval and Modern Europe is *the absence of clipping*. Coins were not clipped by greedy users to make a profit (the only example of such a practice is Late Roman Britain but it has been argued that this was done at a public level, Guest 2005). Quite the opposite, the content of many Greek and Roman hoards proves that worn coins could circulate, sometimes for centuries, alongside fresh ones. It has been calculated that tetradrachms (i.e. large silver coins, in the name of Alexander) lost *c*. 0.035g per century but continued to circulate for 150 years (Delamare 1994: 177; 183). Actually, we are not informed about any issuing power recalling old coins back to the mint because they were too light (but the absence of proof is no certain proof of the absence, since such a technical measure is unlikely to be reported by literary sources).

When compared to Modern Europe, coin circulation in the Greco-Roman world appears much more controlled and less open, with only a small percentage of mixed hoards combining coins issued on various weight standards. Gresham's law (better called "Copernicus' law"), "bad money drives out good," was not so much a reality in the Greco-Roman world as in Medieval and Modern contexts (de Callataÿ 2006). The free choice of users in monetary concurrency may be qualified as feeble in Greco-Roman times.

An additional argument for characterizing Greco-Roman coinages as highly controlled by strong issuing structures is provided by the production of bronze coins (i.e. coins with a high fiduciary value, on a grand scale). This necessarily implies the capacity of the issuing powers to create a high level of confidence for their coins and their use within the restricted polity of the issuing authority. From a third-century BCE inscription of Gortyna (Crete, SIG^3 I 525), we know that the introduction of bronze coins sometimes provoked turmoil in a population which was not ready to accept these grossly over-priced tokens. None the less, bronze fiduciary coinages are a main characteristic of the Greco-Roman world as well as the Byzantine, in stark contrast to the Merovingian, Carolingian, and/or Medieval periods, not to mention much of Modern times. Put into perspective, as far as trust (*pistis* in Greek, *fides* in Latin) is indeed the ultimate foundation of financial matters, the results achieved by the Greco-Roman world seem remarkable. It was a world where coins were mostly accepted as legal tender within the boundaries of the issuing power.

WHY? TO MATCH STATE EXPENDITURES (FIRST MILITARY EXPENDITURES) . . . AND MAKE A PROFIT

Most mainstream economists still believe that coinage was invented to replace barter and to facilitate transactions. They were encouraged by Aristotle himself who explains that coinage ("nomisma" in Greek, coming from "nomos", the law) was created as a conventional standard to measure the price of any commodity or service. There are two key passages where he explains his ideas using the example of a farmer and a shoemaker trying to exchange their products (Aristotle, *Ethica Nicomachea* 5.5.10-16 = 1133a–b and Aristotle, *Politica* 1.3.12-17 = 1257a–b). In *Politics*, he wrote: "Once coinage has been invented because of the need of exchange" (transl. Melville Jones 1993: 13). Economists took this statement for granted and integrated it into a general theory of money, disagreeing about who was originally responsible: private individuals, as proposed by Carl Menger (1892), or the state, as argued by Georg Friedrich Knapp (1905). For numismatists, however, while such a statement is highly significant about the perception of coinage in the second half of the fourth century BCE, this is to confuse cause and effect.

Working with literary sources, some cultural historians have argued in favor of a link between coinage and democracy, not so much in their intentions as in their consequences. Before the invention of coinage, richness was fundamentally visible and made by real property. As illustrated by the theme of *aphanes ousia* (the invisible property, Gabrielsen 1986) recurrent in the orations of Isokrates (436–338 BCE), coins modified the rules. Precious metals could be accumulated by self-made men, sometimes arising out of the aristocratic circles where these metals were confined so far. This is, in principle, true but, despite a good deal of wishful thinking, it remains difficult to prove a link between coinages and democracy (despite Seaford 2004).

Turning to numismatics, another picture emerges. We need first to clearly distinguish between the initial purpose (the first beneficiaries) and the subsequent uses (the secondary beneficiaries). The question "Why was coinage invented?" is to consider its initial purpose, a question that has received different answers over the course of time. As most Greek coins display a religious iconography, it was long believed that coinage was created in the precincts of temples (cf. Burgon 1837; Curtius 1870), so that the fiduciary share of these means of exchange could be guaranteed by gods and goddesses. Later on, and for most of the twentieth century, it was implicitly (more than explicitly) considered that coinages were naturally issued to facilitate economic transactions: heavy coins in precious metals for external trade, small denominations and bronze coinages for daily purchases.

This way of thinking has been severely challenged by modern scholarship. Chronologies have been tightened and the size of issues has been estimated, with the result that for many Greek coins, much-more-condensed periods of minting have become evident than were previously supposed. This creates a structural difficulty for any explanation of coinage as issued for economic purposes in so far as it does not fit with regular long-term activities such as trade and free minting, but also regular civic expenses such as the payment of jurors or building and maintaining public buildings.

Military expenditures first

What was already pretty obvious to the Romans became clearer for the Greeks: coinages were primarily struck for military purposes. This should not surprise us. Before the recent advent of the welfare state (really implemented only in the first half of the twentieth century), military expenditures have always been— and by far—the most expensive item in any civic or state budget. So, to link coinages with state expenditure is to link coinages with military expenditure. This is not to say that these were the only expenditure or that no other issues played a significant role (Howgego 1990) but, proportionally, they generally dwarfed all the others. Estimates vary for Imperial Rome in 150 or 215 CE, but even the less-generous attribute more than 70 percent of all expenditures to the army (Duncan Jones 1994: 45). The same proportion is found when looking at the revenue stratagems evoked in the second book of the *Economics* by pseudo-Aristotle in the last quarter of the fourth century BCE (de Callataÿ 2000: 346–7).

Not all the expenditure was paid in coins, even less in fresh coins. For the Ptolemies or the Seleucids, coin production approximated to only a tiny fraction (1/40 or 1/80) of their annual expenses (Le Rider and de Callataÿ 2006). While it remains difficult to estimate how far state payments were monetized, the evidence strongly points to a privileged link between coins and the army.

First, large-scale coin issues, as a rule, are linked with conflicts. To quote a few: the Second Punic War (c. 218–201 BCE) and the Social War (c. 91–87 BCE) for Republican Rome; the generational cycle of wars initiated by Alexander the Great (c. 334–301 BCE) and the Mithradatic wars (c. 89–71 BCE) in Hellenistic times, or the fifth and fourth century BCE conflicts in Sicily between Greek tyrants or cities and the Carthaginians. It is hard, then, not to link the absolute peak in Athenian production during the second half of the fifth century with the Peloponnesian War (c. 431–404 BCE) (on Athenian coinage and war, see now Pritchard 2015).

Second, if we turn to the details, possibly the best case study ever for ancient coinages is provided by the coins of Mithradates Eupator, king of Pontus (120–63 BCE), which, exceptionally, are dated by year and month. It turns out that the rhythm of their production entirely matches the various conflicts Eupator fought against the Romans (see Figure 2.1). To focus on the major operations (although other issues are strongly connected with military purposes), Eupator armed shortly before he invaded Bithynia at the end of spring 89 BCE. Defeated by Sulla, he none the less managed an honorable exit, forcing him to pay his troops in the autumn of 85 BCE. The emerging pattern is a commander-in-chief who struck coins before and after the war, not during. The third and last war offers a different example. As shown in the graph

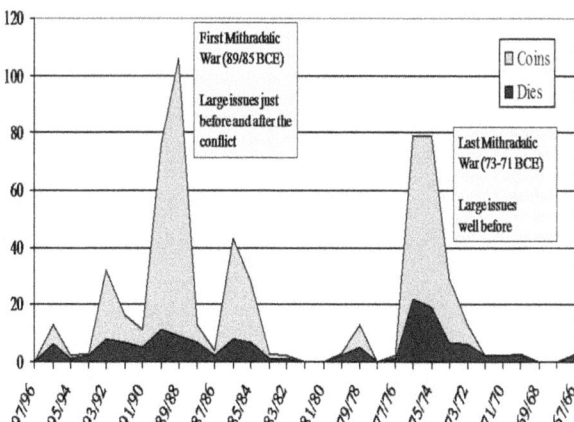

FIGURE 2.1: Recorded numbers of coins and dies for the dated *tetradrachms* of Mithradates of Pontus (de Callataÿ 1997; 2014).

(Figure 2.1), Eupator made intensive preparations years before to invade Bithynia again in spring 73 BCE. This time, defeated on the battlefield, he fled to Cimmerian Bosporus and left his troops unpaid.

Third, coin circulation for precious metals often argues for a military purpose. Out of some 5,000 recorded Greek coin hoards, nearly one-tenth (*c*. 400—a unique phenomenon) are for the late Hellenistic tetradrachms struck in the name of the inhabitants of Thasos and Maroneia. Recovered in large quantity in modern Bulgaria and Romania, these coins have long been interpreted as civic coinages related to trade (slaves, wine, or furs). They are now firmly recognized as the tool used by the Romans to pay their Thracian auxiliaries (de Callataÿ 2009). In addition, their absolute and relative numbers (with a strong overrepresentation of round-numbered sets of twenty, forty or two hundred coins) suggest that they were immediately buried back home, kept as a reserve of value, and saw little use in domestic markets. For the Roman Empire, Keith Hopkins famously modelled a "recycling machine" in which coins were struck in Rome or Lyon and immediately sent to the garrisons on the borders of the empire (Hopkins 1980). Some coin distribution maps dramatically illustrate this pattern (see Figure 2.2). This argues both for the military connection and for the limited circulation of these issues.

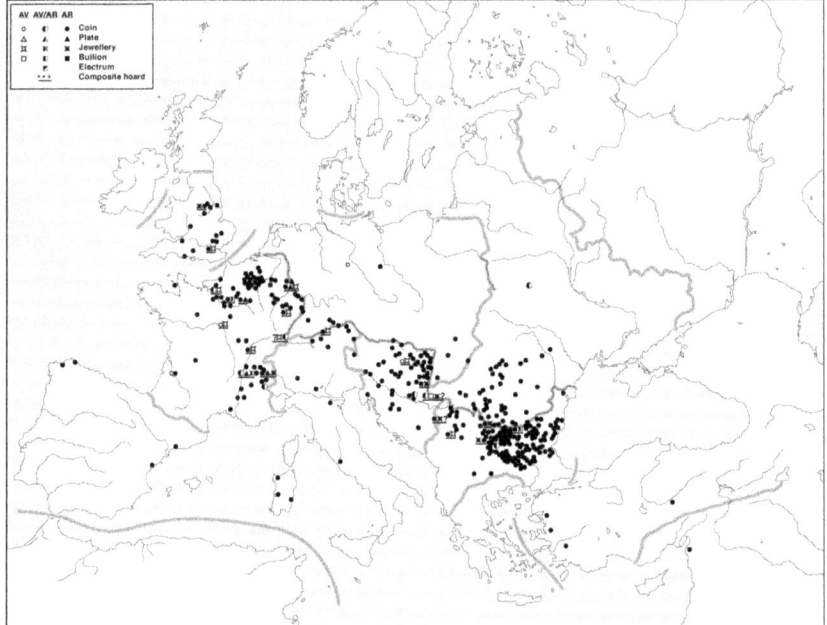

FIGURE 2.2: Precious metals deposits for the years 238–59 CE (Hobbs 2006; Bland 2013: 225).

Compared with the Roman Empire, the military purpose of coinage is less clear for the Greeks due to the smokescreen of hundreds of civic coinages which were long taken as a mark of political autonomy related, implicitly or not, to some economic achievement (external trade or internal monetization). The idea that any coinage is an expression of political autonomy derives from modern thinking, from the Middle Ages onwards: it is attached to the concept of "seignorage," linking profits to power.

Long admitted for Classical antiquity, this way of thinking has been challenged by good arguments (Martin 1985). Military powers, such as Republican Rome in Greece or Asia Minor, may have resorted not only to the use of foreign coinages to sustain their military campaigns (de Callataÿ 2011c), but also to prolonging the issues of their defeated enemies. This does not mean that coin production was considered a minor responsibility; on the contrary, coinage was of such importance that strong issuers were not afraid to sacrifice the potential advantage of using their own to guarantee the acceptance of their coinage. Recognizing this fact is to reduce the role of iconographic propaganda and to enhance monetary pragmatism, which is precisely the current trend of research.

In the 1980s, Colin Kraay (1985) published a paper entitled "Greek Coinage at War" where, not trying to be exhaustive, he listed two dozen examples for which a military explanation is certain or highly probable. Since then, the list has expanded dramatically, largely because it has been recognized that (1) coinages with a strong civic flavor (by the iconography and/or the epigraphy) could have been instrumented by a higher level of power to match military expenses, and (2) bronze issues may have served to pay troops, especially garrisons (Psoma 2009). As a consequence, many issues which were formerly held to be "civic and commercial" are now conceived as "pseudo-civic and military" (e.g., in Thasos and Maroneia mentioned above).

For a large area (continental Greece from Macedonia to Peloponnesus) and over nearly a century (*c.* 150–50 BCE), a recent inquiry estimates that the monetary mass (not taking into account the bronze and small silver issues) which was put into circulation was by far mostly military oriented, leaving a residual part (*c.* 10 percent?) for truly civic issues (de Callataÿ 2016a).

However, the statement that issuing powers were never concerned with facilitating daily transactions is too categorical. When considering the monetary stock, whatever the value of the coins, it is highly likely that a part of the low-value issues must have been intended to feed the demand for usable monetized instruments related to the army. Moreover, some episodes of massive coin importation may also be explained by the need to feed the market.

The Role of Mercenaries

For Greek coinages, the general pattern offers an encouragement to go further than a simple link between coinage and military purposes. Recurrently, the link

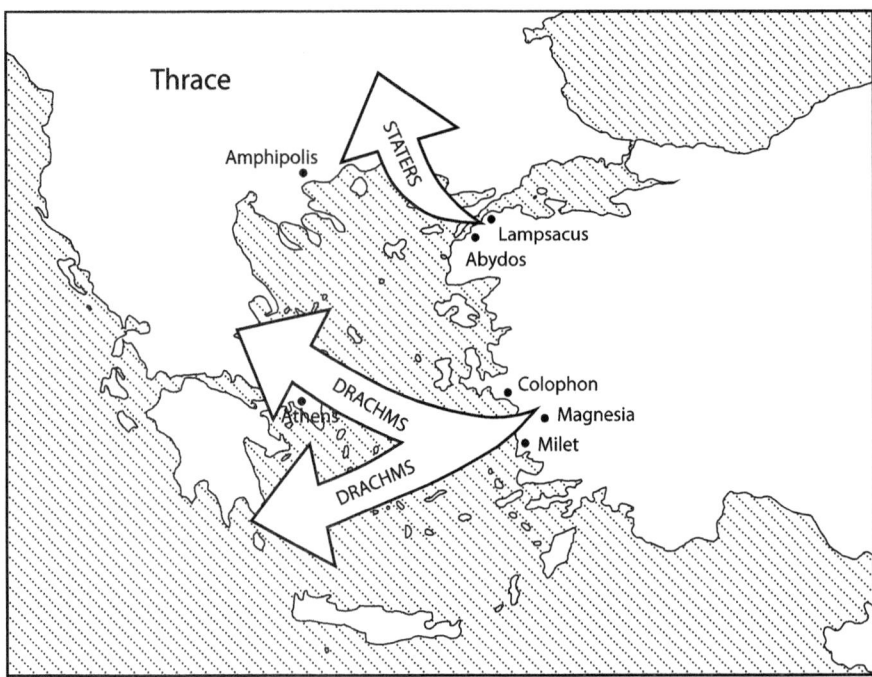

FIGURE 2.3: Map showing the nature and the purpose of the heavy strikes of Alexanders in some harbors in 325–323 BCE (de Callataÿ 1999b, after Thompson 1984; Drawing: Katy Opitz).

is with one category of troops: mercenaries. In a paper entitled "Paying the Mercenaries," Margaret Thompson (1984) convincingly reconstructed the rationale of the particularly abundant issues in specific harbors at the end of Alexander the Great's life (325–323 BCE) (see Figure 2.3). The time corresponds with the return of substantial numbers of troops from Babylonia. It is suggested that, to prevent incidents on the way back, soldiers were told that they would only be paid in certain coastal mints before they embarked for their homeland. To make the measure more effective, these mints were commissioned to produce denominations that appealed to those receiving them: gold *staters* for Thracians and silver drachms for continental Greeks.

The Mithradatic wars offer various additional cases along this line. Mithradates Eupator himself fought the so-called "Second Mithradatic War" (83–81 BCE) using a local army. Here, the absence of mercenaries typically corresponds to an absence of monetary issues, very much in contrast with the preparations of the third war (75–73 BCE) when sources inform us that he gathered many troops from abroad in his kingdom. A very significant case is provided by Tigranes the Great of Armenia who, despite a warlike reign, only began to issue coins when, after seizing Antioch in 83 BCE, he enlarged his army with the mercenaries employed by the last Seleucid kings. In neighboring Cappadocia, kings struck drachms, except the usurpers who were the only ones to produce tetradrachms. It is tempting to link this change of denomination with the habit of paying mercenaries in tetradrachms.

Beyond these specific cases, the careful quantification of the coinages issued during these wars allows us to offer an asymmetric proposal: (1) yes, nearly all coins were struck for military purposes, but (2) no, not all military expenditures were paid with coins. Some, as the building of a Pontic fleet during the winter 90/89 BCE, are not documented by any strike and there is simply not enough evidence to assume all the troops were paid in coins, even less so in fresh coins. So, for the Mithradatic wars at least, mercenaries look like the best differential parameter. It is probable that we could extend the statement to Hellenistic times as a whole. For the Archaic and Classical world, we certainly need to show prudence, but it will be no surprise if the mechanism proves to be the same. It is notable to observe that Phoenician cities, so famous for trade, started to strike coins only in *c.* 450 BCE (i.e. at a time when they were reached by Greek mercenaries) or that Sparta, so famous for fielding her own forces (not hiring mercenaries), refrained from striking coins during the Peloponnesian War.

For a Profit?

The simple idea that the issuing power makes a profit on the coinage generally needs no argument. It comes from medieval practice which postulates that the value of a coin (*rendage*, in old French) combines the value of the metal + the cost of production (*brassage*) + the benefit of the issuer (*seigneuriage* = segnoriage). The problem to solve is thus not so much a binary question (yes or no) than an estimation of how profitable each system was.

In an oft-quoted book, Sture Bolin (1958) made a strong distinction between the Greco-Roman world, where profit was high for the issuer, and Medieval and Modern times where profit was near to zero (hence the full application of Gresham's law). Indeed, considering the broad picture (see above, "Who? A highly state-controlled process"), it seems that Greco-Roman structures were more likely to create a profit for issuing powers.

Explicit evidence is none the less meager in the extreme. An honorific decree of Sestus, dated *c.* 120 BCE, is the only positive statement one can invoke. It declares that: "when the people had decided to use its own bronze coinage, in order that the city's type might have currency, and the city might receive the profit ($\pi\rho o\sigma \acute{o}\delta o\upsilon$ $\lambda \alpha\mu\beta \acute{a}\nu \epsilon\iota\nu$) which would accrue from a revenue of such a kind . . ." (OGIS 339, lines 43–5; transl. by Melville Jones 1993: 277). With this text in mind and endorsing the ideas of Sture Bolin, Georges Le Rider has repeatedly argued that coinage was not invented to facilitate transactions for the users but rather to enrich the issuers by monetizing society (Le Rider 2001: 239–66; Callataÿ 1999a). He developed his ideas using many attractive case studies for the Greek world, pointing out two kinds of situations which were profit-oriented: (1) several cases of closed monetary economies with a forced and unfavorable change at the entrance (Magna Grecia in *c*. 540–490 BCE with the incuse coinages, Ptolemaic Egypt, Byzantium, and Chalcedon at the end of the third century, or the kingdom of Pergamum with the cistophoric coinage); and (2) several cases of double currency production with, as for Macedonia under Cassander, one for abroad with a low rate of profit, and another for "the internal market" with a high rate of profit (i.e. a higher fiduciary part of the coins).

In addition to the immediate profit at the time of production, we should not forget that coins could be loaned with an interest rate, a major distinction in comparison to other commodities. Recent research has emphasized how some not-too-rudimentary financial engineering is reported both for Greece (e.g., at Delos and Delphi, see Chankowski 2001; Sosin 2000; 2001) and Rome (at Pompeii and Puzzuoli [Puteolanum], see Kay 2014).

However, it does not seem that profit was the true cause of coinage, more a peripheral benefit. If one looks at the great coinage produced by Alexander the Great, a commander who was constantly required to pay his troops, it appears more as a necessary expedient than as a structural means of increasing wealth. To get rich, nothing equals the defeat of the enemy and the plunder of his treasuries and his country.

HOW MUCH? A HIGH LEVEL OF MONETIZATION

Although any estimate is conditioned by high levels of uncertainty, we are strongly encouraged to think that the Greco-Roman world was comparatively highly monetized. Conversely, it seems that barter, which never disappeared, was a minor reality for centuries (Howgego 1992: 16–22) before reemerging in Late Antiquity. What had long been considered as inferior in nature is "barter v coinage" as proclaimed by the jurist Proculus. It is interesting to observe from Roman legal texts how barter was redefined at the end of the Roman Empire as being equal to monetized exchange (Aubert 2014), as argued by the Sabinian school.

Hard cash

Coin databases launched at a national level in several northern European countries allow us to calculate the number of recovered coins for each period. Particularly useful because of their robust samples are the Portable Antiquities Scheme (PAS) for Britain and the NUMIS project for the Netherlands (see

Tables 2.1 and 2.2). For Britain, it turns out that more than 70 percent of all coins introduced in the database are classified as Roman. This dwarfs any other period established as by the PAS; Medieval coins come in second with a mere 10 per cent. Due to the huge number of coins recovered from the thirteenth to the seventeenth century, results for the Netherlands are less impressive but still put Roman coins first. As the system allows for the modulation of chronological terms, it appears that coins of the first century CE are by far the most abundant (7,607 coins).

No such tool yet exists for Mediterranean countries with a continuity of occupation between the Greek and Roman periods, but we may already put into chronological perspective coin finds made on several sites. Figure 2.4 gives the percentage per century of production (from fourth to first century BCE) of coins recovered in Athens, Susa, Seleucia-on-the-Tigris, and Delos (House of the Comedians). The general trend is clear: the number of coins found on these four sites increased over time regardless of political circumstances (e.g. there is no decrease at Seleucia when the city passed from the Seleucids to the Parthians around the middle of the second century BCE).

TABLE 2.1: Coins registered by the Portable Antiquities Scheme for Britain. Available online at: https://finds.org.uk/database (accessed March 1, 2016). François de Callataÿ

	Results	%	Quantity	%
Iron Age	43,841	13	49,963	9
Roman	215,058	62	398,711	71
Early medieval	3,462	1	9,016	2
Medieval	49,661	14	54,131	10
Post-medieval	35,890	10	45,802	8
Modern	321	0	713	0
Total	348,413	100	558,336	100

TABLE 2.2: Coins registered by the Numis database for the Netherlands. Available online at: https://nnc.dnb.nl/dnb-nnc-ontsluiting-frontend/#/numis/ (March 1, 2016). François de Callataÿ

	Results	%
500–51 BCE	977	2
50 BCE–400 CE	18,369	34
401–800 CE	4,252	8
801–1200 CE	4,605	9
1201–1600 CE	16,748	31
1601–2000 CE	8,926	17
Total	53,877	101

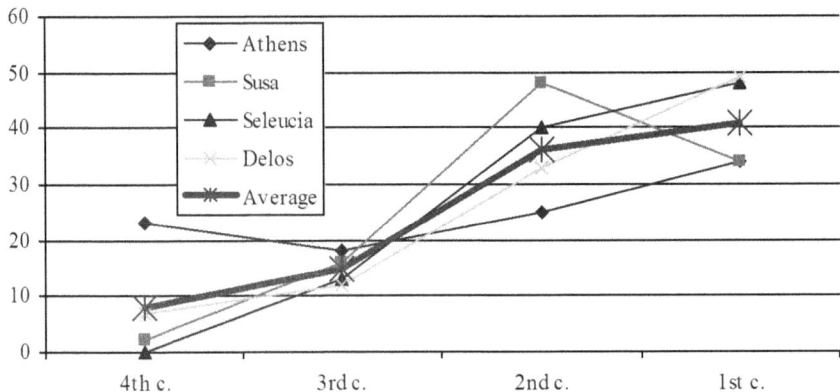

FIGURE 2.4: Percentages of coins recovered at Athens, Susa, Seleucia-on-the-Tigris, and Delos (fourth to first century BCE) (Athens-Kroll 1993: XXVI; Susa-Le Rider 1965: 234–41; Seleucia-Le Rider 1998: 72; Delos-Hackens: 1970). Francois de Callataÿ.

Another way to measure over the long term is to look at the number of extant coins. There exist today many millions (c. 5–10?) of Greek coins and dozens of millions of Roman coins. These numbers appear gigantic in comparison with the c. 10,000 Merovingian coins or the c. 30.000 Carolingian coins, not to mention the few thousands for the Ostrogoths or the few hundreds for the Lombards. For the years 800–1130 CE, the biggest accumulation (c. 700,000 coins) is found in Scandinavia, particularly on the island of Gotland (c. 166,000). A large part of it was struck in Mesopotamia or further east and came to Gotland because of trade with the Muslim Abbasid Empire via the rivers of northern Europe. As most of the coins known today from western European issues have come from these Scandinavian provenances, we are entitled to estimate the number of surviving coins for Western Medieval Europe as fewer than 1 million.

It must be noted, however, that we have available today proportionally more Greek and Roman coins than medieval and early modern. Indeed, as an average, the survival ratio for ancient coinages approximates 1 out of a few thousands (between 1/1,000 and 1/5,000). This is comparatively better than what could be established for medieval coinages (between 1/3,000 and 1/10,000) (de Callataÿ 2000b).

Numismatists have considerably improved knowledge about coin production, much less so about coin circulation. Because literary sources are nearly mute about recalls and the melting down of gold and silver coins (melting of bronze coins was much less frequent), it is extremely difficult to estimate the size of coin circulation for any given time and space. The few attempts to play with the monetary mass in circulation and divide it by the number of inhabitants to compare different systems must be viewed with extreme caution. We reproduce

TABLE 2.3: Per capita equivalent silver as coin at different times and places (Patterson 1972: 216. Numbers for total stock have been divided by two since Patterson is [wrongly] arguing that "one-half of the total stock is assigned to coin;" for 300 BCE: de Callataÿ, Depeyrot, and Villaronga 1993; for 160 CE: Duncan-Jones 1994). Francois de Callataÿ

Time	Region	Population in millions	Total stock (metric tons)	Grams of silver as coins per habitant
450 BCE	Delian confederacy and environs	c. 2	c. 400	c. 200
300 BCE	Hellenistic world	c. 30	(gold) c. 300 (silver) c. 3,000	c. 200
150 CE	Roman Empire	c. 50	c. 5,000	c. 100
160 CE	Roman Empire	c. 55	(gold) c. 880 (silver) c. 5,800	c. 265
800 CE	European and Muslim worlds	c. 50	c. 500/1,000	c. 15
1938 CE	United States	c. 130	c. 100,000	c. 164

the numbers provided by Clair Patterson (see Table 2.3), supplemented by some others (300 BCE and 160 CE), only to show that they do not contradict—quite the opposite—the assumption of a high level of monetization in Greco-Roman times, located one order of magnitude above Carolingian times and not too distant from values experienced in the recent past.

It is also symptomatic that the Greco-Roman world produced some complex tri-metallic systems of hard cash. Yet before Augustus, Ptolemy II Philadelphus already issued coins for no less than twelve denominations: four for gold, two for silver, and six for bronze (from *c.* 100g to 3g). Not only is this number nearly identical with what we experience today (fifteen denominations for euros and thirteen for dollars) but the spectrum between the highest and the lowest denomination is also worth noticing. The highest Ptolemaic denomination, a gold *mnaieion* (*c.* 27.8g), is equal to 4,800 bronze *chalkous* (if not 9,600 hemi-*chalkous*). Again, this is similar to our modern system (from 1 cent to $100 dollars and from 5 cents to €500 euros). Such a high number and spectrum of denominations is not approached again before the second half of the sixteenth century. In France, it is only with Charles IX (1561–74) that we have ten different denominations of coins (two for gold, two for good silver, and six for adulterated silver).

Beyond these efforts at quantification, some literary sources say something about the level of monetization of the Greco-Roman economy. In the *Asinaria* (198–203), a play by Plautus, the courtesan Cleaereta declares

Daylight, water, the sun, the moon, the night, these things I purchase not with money; the rest, whatever we wish to enjoy, we purchase on Grecian trust ("*Graeca fide*"). When we ask bread of the baker, wine from the wineshop, if they receive the money, they give their wares; the same principle do I go upon. My hands always have eyes in them; they believe what they see.

For Plautus, to sell "the Greek way" means to be paid in cash immediately and that covers daily transactions (de Callataÿ 2015). Other passages in Theophrastus and Herodas confirm that the Hellenistic world was a highly monetized society where you had to pay in cash to buy on the market since "as the saying goes, it is not words, but bronze coins, which pay the bills" (Herodas 7.49–50). It was a world where one needed coins to go to the baths (Faucher and Redon 2014), to attend the theater (Theophrastus 6.4, 9.5, and 30.6), to pay the schoolmaster (Theophrastus 30.14; Herodas 3.9–10) or to hire a slave for the day (Theophrastus 30.15).

For the Roman Imperial world, the *Golden Ass* by Apuleius offers an instructive fable whose *realia* have been studied by Fergus Millar. He similarly writes:

It is therefore all the more worth emphasizing that the towns in Apuleius function, not indeed as centres of production, but as the focus for organized exchanges of goods and the hiring of labour. All of this is conducted for cash; whatever else this may be, it is certainly a fully monetized economy.

He concluded that the system "involves cash exchanges . . . down to the lowest levels" (Millar 1981: 72–3).

Credit and elasticity of money supply

In addition to hard cash, credit also existed in Greco-Roman times (Howgego 1992: 12–16). Let us first remind the reader that bronze coinage (i.e. fiduciary coinage) is a form of unilateral credit imposed by the state on the issuers. The vast Augustan reform gave birth to a more bimetallic system (gold–bronze) equaling a *de facto* increase of M1 (the monetary mass as hard cash).

The question to what extent did credit exist: should we still have to follow Moses Finley's strong admonition, "money was coin and nothing else" which dominated the landscape for a generation (Finley 1985: 166)? Or should we endorse the opposite "revisionist view" which let the amount of money created by credit be compared with coinage, as advocated by Ed Cohen (1992; 2008; but see Schaps 2008) for Classical Athens or William Harris (2006) and Elio Lo Cascio (2011) for the Roman world? Neither of them, I am afraid.

There is no question that ample credit was available to Cicero and bankers at Puteolanum. Or that typical intrigues in Plautus's plays are based on the possibility that short-term loans in hard cash between individuals could be obtained. But how is this instructive about real credit with the opportunity to be turned into productive investments? The questions are: (1) At the lower level, what percentage of the population could walk through the city without coins in a purse for paying the barber, the innkeeper, or the prostitute? (2) At the higher level, did credit in Athens or Rome seriously increase M2 or M3—cash plus short and longer-term deposits—beyond hard cash?

Such a "revisionist" view is not only typical of classical economists (after all, classical economics have been built largely against mercantilism and the reductionist idea that money was only hard cash, Smithin 2000); it nearly always coincides with the modernist vision. Looking at several important civic dossiers for the Greek world (subscriptions, loans, and euergetism) we are more inclined to think that money was difficult to find, for states as well as for most individuals, and that it took first the form of hard cash. For Roman Egypt, François Lerouxel shows that banks did not make loans in cash; they were essentially used for the safekeeping of deposits. Conversely, money lending between individuals was everywhere and not restricted to high social status, but this was mostly short-term and mostly in cash (Lerouxel 2012; 2016).

To briefly sum up: with a higher level of hard cash, some real possibilities of credit, although—in my view—not to be exaggerated, the Greco-Roman world was indeed exceptionally monetized. This said, we could still endorse the statement that "there can be no doubt that the (money) supply was often inadequate for the ongoing needs of the society, let alone for the prospects of economic growth" (Finley 1985: 196). As coins, in terms of monetary mass, were poorly produced to facilitate daily transactions (a reality economists venturing into historical studies have difficulty admitting) and only issued from time to time, shortages must have been frequent. How frequent? It is difficult to tell from the few passages reporting cases of *inopia* or *caritas nummorum* (Verboven 1997; Crawford 1971) but the constant need for cash generating interpersonal loans at every level of society in Roman Egypt may be taken possibly as a better indicator of an endemic situation of shortage. As a rule, coins themselves are not very revealing, except in remarkable circumstances. Halving of coins, as under Augustus with the famous crocodile *asses* of Nemausus (Nîmes, France), may be attributed to a general shortage of small change.

WITH WHAT CONSEQUENCES? ECONOMIC GROWTH VERSUS PREDATORY MODEL

For mainstream economics, coinage is possibly a neutral "veil" over exchanges (though ancient historians do not think so) but it is more fundamentally a necessity for the virtuous circle: division of labor → increase of productivity → accumulation of benefits → productive investments → economic growth. So, implicitly or not, the level of monetization is often used as a proxy for a developed economy. After all, Greek and Roman authors themselves repeatedly marked their surprise at societies ignoring the use of coinage and described them as being less advanced (Howgego 1992: 16).

During recent decades, a substantial and refreshing amount of work on the Greco-Roman economy has been conducted by "economist-historians" and "historian-economists" with a great focus (especially from "historian-economists") on New Institutional Economy (NIE) (see Verboven 2015). The general tone of this literature is optimistic, as if each researcher wanted to prove how modern were the ancients. However, this positive approach is partly tainted by wishful thinking from mainstream economists who have been trained to think the contrary and for whom such a strategy is twice rewarding: to appear as innovative/provocative to their fellow economists and to operate a *captatio benevolentiae* of ancient historians. Ancient historians turning to the NIE generally aim to achieve a more modest goal: to be recognized by their colleagues as bridge-builders dressed in an attractive costume.

The incursions of neoclassical economists into the realm of ancient history are becoming frequent and generally lead to a mutual better understanding. An example of this is provided by a recent book about monetary and financial innovation (Bernholz and Vaubel 2014). While the two economists who coordinate the project fully endorse the statement professed by David Hume that competition between neighboring states, connected by commerce, creates the most favorable conditions for emulation, hence innovation, they are *de facto* contradicted by the specialists of the ancient world they asked to contribute who all insist that war is the fundamental driver for monetary innovation (Schaps 2014; Meadows 2014; Woytek 2014; on monetary innovation, see also Picard 1989; Amandry 1993).

A poor capacity to anticipate economic consequences

Before considering the role of coinage in economic growth, something must be said about economic rationalism. Here, too, the pendulum has oscillated over a large spectrum, from Finleyan primitivists who long denied any independent thinking on economic matters, to the recent flowering of papers assuming surprisingly sophisticated financial knowledge. Now that primitivism has nearly everywhere lost its dominant position, it seems more appropriate to temper the excesses of classical economics with its confidence in universal rules and its over-rigid chartalist view.

First, it seems important to stress that, strictly speaking, no ancient issuing power had any monetary policy (i.e. the capacity to regulate prices through the monetary mass (despite Lo Cascio 1981)). This is not to say that Greeks and Romans did not realize that a sudden increase of the monetary mass (as with the generation after Alexander the Great or Rome after the transfer of the gigantic Egyptian wealth under Augustus) was responsible for an increase in prices (see Suetonius, *Divus Augustus* 41.1–2; Nicolet 1971 and 1984) but there is no chance that they could finely tune this monetary mass because its perception, as was still the case in Napoleonic times, was vague and too imprecise to take efficient measures. The very concept of "replacement issues" (i.e., issues produced to keep M1 at the same level) is anachronistic.

Second, the most effective principle experienced by the Greco-Roman world was the law of demand and supply with, as a rule, a poorly elastic demand and an irregular supply. By contrast, and even if much has been written on the subject, the quantitative theory of money (Irving Fisher: M[onetary mass] × V[elocity] = P[rices] × T[otal volume of monetized transactions]) is unlikely to have played any part in the monetary decisions of ancient polities. For Greek times, the only documented case of a general increase in prices linked to an inflow of cash is the last quarter of the fourth century BCE after the substantial monetization by Alexander of the Persian treasuries (de Callataÿ 1989). We do not know for sure if this increase of prices is not better explained by an extension of monetized transactions and we are at pains to explain why prices fell back to their original levels at the beginning of the third century BCE. The same mechanism in which prices were more affected by an increase of T (the amount of monetized transactions) than by a raise of M (the monetary mass) has been argued for Republican Rome (Hollander 2008) and Roman Egypt during the third century CE (Rathbone 1996).

Third, one should keep in mind the fact that only a small part of precious metals were turned into coins. This has been estimated at under 20 percent for Hellenistic times (de Callataÿ 2006b). In other words, issuing powers, whether civic, royal, or imperial, did not push as far as they probably could the monetization of precious metals. This contradicts the view of Hellenistic kings eager to convert any gold or silver to sustain their *Weltmachtpolitik*.

All in all, monetary matters in Greco-Roman times offer a range of situations defying mainstream economic analysis. That coin production was embedded in the larger cultural frame is typically illustrated by the unprofitable (and failed) attempts driven by moral values (and totally against economic rationalism) made by several Roman emperors to restore a high degree of fineness for gold coins (Howgego 1995: 119–20).

Economic growth or predatory model

The late, but substantial, incursion of trained economists, coupled with the general obsession of the last decades for economic growth on one side and the domination of cultural history on the other hand had an influence on how Greco-Roman coinages are perceived. In both cases, the agenda looks pretty optimistic: to prove that coinage is partly responsible for economic growth or for democracy, and the more the better. As already noted, beyond general and appealing ideas (Seaford 2004), the link with democracy is hard to trace from the factual evidence. It has not even been argued seriously by coin specialists. The link with economic growth is a much stronger case.

Coins in precious metals were mainly struck to match state expenditures, but there can be no question that they were mostly used afterwards in economic circuits and perceived as such (Lo Cascio 1996). In addition to the passages of Aristotle, Plautus, and Apuleius quoted above, archaeological site maps of recovered coins clearly show a concentration in or near places of transactions (at the agora in Delos or corner shops in Pompeii: Hobbs 2013). The recent renewal of interest in extra-economic uses of coins, as votive offerings, gifts for the dead, amulets and so on is extremely interesting (see Kemmers and Myrberg 2011; Haselgrove and Krmnicek 2012) but only deals with a minor reality.

As argued above ("How much? A high level of monetization"), the Greco-Roman world experienced an exceptional monetization, well beyond what followed for a millennium. In terms of monetary mass, it seems most appropriate to place the peak of coin production between c .300 BCE (after the converting of Persian treasuries into coins by Alexander the Great), through the transfer to the Roman Republic of much of the silver stock of the East, and 200 CE (before the "crisis" of the third-century CE).

It turns out that such a chronology fits with another peak: the economic performance of the Greco-Roman world. There is a growing consensus that this world experienced a kind of sustainable growth from $c.$ 200 BCE–$c.$ 200 CE. Besides monetization, economic activities were responsible for increased levels of lead and copper atmospheric pollution, a number of shipwrecks, sizes of bones (tibias), fish-salting vat capacities, the amount of animal bones or wood pieces found on regular excavations, average house sizes, and the overall level of different occupations viewed through archaeological surveys. The cumulative evidence is so strong that no recent voice has tried to contest this major phenomenon.

So, how to interpret the concomitance of these two peaks? Did the abundance of coins promote exchanges, hence growth? In what measure did economic growth promote coins in return? These are questions for the economist to whom historians are at pains to provide firm answers. For example, the massive production of gold coins by Alexander the Great deeply modified the monetary landscape: it lowered the ratio of gold to silver (from 13.3:1 to 10:1) and it increased prices, but we may seriously doubt that these high-value coins spent in lavish conspicuous consumption had any serious effect on economic growth (de Callataÿ 2016b; for another case and a more optimistic view, see Chankowski 2013).

Moreover, "the voice of the coins" offers a much more convincing alternative to the virtuous economic model, even if it is far less sympathetic: the predatory model. Coins were struck to make war which, in return, allowed strong political powers to plunder (the much-debated theme of center and periphery) and to get richer. But this sudden richness (translated temporarily into economic performance) is fundamentally due less to structural improvements, being technological, legal, or organizational (a lowering of transaction costs for the NIE), than to circumstantial and extra-economic reasons. In this predatory model, economic growth is doomed to vanish, considering some dissipative inertia, once the process of conquest has stopped.

Let us conclude that in the debate between exogenous (the Antonine plague) or endogenous (the end of the predation) reasons for the first fall of the Roman Empire in the second half of the second century CE, monetary matters—although certainly not in an univocal manner—are in support of the latter. As such, the predatory model is to be favored against economic growth as stated by Philip Kay who argues that the period of 150–50 BCE saw the greatest growth in the economy of peninsular Italy, greater even than in the Empire, and that this was due to the transfer of wealth through successful warfare, rather than sustainable growth of production *per se* (Kay 2014; on the general increasing of luxury due to Republican imperialism, see Wallace-Hadrill 2008).

ACKNOWLEDGMENTS

The author is much indebted to Clive Stannard for the comments he made on an earlier version of this paper and to Oliver Hoover for correcting his English.

CHAPTER THREE

Money, Ritual, and Religion

Noneconomic Qualities of Coinage

STEFAN KRMNICEK

The market-place of Pharae is of wide extent after the ancient fashion, and in the middle of it is an image of Hermes, made of stone and bearded. Standing right on the earth, it is of square shape, and of no great size. On it is an inscription, saying that it was dedicated by Simylus the Messenian. It is called Hermes of the Market, and by it is established an oracle. In front of the image is placed a hearth, which also is of stone, and to the hearth bronze lamps are fastened with lead. Coming at eventide, the inquirer of the god, having burnt incense upon the hearth, filled the lamps with oil and lighted them, puts on the altar on the right of the image a local coin, called a "copper," and asks in the ear of the god the particular question he wishes to put to him. After that he stops his ears and leaves the marketplace. On coming outside he takes his hands from his ears, and whatever utterance he hears he considers oracular.
—Pausanias 7.22.2–3, transl. Jones 1933

The detailed description of the Oracle at Pharae and its cult practices penned by the Greek travel writer Pausanias in the second century CE gives us a vivid image of the rituals performed there. The offering of a bronze coin of the lowest possible denomination was embedded in the performance laid out step-by-step when consulting the oracle. Pausanias' description also demonstrates that a specific coin deposited in the right location ("on the right of the image a local coin, called a 'copper'") was essential to enact the ritual and for the procedure to follow its correct course. Yet it is not just literary sources that tell us about the use of coinage in ritual and religion. Far from it. The archaeological evidence constitutes the richest source of information concerning the use of coins in the Greco-Roman world; it indicates that coinage was used as payment for performing rituals, as an offering, as a substitute for other values, and as an indicator for ritual standards. Given that there are so many possible uses of coins in cultic and ritual contexts in antiquity (see Thüry 2006; Rowan 2010; Gorini 2011), only a few of the most significant and archaeologically best-documented kinds of ritual practices involving the use of coinage between the seventh century BCE and fourth century CE will be sketched out in the present chapter. The coins from the Magdalensberg (Carinthia, Austria), which date to the Iron Age–Roman transition period and are archaeologically well documented, will be presented as a case study in the concluding part of this chapter to better illustrate the relationships that existed in antiquity and the potential of modern research.

INTRODUCTION

In the ancient world coinage was primarily used in a monetary sense, similar to our Western conception of money. The impact such money had on society and its perception was also not all that different from the effect it has today. Coinage was used to pay for goods, money was hoarded, wealth accumulated, and money meant power. The Roman author Petronius, writing in the first century CE, illustrates this situation most aptly in his satire, putting the following words in the mouth of the nouveau riche Trimalchio—a former slave who had become a wealthy freedman:

> If you have a penny, that is what you are worth; by what a man hath shall he be reckoned. So your friend who was once a worm is now a king.
> —Petronius, *Satyrica* 77, transl. Heseltine 1956

Yet, despite the presumed proximity of Greco-Roman and modern mental attitudes toward money, the written sources also refer to positions that clearly show considerable differences in its perception, reminding us that caution is needed and that we should not consider as equivalent two systems over 2,000 years apart. So, for example, in his account of the teachings of Epictetus, Arrian of Nicomedia refers to the characters of the emperors Trajan and Nero when reflecting on value, stating that a coin issued by Trajan was to be preferred to one struck by Nero:

But his personal qualifications as a man, the impressions which he brought into the world stamped upon his mind; such as we look for in money, accepting or rejecting it accordingly. What impression has this piece of money? Trajan's. Give it me. Nero's. Throw it away.
—Arrian, *Epicteti dissertationes* 4.5.15–18, transl. Higginson 1890

Methodologically, archaeological research has treated ancient coinage as similar to modern money right from the outset, considering it to be a purely monetary medium. The rich body of ancient written sources referring to the economy, trade, and circulation of coins and the spectacular archaeological discoveries (money boxes, hoards, etc.) made in the extensive excavation campaigns of the nineteenth century (especially in Pompeii) have reinforced the impression that there was a conceptual similarity between ancient and modern (Western) coinage. These small, mass-produced, circular pieces of metal resonated with our modern ideas of value, promoted by the international trade in coins; put simply, it meant that "ancient coin = modern (value in) money." The numismatic research of the nineteenth and early twentieth centuries which stemmed from an approach which prioritized typology, seriation, and iconography, perpetuated this uncritical attitude toward the meaning of money in antiquity. Even the later shift in ancient history toward questions of monetary history did not target coins in their archaeological context, preferring instead to focus on the chronology and frequency of issues and their sequence, and their relationship to the political–economic environment. It is only thanks to Iron Age numismatics, which is institutionally much closer to archaeological fieldwork and to the methodologies of Anglo-Saxon prehistory, that a shift in the study of coins took place in the last third of the twentieth century (Haselgrove and Krmnicek 2012). The impetus for archaeologically based research of coinage came from Iron Age studies, not least because the European Iron Age cultures did not themselves produce written accounts which could have contributed to answering certain questions relating to the use and meaning of Celtic coins (Haselgrove and Wigg-Wolf 2005). Over the last fifteen years, ancient numismatics has adopted a contextual approach within Roman archaeology (Hingley and Willis 2007) as well as developed its own innovative ways of tackling the material. This new emphasis has so far remained limited to Roman numismatics, whereas the study of coinage and money from an archaeological perspective has had little impact on ancient Greek numismatics. There, research has focused anew on questions of economic history and typology (see Arnold-Biucchi and Caccamo Caltabiano 2015). The principal reason for the difference in methodological emphasis lies in the fact that the countries of northwestern Europe have had the adavantage of large-scale archaeological excavations (and detailed reports) and finds databases at a national level, which have promoted a context-oriented approach to Roman material culture.

Contextual numismatics, although employing different methods and asking different questions when applied to Iron Age or Roman archaeology, demonstrates how an approach favoring archaeological contexts can shed new lights on past concepts of money. It was only by investigating coins in their original circumstances of use (or rather, by examining the archaeological contexts and assemblages in which the coins were embedded) that it was established that money in the Iron Age and Mediterranean spheres was not simply a monetary instrument but a much more multi-faceted medium with non-monetary uses (Haselgrove and Krmnicek 2016b). Ancient coinage appears to have exercised the most influence and been most active in the cultic, ritual, and religious sphere. The material properties of the objects and the different meanings their users would have attributed to them are among the reasons for this prominence. Indeed these attributes allow coins to move between different functional contexts: they were easily available; they were an everyday object invested by society with a specific value; they were hand-made in a metal alloy (within a relatively metal-poor civilization—thus the importance of recycling); their color, smell, and sound varied depending on the raw material used (gold, silver, bronze); they had a special shape (flat, circular, and with two sides); they were anonymous bearers of messages in words and images while at the same time active means of communication (see Kemmers and Myrberg 2011). In addition, coins have a rich pictorial content, which itself reflects religious beliefs in daily life (Williams 2011).

RITUAL AND RELIGION

Even when coins from well-documented archaeological contexts are thoroughly examined, we still encounter difficulties when it comes to reconstructing past ritual and religious activities from the material record. While ethnographic research can observe dynamic processes, and historical research of recent periods makes use of written and oral evidence concerning the vast array of immaterial testimonies to human interactions, archaeology and numismatics only have (except for a few written sources applicable in specific cases) the material record and the circumstances of the deposition of a given find or assemblage to work with and from which to argue for a belief system. Inevitably, this raises the question of whether (or if at all) ritual and religion can be inferred from archaeological findings.

In archaeology, ritual is commonly used as a general concept referring to more-or-less repeated, formalized, and regular transactions in a religious and non-religious context, whereby social, communicative, symbolic, performative, and aesthetic dimensions come into their own (Sundqvist 2003, 32). Defining religion is far more difficult; this is discussed differently among anthropologists, sociologists, scholars of religion, and archaeologists. Approaches range from simple descriptions to the elaboration of highly complicated constructs, in which religion is seen to be made up of different elements (beliefs, rituals, practices, experiences, social factors, etc.; see Insoll 2005). In some recent religious studies, the term "religion" has been criticized because of its Eurocentric perspective and its prevailing impression of a coherently codified (and thus literate), authoritative system of belief (often operating in an urban context) (Renfrew 1994: 47). The study of religions outside the great world religions or those codified in writing has shown that in such areas and at different times religion is used as an overarching term to describe a whole series of phenomena (collective as well as individual) and cultic practices that refer to a supra-human dimension of reality. This supra-human world includes not just deities, but a wide spectrum of spiritual beings with different meanings, including ancestors (Hultgård 2003: 430). Such an approach also applies to the equally important observance of practices and performances which are usually subsumed under the term "household religious practices" (Insoll 2011; Bowes 2015); the boundaries between religion, magic, and enchantment are fluid. This makes it all the more difficult to draw clear-cut distinctions when the aspect or object under investigation belongs to a past culture where direct observation is no longer possible.

While in his seminal work of 1985 Renfrew put forward the idea that archaeologists can effectively identify the material remains of religion, the concept of religion has become less common in post-processual, contextual, or interpretative archaeology. Indeed, recent archaeological scholarship has largely abandoned the term "religion," focusing instead on the "ritual" or "symbolic" dimensions of material culture (Insoll 2005: 47; Fogelin 2007: 62–3). Hence the term "ritual" has become much used and has been given a variety of meanings. Not least because of its unsatisfactory definitions, archaeologists tend to avoid the term "religion" altogether, unless it refers to the large world religions codified in books. Instead, the word "ritual" is generally preferred in archaeological studies to describe material and situations which elsewhere would come under the umbrella of religion. The exponential increase in the term "ritual" in the titles of archaeological publications from the later 1990s onward clearly reflects a turn in (initially prehistoric) research toward interpretative models in a non-profane context; at the same time, it indicates that the idea of ritual has been modified (see Hänsel and Hänsel 1997). The concept underwent a semantic shift, in the sense that "ritual" came to be used to describe any archaeological context which could not be fully understood. Hence the term has become an alternative for anything that cannot be explained, a synonym for the "odd," whether secular or sacral in intent (Fogelin 2007). Yet the weakness of this approach (i.e. an inability to separate the sacred from the profane) is also one of its strengths. The definition (or lack of definition) of "ritual" has great potential, in particular for domestic or other small-scale rituals (Bradley 2003), where religious and secular rituals are neither distinct nor clearly identifiable. It blunts the edges of the dichotomy between sacred and profane, letting the blurred areas between religious rituals, secular rituals, and everyday life become visible, and promotes a perspective that considers how a seemingly ordinary action becomes ritualized (Bradley 2005; Fogelin 2007).

GOD'S MONEY

The so-called pot hoard of Ephesus figures among the earliest deposits in the history of the ancient world of struck coins in a "religious" or ritual context. During excavations in 1904/5 around the foundations of the Temple of Artemis—one of the Seven Wonders of the Ancient World—a group of at least ninety-five coins made of electrum, including seventeen (Kerschner and Konuk forthcoming) contained in a small jug (hence "pot hoard"), came to light. David G. Hogarth, the excavator of the remains of the layer in which the coins were found, interpreted the evidence as the foundation of a building that had preceded the late Archaic marble temple of Artemis, the so-called Croesus' temple. The most recent reexcavations of the complex stratigraphic sequence and of the context of the discovery have yielded new information about the assemblage (see Figure 3.1). The votive deposit had been placed in a clay make-up layer under the floor of the so-called Naos 2, presumably as a foundation deposit: it consisted of a jug with the electrum coins (the so-called pot hoard) deposited upright in the southwestern corner of the structure; to the

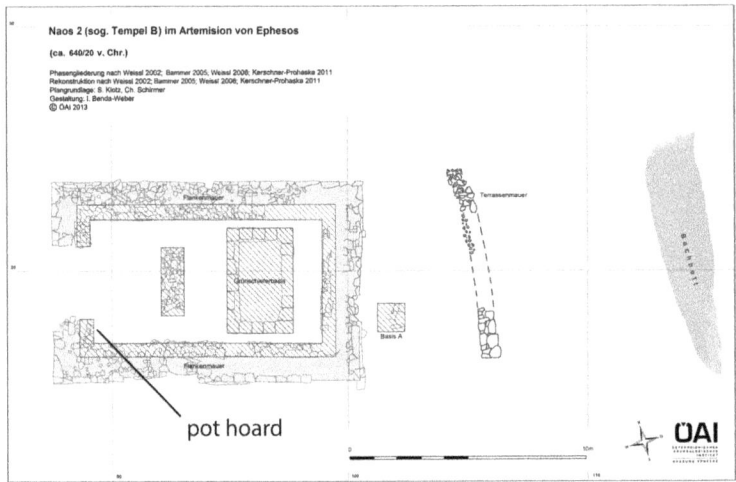

FIGURE 3.1: Excavation plan of Artemision (Naos 2) with findspot of pot hoard (Kerschner 2015: fig. 14, with additions). Image courtesy of Michael Kerschner, Austrian Archaeological Institute, Vienna.

north there was another deposit of nearly 1,500 objects consisting mainly of jewellery and other small votive objects, some made of precious materials like gold, silver, ivory, or amber (Kerschner and Prochaska 2011: 83). According to the most recent research, the chronology of the stratigraphic sequence indicates that the electrum coins and other votive objects were placed in this foundation deposit around 640/620 BCE. It suggests that the early electrum coins were viewed as appropriate offerings in a ritual context at Ephesus very soon after their first appearance in the middle or the second quarter of the seventh century BCE (Wartenberg 2016).

A similar instance of coins used in a context with "religious" or ritual connotations has been recorded at the Sanctuary of Hemithea at Kastabos. Kastabos, a religious and political center in the "Carian Chersonese"—a peninsula in the southwest of present-day Turkey—acquired its monuments during the period of Rhodian power in the third century BCE, including a new temple and a theater (Held 2015). In two excavation campaigns in 1959 and 1960 the archaeologists John M. Cook and William H. Plommer uncovered large parts of the temple terrace. Below the *cella* (i.e., the inner chamber of the temple), a deposit of 175 coins was discovered in a fill of earth and marble chips that was sealed by a layer of stones and the temple floor, which consisted of a layer of white lime plaster. The four silver coins and 171 bronzes—all but two pieces from Rhodes—were clustered on top of the fill in an area not exceeding a square meter on the surface and about 30 cm deep. Numerous sherds of at least two fine tableware *kantahroi* (cups used to hold wine, for drinking and for ritual use or offerings) were also found there (Cook and Plommer 1966). The stratigraphy of the coin and pottery deposit underneath the temple floor clearly indicates that the material was not only deposited deliberately, but that it was also intended to be permanent at the time the temple was constructed. The position of the deposit in the center of the *cella* is also significant, about a meter in front of the northern half of the threshold of the earlier shrine.

A further assemblage is documented at the Temple of Artemis at Sardis and was likely of a "religious" or ritual nature. Between 1910 and 1914, excavations conducted by the Princeton Expedition under Howard C. Butler uncovered the base of a cult statue made of two courses of sandstone masonry in the eastern *cella* of the temple. In the vertical joints between the stones of the upper course of sandstone, 126 Hellenistic silver and bronze coins were found. The coins differed so widely in date (between the mid-fourth century BCE and around 200 BCE), and many of the earlier coins were in such a perfect state of preservation, that Harold W. Bell, who published the coins from the excavation, convincingly argued that they were not placed in the base at one and the same time (Bell 1916: vi). Furthermore, an important aspect of the deposit is that fifty-four silver coins were found in the vertical joints of the stones along the eastern side of the base (see Figure 3.2), as if carefully laid at the foot of the

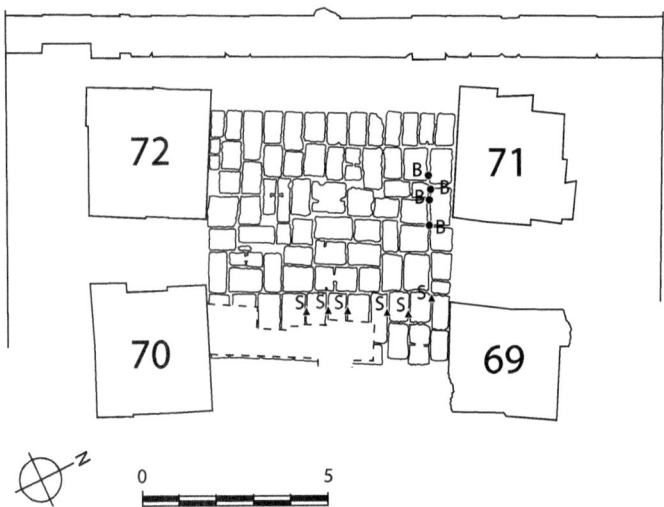

FIGURE 3.2: Coin finds in the basis of the temple of Artemis at Sardis after Butler 1922: ill. 71 and Hanfmann and Frazer 1975: fig. 127 (Drawing: Katy Opitz).

statue's pedestal (Butler 1922: 74), while seventy-two bronze coins were found along the northern side of the base (Hanfmann and Frazer 1975). Should we see this assemblage as an actual ritual deposit made at the time the statue base was erected in Hellenistic times, in a manner similar to those of Ephesus and Kastabos? Or is their position between the vertical joints of the stones the result of coins being deposited in ritual practices around the statue, and then (accidently) slipping between the stones? In addition to this specific instance, Sardis is further distinguished by another unusual find of a sixth-century BCE silver coin of Croesus, found near the center of the statue base. The accounts of its position differ, however: it was either between the upper and lower rows of masonry (Bell 1916: vi; Butler 1922: 76) or below the lower course of the sandstone base (Butler 1911: 454), which is why its functional use cannot be determined.

Literary sources also record instances of coins being offered to the gods for the protection of sacred or public buildings (e.g., under floors or inside walls). The Roman historian Tacitus (*Historiae* 4.53) gives a detailed description of the rebuilding of the Capitolium in Rome under Vespasian. In a public ceremony, the foundation stone of the new temple was dragged into place, and only unstruck gold and silver was thrown into the foundations as ordered by the haruspices. The only plausible explanation for Tacitus' explicit reference to unstruck coins of gold and silver as a foundation offering at the Capitolium is that minted coins were normally used in rituals involving other, less prominent, public and private buildings (Donderer 1984). Among Roman cult buildings, Mithraea and the coin offerings recovered in them have been particularly well studied (see Sauer 2004). The so-called Mithraeum II in the Roman *vicus* of Güglingen (Baden-Württemberg, Germany) provides an excellent example of multiple deposition rituals and the kinds of material used in a sacred building: its large cult image was seated at the east end, set on two sandstone pedestals with reliefs of the god Mithra. Dedicatory offerings consisted of a small ashpit under one of the plinths and the skull of a calf under the other. On the steps of the podium and in the central aisle there were small pits containing charcoal and chicken bones as well as a vessel. A single, almost freshly minted, coin of Faustina II was found in the fill of the podium (Kortüm and Neth 2004).

The site of a cave used for rituals near Zillis (Grisons, Switzerland) illustrates that coin offerings need not be found exclusively in Greek and Roman temples and cult buildings. In the 1990s, the archaeological services of the canton of Grisons excavated a natural cave located on the banks of the river Rhine a little to the south of Zillis. The site had been used in Late Roman times (third to fifth century CE) for an Eastern cult and as a funerary site in the sixth century CE (Liver and Rageth 2001). Cult vessels, including a richly ornamented ring vessel and food remains, especially chicken bones, were found both in the cave and in front of it; no doubt they were left there by the community taking part in the cult. Numerous votive offerings such as votive plaques, rock crystal, and some 600 coins were also recovered. The distribution of the coins gives the impression that they were thrown into the cave from outside (Rageth 1994). This corresponds to a Greek practice, whereby a participant would throw his offering from the temple's threshold—which he was not allowed to cross— onto the floor of the *cella*, where it would remain.

Finally let us mention the temple of Apollo Grannus at Neuenstadt am Kocher (Baden-Württemberg, Germany). It is an impressive example of how our understanding of the ritual use of coinage in sanctuaries depends on well-recorded fieldwork and interpretation (Krmnicek and Kortüm 2016). The excavation of the temple, carried out between 2007 and 2013 by the archaeological services of Baden-Württemberg (Landesamt für Denkmalpflege), uncovered an unusual complex of buildings consisting of a peristyle temple and a hall-like annexe joined to the temple by a passage. There was an open square at the foot of the temple terrace with springs whose water was collected in two hexagonal sandstone basins. A locus with several hearths dedicated to the burning of offerings was sited in the open space between the ancillary building and the temple. The sanctuary was dedicated to Apollo Grannus, as documented by fragments of dedicatory statues and inscriptions (Kortüm 2014). The coins that were found in the area next to the capture point of the spring at the foot of the temple show the potential of a close study of coin finds: a surface of some 10×7 meters was paved with sandstone slabs, some of which had remained *in situ* in the northwestern corner. Two coins (nos. 1046 and 1221) were found under the original paved surface around the eastern spring outlet; three coins

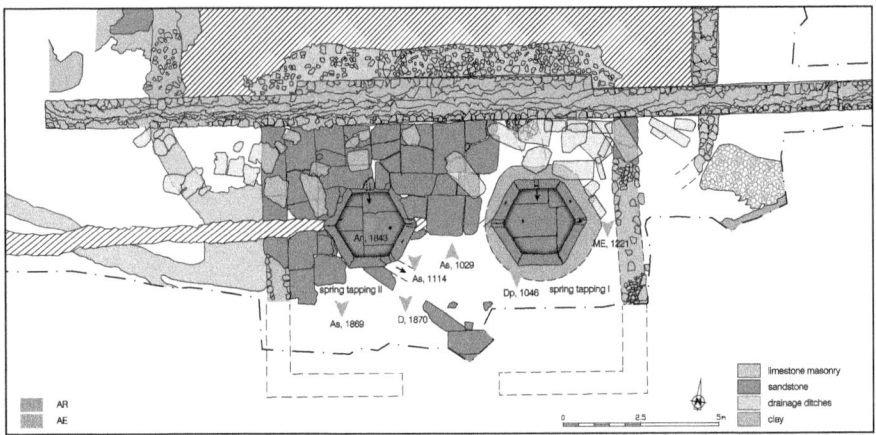

FIGURE 3.3: Coin finds around spring tappings at the temple of Neuenstadt. Image courtesy of Landesamt für Denkmalpflege, Esslingen am Neckar (Drawing: Marion Vöhringer).

(nos. 1114, 1869, and 1870), among them a *denarius* of Titus for Divus Vespasian, were recovered in the ancient make-up level for the paving around the western spring capture point (see Figure 3.3). The position of the two coins immediately under the flagstone paving is unusual. Are we dealing with a deliberate deposition, intended to be permanent, performed during the structural rearrangement of a sacred spring and the paving of its courtyard? Given the sacred character of the area around the capture of the two springs in the sanctuary of Apollo Grannus, we should consider whether all the coins found in the vicinity were left there for a special purpose. The area of the spring capture was undoubtedly of paramount importance in a cult setting that made use of water in a variety of ways. The findspot and context of a radiate coin of Tacitus (no. 1843) in the western basin (on the stone base under the final backfill of the basin) exclude the possibility that this was an unintentional loss; rather, they indicate that the coin was a deliberate deposit. We shall devote the next section to examining in greater detail the presence of coins in springs, fountains, and other watery places.

COINS IN THE FOUNTAIN

What tourist does not dream of returning to Rome? For this wish to come true, he or she tosses a coin into the Trevi Fountain; the custom dictates that this should be done over the shoulder facing away from the fountain (Travaini 2000). Just about every guide to Rome mentions this in connection with the *Fontana di Trevi*. The custom gained popularity after the release in 1954 of the American film *Three Coins in the Fountain*; in 1960, Anita Ekberg and Marcello

Mastroianni took a moonlit dip in the fountain in Fellini's *La Dolce Vita*. This, one of the most famous scenes in the history of cinematography, has contributed in no small measure to the popularity of the fountain and the adoption of the ritual among tourists. As a matter of interest, the act of tossing a coin into the fountain is documented only from the late nineteenth century onwards (Wünsch 1900), whereas taking a sip of water from the fountain was the done thing in the middle of the century, if one were to have one's wishes fulfilled (Krist 2015: 43–6).

A multiplicity of such transactions is also known from Roman antiquity, among travelers, believers, and pilgrims who had various reasons for discarding coins in watery bodies (springs, fountains, lakes, and rivers). Most archaeologically recorded assemblages reveal that it was not exclusively coins that were deposited, but also other offerings and sacrificial gifts including weapons, tools, vessels, jewelry, pieces of personal adornment, cult objects, etc. The coincidence of different artefact classes indicates that, over time, coins would become substitutes for other objects and that the choice of objects and projection of function behind the rituals and mental processes had become increasingly complex (Teegen 2003). The power of the suprahuman sphere that watery places and water sanctuaries had over people in antiquity (Edlund-Berry 2006) is described by Pliny the Younger himself:

> Have you at least seen the source of the river Clitumnus? As I never heard you mention it, I imagine not; let me therefore advise you to do so immediately. It is but lately indeed I had that pleasure, and I condemn myself for not having seen sooner. At the foot of a little hill, covered with venerable and shady cypress trees, the river head is sent up out from the ground in several and unequal rills, and bursting forth forms a broad pool so clear and glassy that you may count the shining pebbles, and the little pieces of money which are thrown into it.
> —Pliny, *Epistulae* 8.8, transl. Melmoth 1963

Nearly all the archaeological finds from watery contexts have in common that they were discovered very early, in the eighteenth and nineteenth centuries, hence lack the kind of documentation that would be expected from modern scientific recording and analysis. For example, the excavation in 1836 of a mineral source known as the "Roman spring" of Niedernau (Baden-Württemberg, Germany), in the vicinity of the Roman town of Sumelocenna (Rottenburg), yielded, at a depth of 5–6 meters, a relief of Apollo (a god with healing powers), numerous rings, fibulae, beads, keys, and some 300 Roman coins dating between the first and fourth centuries CE. Judging by the coins represented in the assemblage, it seems that the cult site and sacred spring were of regional importance within the catchment area of the Roman settlement of

Sumelocenna (Paret 1932: 177–8, 351). The fact that from the second half of the third century CE onwards (i.e., after the Roman frontier was relocated westward) Niedernau and its spring were located a good 70 kilometers beyond the frontier of the Roman Empire is of particular interest. The presence of coins of the late third century and entire fourth century CE attests to the continuity of ritual activities by local communities and suggests that these practices may also have been adopted by the Alamanni who had moved into the region from the 260s onward. In 1842, the construction of waterworks at a spring located on the Brenzkoferberg near Sigmaringen (Baden-Württemberg, Germany) revealed the remains of walls, posts, many shards of pottery, especially Roman finewares, and around 200 Roman coins. The buildings recorded in this location may have served a cultic purpose (Paret 1932: 178, 375). A similar assemblage is known from the Roman *vicus* of Aquae Helveticae, present-day Baden (Aargau, Switzerland), located close to the Roman legionary camp of Vindonissa (Windisch). Refurbishment work in 1967 and 1968 affected the spring known as the "Grosser Heisser Stein" ("Great Hot Stone"), located next to other thermal springs on the bend of the river Limmat north of the Old Town of Baden; this spring had to be pumped dry several times and reinforced structurally. Over 300 Roman coins (see Figure 3.4), two bronze pans, two

FIGURE 3.4: Bronze coin (*dupondius*) of Trajan from the thermal spring "Großer Heißer Stein" fused with pebbles. Image courtesy Schweizerische Numismatische Gesellschaft (Photo: Susanne Schenker).

handles from such vessels, and various objects made of lead were recovered. The "Grosser Heisser Stein" spring yielded a remarkable quantity of coins dated to the end of the first century and beginning of the second century CE. The curve then flattens out. The most recent finds show that the spring was open and that its water was used at least until the end of the fourth century CE (Doppler 2007). The question of whether, and how often, the spring shaft was cleared out in antiquity, remains unresolved here as in many other sites with coin deposits discovered early in the history of archaeological research. An inscription (CIL XI 4123) from Narni in Umbria (Italy) nevertheless tells us that offerings of money were periodically removed from watery places and used to finance a cult image of the deity venerated there. Similar circumstances must have existed for offerings in springs and temples elsewhere, as recorded for example in an inscription on a mosaic from the Roman temple of Lydney Park (Gloucestershire, UK) which states that the mosaic was financed by money offerings (*ex stipibus*; CIL VII 137).

Recent studies dedicated to re-assessing in detail old discoveries and early records have demonstrated the great potential of researching the deposition of coins in watery places and springs (see Sauer 2011; Erdmann 2014). The broad time span and wide spectrum of coins clearly shows that each site requires detailed archaeological (re)investigation (Facchinetti 2010) even when, in most cases, the surrender of coins is presumed to reflect similar concepts in the Roman world (Facchinetti 2003). The example of the coins found near the Roman bridge at Trier illustrates the type of methodical approach required to exclude the possibility that factors other than deliberate deposition (e.g. unintentional loss) were the reason why artefacts were left in watery places. Since the early 1960s more than 500,000 ancient coins have come to light in the wake of engineering works on the River Mosel in areas under the former Roman bridge and downstream from it. Three-quarters of the coins dating to Roman times belong to the Late Roman period. Such a large assemblage of coins can hardly be explained by normal, casual loss incurred while using the bridge. It is possible that the practice of making offerings to the river goes back further than the foundation of the Roman city, to Iron Age (Late Celtic) times, since the earliest coins were deposited near a ford or older bridge. These Iron Age coins, some forty in all, were, in the majority of cases, no longer in circulation in the early first century CE; at least some were most probably consigned to the river in (pre-)Caesarian times (Gilles 2001).

The sites of Bath (Cunliffe 1988), Bourbonne-les-Bains (Sauer 2005), and Coventina's Well (Allason-Jones and McKay 1985) have yielded the best-known and best-researched large coin assemblages from water sources. Coventina's Well is located to the west and outside the auxiliary fort of Carrawburgh on Hadrian's Wall in Britain. It consisted of the capture of a spring combined with a shrine dedicated to the healing goddess Coventina. In addition to the many objects made of bronze, bone, ceramic, glass, leather, and lead, just over 13,000 ancient coins were found, one of the greatest collections of alienated objects. The cult site and its votive deposits are particularly significant given its location in a military context right on the frontier of the Roman Empire, as well as the presumably military milieu of the actors involved, who would have had a non-local cultural identity. The goddess or water nymph venerated at Coventina's Well was apparently a local spirit, although her cult is not attested before the Roman period. Thus, we witness here—as a result of the spread of Roman religious practices—soldiers blending elements of Roman religion and local tradition into their existing religious beliefs, modifying both to create new and variable traditions (Hingley 2011). The overview of the finds from the sacred spring of Sulis at Bath is also relevant for our discussion. More than 12,500 Roman coins were recovered in the excavations of 1979 and 1980, as well as personal objects like jewelry, pottery, and unexpected items such as priestly equipment and even a washer from a Roman army catapult. The lead curse tablets, more than 1,500 of them, are amongst the best-known objects from the sacred spring, highlighting the different shades of intentions behind the various objects deposited (Cunliffe 1988). The few precious metal coins from Bath and those from Coventina's Well emphasize that, in Roman times, objects destined to be alienated were deliberately selected from the coinage circulating locally. The ritual deposition of precious metal coins, especially silver coins, in the Iron Age stands in complete contrast to the Roman situation. The finds from Bourbonne-les-Bains offer insight into yet another dimension of coins as votive deposits, namely ritual mutilation (bent coins, cuts, bent edges) (Sauer 2005: 79–86). This phenomenon is recorded in the majority of cases at sanctuary sites in Gaul, indicating that in Roman times ritual practices could remain confined to local or regional custom (Kiernan 2002). It would suggest that the practice of destroying coins is analogous to the bending and breaking of weapons in the European Bronze Age and Iron Age.

CASE STUDY: MAGDALENSBERG

Given the exceptionally large dataset of coins recovered from features in stratigraphic context during systematic archaeological excavations, the Roman settlement on the Magdalensberg offers an ideal case study for examining the different spheres of coin use and practices of coin deposition in domestic or small-scale rituals during the Late Iron Age–Roman transition period, on the fringe of the Mediterranean World (Krmnicek 2010). The settlement, situated on a step-like terrace beneath the hilltop of the Magdalensberg at about 1,000m altitude, became a center for the production and trading of metal products in the first-century BCE kingdom of Noricum. After the Roman conquest of Noricum in 16/15 BCE, the settlement became the administrative center of Roman control and the economic hub for the region, before systematic abandonment some sixty years later. Key features of Roman urban architecture such as a basilica and a forum are well attested from the early phase of occupation, augmented later by other public buildings such as a temple and baths. The house blocks around the city center were filled by tabernae, rectangular units accommodating workshops for metal production (including bronze and iron foundries), commerce and domestic space (Piccottini and Vetters 2003). Epigraphic data collected from funerary monuments and public inscriptions found at the site provide good evidence for the residents' cultural background. Both Romans and indigenous people inhabited the settlement from the very early phase until its final abandonment, an observation that correlates with the archaeological data, although all sources are heavily biased toward Roman evidence. The settlement was a central place for cultural interaction and a port of trade until the Roman conquest of Noricum, when Rome imposed her rule on the area, installing Roman authority and Mediterranean life-style.

Coin finds

Over the course of five decades of archaeological fieldwork, the settlement has been systematically excavated, providing a comprehensive stratified and contextualized dataset. An uncommonly rare methodological factor affects the interpretation of the 1,434 Greek, Roman, and Iron Age coins found on the site: thanks to the unique topography of the settlement, extending over a steeply sloping hill, standing walls and other architectural elements have survived for almost all excavated buildings of the ancient town. This very rare feature for an archaeological site provides excellent opportunities to study the finds using a three-dimensional approach. Of all 1,407 attributable Greek, Iron Age, and Roman coins, 1,010 coins (71%) were recovered in stratigraphic contexts; of all ancient coins found, 758 are (mostly local) Iron Age issues, 642 are Roman and seven are Greek coins. The composition of the Roman coins is less homogeneous, though distinct patterns emerge. In more than sixty years of archaeological fieldwork, only two aurei were found. This is remarkable, in so far as one would expect high-value denominations in the archaeological record given the settlement's character as a prominent commercial center.

Pits, foundations, and watery places

Thanks to thorough recording of each coin find, archaeological contexts of 578 coins could be identified which imply a deliberate "deposition" as opposed to those coin finds for which we must assume accidental loss or where the archaeological evidence simply does not provide further insights into the coin's character. Figure 3.5 displays all sixty-four archaeological features in which 578 coins were deliberately deposited, grouped according to their archaeological

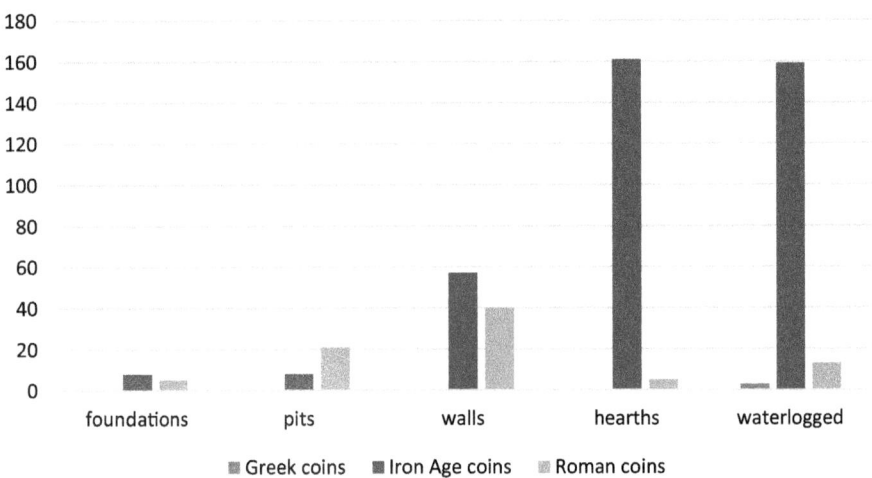

FIGURE 3.5: Deliberately deposited coins grouped according to their archaeological context (n = 578). Stefan Krmnicek.

context. In total forty-two coins out of twenty-six features were recovered from pits and foundations. It has long been recognized in Iron Age (and recently in Roman) archaeology that deliberately discarding objects of value in artificial or natural features underneath the visible surface with no intention of recovery conveys a symbolic dimension (Woodward and Woodward 2004; Schäfer 2013). The identification of a deliberate deposition of coins as opposed to deposition deriving from rubbish disposal is built on the observation of precise locations of the numismatic material within features, as well as the associated finds (cf. Curteis 2005). From the features providing good archaeological data, it appears as if the positioning of coins in pits and foundations was deliberate and carefully chosen in the settlement on the Magdalensberg. Most coins come from the bottom of foundations and pits; only a few derive from the top of the filling, suggesting that they may have functioned as termination deposits.

Studies on the ritual deposition of Iron Age coinage are still predominantly concerned with sacred and supposedly sacred structures such as temples, shrines, and enclosures; the above-mentioned coin finds in pits and foundations on the Magdalensberg, however, come from domestic and private workshop contexts of the urban center, differing fundamentally from public sites. There is but one instance of presumably sacred deposition in the context of religious cult; a denarius of Tiberius was recovered from a pit ("Felsheiligtum") at the edge of the hillside behind the Roman temple precinct, which seems to indicate deposition in the context of ritual feasting, given the vast number of associated finds of bones (Görlich 1950). Feature no. 59 T/O also stands out from other deposits, as a gold coin (aureus) of Augustus was recovered, together with fragments of glass from the bottom of the foundation pit of the room's northern wall. The prominence of the coin is further emphasized by the absence of any other metal or pottery finds. Given the scarcity of gold coins found on the site, the deliberate discard of an aureus in a foundation pit, preventing any recovery, is a unique example for deposition of high-value denominations. A deposit of two small silver Iron Age coins has been recovered from the foundation under the stone threshold of the south wall in room OR/16. It is widely recognized that thresholds functioned similarly to ditches in European Iron Age societies, as symbolic divisions of space between the interior and the outside world (Beilke-Voigt 2001: 180–1). The selection of Iron Age coins for deposition under the threshold of a workshop unit dated to the Roman period may indicate the survival of an Iron Age tradition. The absence of other small finds in this instance gives further weight to the non-economic function of the coins. Similarly, the deposition of coins in postholes seems to be rooted in a tradition of ritually placing objects in such contexts. Several examples in Britain and Germany attest to the widespread custom of deliberately depositing coins in postholes from the Iron Age into Roman times (Haselgrove 2005). At the settlement on the Magdalensberg, there are three examples in which coins were recovered from postholes that had no other associated finds in the fill.

The coin finds in waterlogged contexts in the settlement on the Magdalensberg belong to a widespread pattern of ritually placing objects, exhibited by the careful selection of Greek coins used for deposition in watery places. When comparing all coin finds in watery contexts with those that indicate no deliberate deposition, the distribution pattern emphasizes a preference for depositing Greek coins. Three of the seven Greek coins found on the Magdalensberg (of which one is an unstratified find) were deposited deliberately—and they occur only in waterlogged contexts. Perhaps their exotic and ancient nature required their deposition in wet places? The archaeological data of coins deposited in wells and fountains in the northwest provinces of the Roman world has increased dramatically in recent decades, but the personal intention and meaning of the individual depositions in such places remains unknown (Facchinetti 2003; Facchinetti 2010). The same holds true for the coins from the Magdalensberg, where predominantly modest numbers and values of coins were deposited in small profane watery contexts, as opposed to finds of vast material for ritual offering at focal sites such as Bath, Bourbonne-les-Bains, or Coventina's Well.

Walls

In the settlement on the Magdalensberg, nine features containing coins and associated with standing walls have been discovered. The features contained fifty-seven Iron Age and forty Roman coins and are dated from the earliest occupation period in the second half of the first century BCE until 50 CE, when the settlement was eventually abandoned. All but four of the nine features contain only a single Iron Age or Roman coin. An *as* of Claudius was recovered from a building joint of the south and north wall of rooms AA/27 and AA/24, a situation which demonstrates that the object could only have been intentionally placed in this position. A Republican *quinarius* and a Republican *as* stuck in the mortar surface between stone bricks of the south wall in OR/1 and north wall of OR/11 respectively seems to indicate that these coins were deliberately built into the wall during construction. Two coins, an Iron Age large silver unit and a Republican *as*, were recovered on top of a sill beam of the demolished timber building in OR/40. From the evidence presented above it becomes clear that the coins could have arrived at their precise position of modern discovery only by intentional human action. While for the characterization of coin finds below floor level secondary dislocation or accidental dropping from an elevated position cannot be entirely ruled out, the position of coins in walls well above floor level is clearly a product of a deliberate action. Although the exact meaning of coins concealed in walls or plunged into the surfaces of walls remains hidden to us, the deposition of single coins in walls without intention of recovery is likely to have exercised a function in the ritual sphere. Given the scarcity of standing structures surviving from ancient urban settlements, it is difficult to obtain relevant archaeological data for comparison.

Across the Roman Empire, we encounter several instances in which coins were recovered from walls in domestic contexts, suggesting that they were deliberately built into the structure. For instance, at the Roman Villa Chilgrove 2, in West Sussex, a radiate of Victorinus was built into the north wall of Room 7 of Building 2, a coin of Magnentius was found on top of the demolished wall footing in a central room (Room 12) of the villa's bath, and a coin of Constans was found in the east wall of the neighboring Room 13 in the same building (Down 1979: 86, 88–9). The Roman Villa at Dunkirt Barn, Abbotts Ann, produced a radiate of Carausius in the west wall of Room 3 in the southeastern wing (Cunliffe and Poole 2008: 53). The most significant coin find at the Roman house with wall painting in Dover is a little-worn denarius of Severus Alexander found inside the Phase II replacement wall; the light wear suggests minimal circulation before deposition (Philp 1989: 48). A coin of Emperor Hadrian and one of Emperor Antoninus Pius were also found in the Casa del Planetario (Italica, Spain) at half a meter above floor level in the mortar of the wall separating the southern domestic area from the tabernae (Luzón 1982; 456). Even in the Mausoleum of Empress Helena a bronze coin (nummus), dated 324–6 CE, was found in the mortar of the circular wall (Deichmann and Tschira 1957: 64). At Trier, a late Roman bronze coin (looking rather uncirculated) of Severus II from 305 CE was discovered in the wall at the southeastern corner of the vestibule of the Basilica of Constantine (Aula Palatina) (Reusch 1956: 35).

While the coins built into the wall of the Mausoleum of Empress Helena and in the corner of the Basilica of Constantine might reflect a ritual intention, the literary evidence of coins and jewelry concealed in a wall in Roman Egypt seem to indicate a secular hoard. A papyrus in the John Rylands University Library at Manchester mentions the accidental discovery of jewelry and coins in a wall by workmen during demolition works in the reign of Tiberius (Hunt and Edgar 1933: 259). At first glance, four coin deposits in walls on the Magdalensberg appear to be similarly disposed in economic intention. Two deposits were recovered from two neighboring rectangular beam sockets in the east wall of room OR/15. During occupation of the two-story taberna, both beam sockets would have been blocked by beams supporting a second floor, leaving the coins inaccessible for retrieval. This permanent abandonment of the objects due to the long-term occupation of the building until the end of the settlement makes an interpretation of simple economic saving less likely. The exact intention behind the deposition remains unknown, but the evidence presented above suggests a function in the ritual sphere, similar to the variety of single coins built into walls. The prominence of both deposits is further emphasized by the graffiti LATIN and F incised on two denarii in one of the deposits—which reminds us of the well-documented Iron Age tradition of curating and modifying coins before deposition, such as breaking, folding, bending, cutting, etc. (cf. de Jersey 2005).

Room NG/32 produced the second aureus of the two gold coins found on the Magdalensberg. The aureus was recovered from the mortar surface on the bottom of the west wall just above floor level. Imprints and remaining fragments of a wooden board on the lowest part of the wall reveal that the coin was once concealed behind a base board during the period of occupation. Given the high value of a Roman aureus and the scarcity of gold coins found in the settlement on the Magdalensberg, the deposition of this coin is very likely to have held a particular meaning. The place of deposition behind a base board was clearly accessible for recovery without great effort; interestingly, the coin remained at its original place until the house unit was abandoned, suggesting a ritual meaning behind the act. A similar phenomenon was discovered in the Artemis precinct (Monument 10, Exedra D) of the second century BCE in Sardis, Turkey. There, Hellenistic coins were placed intentionally under the ivory-white water-impermeable stucco floors and in the wall footing before three coats of impermeable stucco were applied (Hanfmann and Burell 1981: xxi).

Material vs. intangible rituals

A wealth of textual evidence surviving on Roman wall plaster on walls at the Magdalensberg illustrates commercial practices such as stock lists, schedules, and traders' notes (Egger 1961). A small fraction of textual evidence relates to the inhabitants' ritual activities, including a number of Roman graffiti mentioning vows and votive offerings ("vota suscepta" and "sacrum"). Two clusters of interesting graffiti referring to vows and votive offerings were discovered around niches in two workshops. These occur in several houses on the Magdalensberg and appear to be features for the worship of guardian deities or household gods. In most graffiti, the authors invoke Mercury, the god associated with the profane sphere of trade. This fits well with the local context of the settlement as a center for production and trade. Two other graffiti from the workshop and domestic sphere (AA/27 south wall and OR/23 west wall) refer to votive offerings to the chthonic gods, deities associated with a belief in supernatural powers in the underworld, and the interior of the earth (Antonaccio 2005: 102–11). The graffito on the west wall in house OR/23 explicitly records a libation, citing several cups of wine offered to the chthonic gods. These votive graffiti and the graffiti around the niches are of great importance in providing explicit evidence of ritual performances that took place there, of which no material culture has otherwise survived. Many of the coins from the Magdalensberg were found in positions that imply deliberate deposition. Most of them do not appear to be secular saving hoards and it seems reasonable to identify them as material remains of a ritual of which no other evidence (e.g., textual evidence) but the material objects (i.e., the coins) has survived.

A good example of this is the coin finds in house NG/41. There, the coins were recovered from a man-made cavity in the west wall at floor level. The cavity is located below and half a meter to the left of a niche and was carefully sealed with a carved stone block. It contained three Iron Age large silver coins and thirty-five small silver coins. According to the sequence of the construction of the house block and its chronology, the deposition must have been executed after the Roman occupation in the first half of the first century CE. The exclusive selection of Iron Age coins in a deposition dated to the Roman period might underline its non-mundane character. An argument could be made to suggest that the deposition near the niche had a relevant association, for such niches were key places for religious worship and ritual performance in the private and personal sphere of people in the settlement on the Magdalensberg. When considering the spatial context of the deposit near a potential place of religious significance, a purely economic meaning for the creation of the deposit becomes less likely, even if the exact meaning and intention will remain unknown.

The deposition patterns described here suggest a value beyond profane function for the majority of deposits and make it plausible to identify them as material traces of ritual performances. The evidence of Iron Age and Roman coins equally deposited in a supposedly ritual manner in foundations and pits highlights the impact Roman coinage had during the Iron Age–Roman transition period and how individuals adopted and appropriated Roman objects for use in indigenous customs. When site finds are compared with deliberately deposited coins, we encounter a distinctive difference in coin use over time (see Figures 3.6a and 3.6b). Looking first at single finds, we can trace the development of coin use against the backdrop of major socio-cultural change. In the initial phase of occupation, from *c.* 40–25 BCE, only local Iron Age coins circulated. In the Augustan period, we see a massive influx of Roman coins, accompanied by a subsequent increase in coin circulation, from 25 BCE until 15 CE, by which time Roman coins outnumbered local Iron Age coins. In layers dated to the final period of occupation, Iron Age coins have almost entirely disappeared from circulation. Conversely, the distribution of deliberately deposited coins follows

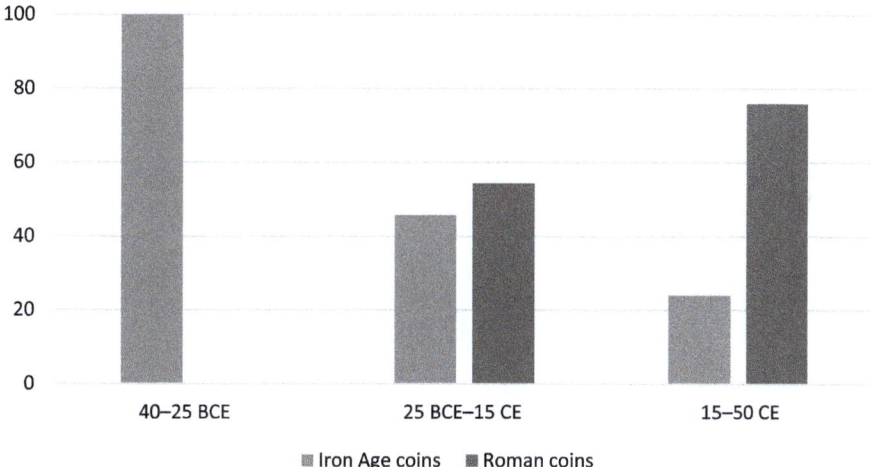

FIGURE 3.6a: Site finds ("accidental loss") in % (n = 491). Stefan Krmnicek.

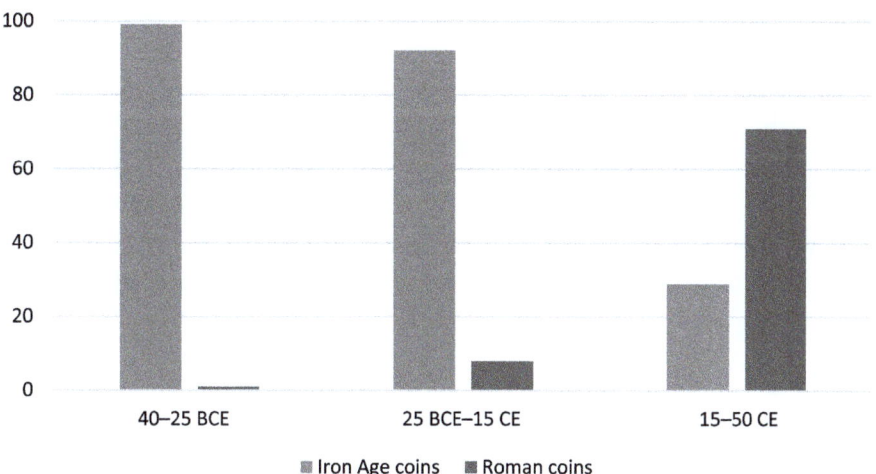

FIGURE 3.6b: Deliberately deposited coins in % (n = 502). Stefan Krmnicek.
https://archive.org/stream/annalesduservice910egyp#page/n57/mode/2up

a different pattern. Roman coins were apparently adopted more quickly for economic transactions but, for ritual performance, people still used Iron Age coins. In the transition period (from 25 BCE to 15 CE), Iron Age coins still predominate in ritual use. Only in the last phase of occupation (15–50 CE), do we see Roman coinage used at a similarly high level in both the ritual sphere and in daily transactions. Apparently, those who actively used coins in rituals had a strong preference for employing Iron Age coins as long as they were available. The differing uses of Iron Age and Roman coinage at the Magdalensberg provides insight into the private and personal spheres of individuals' coin use. It is also a unique source of insight into the cultural identities expressed by people who seemingly negotiated and manipulated their own traditions against the benefit of adopting Roman identity, individuals whom otherwise we normally only encounter though the filter of Roman burial. Instead of focusing on the elite, as many numismatic studies do, an archaeological approach in numismatics allows us to examine coin use at different levels of society and even to trace how individuals actively shaped culturally different objects (in this case coins) through their discrete use and appropriated them for their own needs.

ACKNOWLEDGMENTS

I am grateful to Michael Kerschner (Vienna), Klaus Kortüm (Esslingen), Markus Peter (Augst), and Christian Weiss (Augst) for willingly providing permission to use their excavation plans and images of objects. I am also grateful to Katy Opitz (Tübingen) for her support in the editorial process. In addition, I would also like to thank Sophie Crawford Waters (Philadelphia) for assisting with the English version of this chapter.

CHAPTER FOUR

Money and the Everyday

Multiple Moneys for Multiple Users

STÉPHANE MARTIN

What happens every day and comes back every day, the commonplace, the daily, the evident, the common, the ordinary, the infra-ordinary, the background noise, the usual, how to give an account, how to question it, how to describe it?
—Georges Perec (1973) (translation by author)

INTRODUCTION

One can legitimately agree with French writer Georges Perec that the everyday does not generally receive the attention it deserves. But Perec, at least, could tackle the problem by direct observation. As the practices of ancient money users have hardly been recorded, what is left to us archaeologists, historians, and numismatists are some generally ambiguous material remains, only very partially lit by often ambiguous texts. Any treatment of the subject will, of necessity, be patchy and sketchy at best. The focus of this survey is limited to the territories eventually conquered by the Romans: from Mesopotamia to the Atlantic and from northern Africa (including Egypt) to northern Europe. The spread of monetary practices from the Near-East to Europe and the common use of coinage in later periods lend some unity to the area. Rather than representing a cultural bias against other traditions of money and coinage, this choice has been dictated by practicality and by my own expertise, which lies mainly in the coinages of the pre-Roman and Roman West. Even with these limitations, the area to be covered remains large. Since nothing is more peculiar to a specific time and place than the everyday, an exhaustive overview is out of the question. Less ambitiously, therefore, this chapter will highlight some relevant themes and illustrate them with well-researched examples from recent literature. Sources at our disposal can be classified into four main groups, which partly overlap: literary texts, documentary texts (papyri and inscriptions), material currencies (mainly coins), and archaeological documentation (both objects and contexts).

It has long been recognized that most of our literary evidence devotes very little attention to everyday life. Much of what is to be found on the subject of money and its use does not come from ancient historians but from other genres such as comedy, the novel, or satire. This can raise the question of whether the information is trustworthy. Although this must be judged for each passage by looking at its wider context, both textual and historical, one can often assume that there is much to be gained here (see, e.g, Millar 1981 on Apuleius' *Golden Ass*). Walter Scheidel (2014), after reviewing monetary valuations in ancient sources, believes them to be reliable for quantitative analysis. Sometimes monetary mentions are nevertheless difficult to interpret: the *Historia Augusta*, a collection of imperial biographies written in late fourth or early fifth century CE, is an extreme case, with numerous inventions and anachronisms (Carlà 2007b). But even an apparently more straightforward text can offer pitfalls. Juvenal, for instance, writing in the late first/early second century CE, uses the denomination *triens* to designate the so-called Charon's obol (Juvenal 3.267), an obvious archaism as *trientes* were last coined in the 80s BCE.

Documentary texts do give better insight into ancient practices, but they usually deal either with institutions or with rich individuals. This is particularly true of stone inscriptions, the best-preserved type of documentary text throughout the ancient world. In the East, the situation is a little more balanced. From the third millennium BCE to the Hellenistic period, the cuneiform tablets from Mesopotamia offer, along with various collections of laws (Roth 1997), numerous archives, both public and private (one of the most famous private archives is that of the Murašû family, powerful merchants from fifth-century BCE Babylonia: Stolper 1985). They give a quite detailed picture of everyday transactions from the middle classes upwards. Only in Egypt have inscriptions, papyri, and *ostraca* (texts written on pottery sherds) survived in large quantity during the whole period under study (a review of sources and literature can be found in Menu 2001; Agut-Labordère 2014). Such documents are also preserved in smaller number in other regions, for instance in the northern provinces of the Roman Empire (the Vindolanda tablets are the best-known example: Bowman, Thomas, and Tomlin 2010; 2011 and "Online resources" below). Although graffiti on ceramics or walls are not uncommon, they are rarely extensive (see Figure 4.1). When they are, as in Pompeii, they provide a

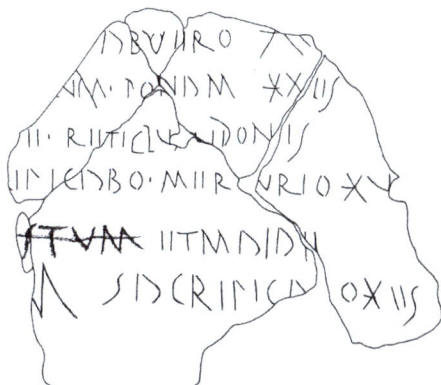

FIGURE 4.1: Graffito from the sanctuary of Châteauneuf (France), with offerings to Mercury and Maia in denarii (first century CE). From Mermet 1993: 106 fig. 10 (image courtesy of Christian Mermet).

fascinating glimpse into everyday life (most of these are available in the *Corpus Inscriptionum Latinarum* [*CIL*], volume IV with supplements, now online).

For the Greco-Roman world, a few projects have tried to gather together the most useful textual evidence. John Melville-Jones has published a selection of texts relating to Greek coinage (1993; 2007) and is preparing a volume on Roman coinage. Wolfgang Szaivert and Reinhard Wolters (2005) have issued a very useful collection of prices and salaries in the Roman world, which can be used with Walter Scheidel's online database on monetary valuations in literary sources (see "Online resources"). Numerous studies are concerned with epigraphic documents; it is hard not to mention the names of Louis Robert for the Greek world and Richard Duncan-Jones for the Roman (along with the books by Melville-Jones, a good starting point for epigraphy is Bérard *et al.* 2010, with online supplements). For the numismatic evidence, the best place to start are the *Surveys of Numismatic Research* published every six years by the International Numismatic Council and divided by chronological period, along with the *Numismatic Literature* published by the American Numismatic Society (some issues are available online, see "Online resources"). For coin finds, the *Surveys* are again useful. For other aspects of the archaeological documentation, one must immerse oneself in the literature dealing with the area under investigation. The importance of archaeology has long been highlighted: Richard Reece has been highly influential in promoting "applied numismatics" that consider the nature of the sites (Reece 2003). But only recently has progress in excavation methods made possible a closer study of where, with what, and—sometimes—why coins were deposited on a given site. This, of course, also applies to other classes of material, including other forms of money less readily recognizable. It is better to start with recent works, then go back to older literature, as standards in archaeological excavation and publication have increased dramatically, allowing for better and more precise interpretations. There is a growing awareness of the value of archaeological context for interpreting money; it is certainly one of the most promising avenues for new research, as demonstrated by the recent work by Colin Haselgrove and Stefan Krmnicek (Haselgrove and Krmnicek 2012; 2016b). (For recent monographs making use of archaeological data see, e.g., Butcher 2003; Krmnicek 2010; Frascone 2013; Hobbs 2013; Martin 2015.) For much of the Ancient world, archaeology is, of course, the only way to explore periods and regions where no texts have existed or survived. But one should not underestimate the value of archaeological data for the better-documented Classical world: for instance, the chronology of the first coinage from Lydia is currently being revised thanks to new excavations and a greater attention to material from previous campaigns (see Konuk 2012 with previous literature).

We have no way to gauge precisely the level of monetization in ancient societies, but it is clear that it was quantitatively and qualitatively different from our use of money. We live in a highly monetized world, one that is much more integrated, from the monetary viewpoint, than it ever was before. Still, the assumption that most people in Antiquity would have lived without money and, particularly in the countryside, would have mainly, if not exclusively, used barter, is being proven wrong. First, progress in archaeological practice makes it clear that coins were much more present than we thought even in the rural areas. Second, we now know that coinage is not the only "real money": communities that did not use coins even after their invention should therefore not be considered as being outside the monetary world. As a result, the aim of the following pages will be to show that money was a much more important part of everyday life than is often assumed. As much as possible, the focus will be on "common people," as the uses of money by institutions, whether states or cities, temples or armies, have to this day received most of the attention. We must keep in mind, however, that, as always, the available written and material documentation does not do justice to the lowest classes of the population. To a large extent, they remain largely out of our reach.

"MULTIPLE MONEY"

For a long time, money meant coinage for most scholars of Classical Antiquity. Moses Finley's statement that "this was a world which never created fiduciary money in any form, or negotiable instruments. Money was hard coin" (Finley 1985: 141) helped anchor this belief. This view seemed to be supported by ancient sources: it is clear from Caesar and Strabo that using currencies other than coins was viewed as barbarous (Caesar, *Bellum Gallicum* 5.12.4; Strabo 3.3.7; 7.5.5; 11.4.4). Similarly, in Late Antiquity, John Chrysostom could write that "The use of coins is inherent to our existence, it regulates everything in life. Each time we want to buy or sell something, it is done by means of coins" (*In Principium Actorum* 4.2 = *Patrologia Graeca* 51.99.36–40). Indeed, once coinage was invented, it acted as "all-purpose money," used in every kind of transaction and widely adopted all around the Mediterranean and beyond.

It is now well accepted, however, that coinage was *not* the only form of money and that there was money *before* coinage (e.g., in Mesopotamia and Egypt: Powell 1996; Menu 2001). It is also clear that uncoined money did not disappear with the advent of coinage. *Hacksilber* (i.e., silver ingots and objects chopped down and weighed) remained in use for decades, sometimes centuries, in both the East and the Iberian Peninsula. Some *Hacksilber* hoards contain chopped coins, indicating that they served primarily as ingots. In the Egyptian oasis of 'Ayn Manâwir, coinage was used as such but became part of the already existing two-tier monetary system. Coins were integrated into the upper tier of silver currency while the lower tier, where barley was the main currency, remained unaffected (Agut-Labordère 2014). Although the 'Ayn Manâwir evidence, dating to the early stages of coin use in Egypt, is exceptionally detailed, one wonders if similar situations were not more common than we assume in the Ancient world. Recent work has argued against an evolutionistic view from kind to cash (see, e.g., von Reden 2010). Jean-Jacques Aubert (2014) has recently reminded us that Roman jurists devoted a great deal of attention to barter, which implies that it was a widespread phenomenon. It is very probable that some transactions involved other currencies than coinage in a situation of "multiple money." This concept was put forward by Georges Condominas (1972; 1989), a French ethnologist who studied the Mnong Gar society in modern-day Vietnam. He observed that goods could be valued in a number of commodities, from buffalo to blankets to chicken, as well as in piasters (the official currency of French Indochina at the time of Condominas' research). Each of these commodities could also act as means of payment. Although each was invested with a different value, none was assigned to a particular type of transaction. They did not function as "special-purpose money," and the choice of use was dictated by convenience rather than by the "sphere of exchange." Although we have much less evidence to show that this was the situation in Antiquity (but see Ramos dos Santos [2008] for Mesopotamia), "multiple money" helps overcome the false dichotomy between natural economy and monetary economy: payments in kind need not indicate barter transactions (for the Middle Ages, see Bloch 1939; English translation in Bloch 1967: 230–47).

If this makes the monetary landscape much more interesting to look at, it also makes its study more complicated. For if it is quite easy to identify coins, other kinds of money are difficult to recognize, particularly in the absence of texts. Cereals always played an important role in the Middle East and Egypt, but ultimately their fate was to be eaten, and organic materials, in general, are seldom preserved. The only practice linked to money that we can trace to some extent in both the material and textual records is weighing (see Figure 4.2). Because it implies agreed standards between the parties, this practice is increasingly seen as a central process in establishing currencies and thus as a crucial step toward the invention of coinage. The control of weight standards was a top priority for all authorities during Antiquity. It appears in the earliest Mesopotamian law texts (Roth 1997) as well as in the Bible ("A false balance is abomination to the Lord: but a just weight is his delight," *Proverbs* 11.1 [King James translation]). One of the tasks of Greek *agoranomoi* and Roman *aediles* was to control weights, and Late Antique and Byzantine monetary weights regularly featured the image of the emperor(s). In the present state of data, the oldest balances and weights that appear in the archaeological records are dated to the first half of the third millennium BCE (Early Bronze Age) in Mesopotamia (Rahmstorf 2016, with reference to previous work by the same author). This accords with the textual evidence of contemporary law collections. The phenomenon then spread out toward the West, reaching Italy and Central Europe a millennium later (Pare 2013). Clear links between standards from different regions demonstrate that commensurability was sought. Furthermore, according to a case study, weighing equipment can be found in varying contexts, public, private, and funerary: the practice appears to have been relatively widespread (Michailidou 2010, a case study on the Late Bronze Age Aegean).

Of course, not all weighing is related to money, but there is a clear thread linking weighing and currency running all through Antiquity. At the far end of the period, Late Antique Roman gold coins were weighed while being used as coins (Carlà 2007a; 2010). Weighing is therefore not an indication of non-monetary exchange but rather of different habits, often implying other

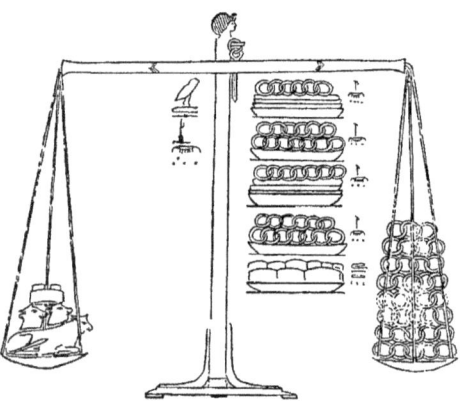

FIGURE 4.2: Weighed money from Egypt. This type of scales is common throughout Antiquity. From Ducros 1908: 49 fig. 2 (public domain https://archive.org/stream/annalesduservice910egyp#page/n57/mode/2up).

currencies than coinage. The widespread appearance of scales in periods when coinage was either not yet invented (Bronze Age) or declining (Merovingian times) can thus be seen as hinting at different forms of money use rather than to non-monetary forms of exchange. Although the remainder of this chapter will deal primarily with coinage, as it is the most readily identifiable form of money and present in a wide array of contexts, the reader should keep in mind that it was probably used in a situation of "multiple money."

PRODUCING MONEY

In the contemporary world, producing currency (in the form of coins and banknotes) is a highly protected and partly secret activity carried out by the state, and we tend to project this state of affairs onto Ancient times. Indeed, the Imperial Mint in Rome, excavated under the church of San Clemente, lends support to this view: it is a massive building with thick walls and no windows (Guidobaldi 1992: 48–69). Although the building itself was in plain view and its function known (it was mentioned on the *Forma Urbis Romae*, the marble plan of the city, and a group of inscriptions was set up by the mint personnel, probably in front of its entrance), what went on inside was well hidden.

But as we have seen, money was not always coinage and was not always produced by public authorities. In the pre-coinage phase of weighed metal, be it silver or gold in the East or in the Iberian peninsula, or bronze in the Italian peninsula (*aes rude*) and possibly in continental Europe, there does not seem to have been any public involvement other than guaranteeing common weight standards (but their adoption could also have been the result of personal initiative). The actual production of the metal objects was in private hands. Although there is general agreement among modern scholars (in line with ancient sources) that coinage was produced by public authorities, this does not always seem to have been the case. There is still no definite proof that there was state monopoly on the earliest electrum coinage from Lydia (Konuk 2012: 48). In pre-Roman Gaul, the case for decentralization appears to be even stronger. In the region now corresponding roughly to the northern half of France, coinage was introduced *c.* 300 BCE. The early faithful copies of golden *staters* from Philipp II of Macedonia quickly evolved into original coins decidedly Celtic in style. From *c.* 200 BCE, copper-alloyed cast coins were introduced; some decades later and in some areas, gold coins were replaced by silver, often bearing Roman-inspired images. Local coinages, mostly struck bronzes, thrived after the Gallic Wars (58–51 BCE) before disappearing completely *c.* 20/10 BCE. Throughout these three centuries, it is rather rare to find coin distributions matching the territories of the various *civitates* (often translated as "tribes" in English). Some coins circulated widely, including low-value cast coins (see various contributions in Gruel 1995), while others appear only at one site (this is particularly true of sanctuaries from modern-day Picardy). Although a growing number of coin types, from the mid-second century BCE onwards, display legends, not a single one mentions the name of a Gallic *civitas* before the Gallic Wars. Even after that date, most legends consist of personal names, some of which are aristocrats mentioned in Caesar's *De Bello Gallico*.

Based on this evidence, it is very likely that a large part of coin production, if not the majority, was in the hands of private individuals. This accords well with the rare traces of Iron Age coin production found in excavations in Gaul. At Migné-Auxances, near Poitiers (France), a rescue excavation on a farm uncovered the remnants of a probable mint dated between 130 and 100 BCE. The production of copper-alloyed blanks was situated in a pit. Although no tools were found relating to the minting itself, it is very likely that this also took place on the farm, as the blanks were of similar composition to coins found during the excavation (Toledo i Mur and Pernot 2008). On the Fossé des Pandours (a hill-top settlement in eastern France), several miscast potin-coins were found in a well very close to rather high-standard dwellings—suggesting direct control of coin production by the local élites. Similar evidence was uncovered on the *oppidum* of Villeneuve-Saint-Germain in France (Debord 1989). These Gallic examples are proof that mints operated in the middle of living quarters: no doubt controls were tight, but it was certainly not a secret process. Furthermore, technological studies have shown that casting and minting—the engraving of dies excepted—were accessible to average craftsmen and did not require extra skills. In the excavated workshops, it is clear or at least suspected that minting was not the only activity. This may also have been the case in the official mint for bronze coins in Athens, where traces of iron working have been found (Camp and Kroll 2001: 144).

These few examples concern official minting. Even more embedded in everyday life was the production of unofficial coinage. It is not always clear if we are dealing with false coins, as some productions are so peculiar that it would have been impossible to be duped (for the Roman period, see Peter 2011). Roman Gaul has been well studied in this respect. Some production sites are indeed hidden, for instance in caves. But most of them are to be found either in towns, in metalsmiths' workshops or in rural settlements. The best-known examples of urban workshops are from Augst in Switzerland (Peter 1990; Straumann 2011) and Châteaubleau in France (Pilon 2004; 2005). It is not always clear if the minting was clandestine. For instance, although the production seems irregular, the second-century BCE mint excavated in the temple of Karnak (Egypt), which was set up against the wall of a chapel, could hardly have gone unnoticed (Faucher *et al.* 2011; see Figure 4.3).

Whatever the status of and the reason for these unofficial productions, they seem to occur in periods of shortage (sometimes only in small denominations) and can be taken as clear signs of the need of currency in everyday life. In the

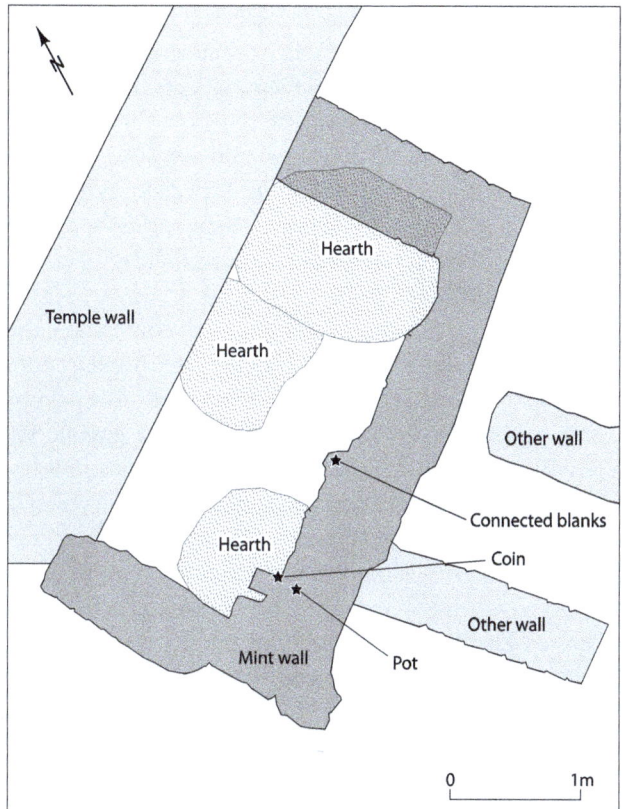

FIGURE 4.3: Plan from the second-century BCE mint of Karnak (Egypt). Redrawn by author from Faucher *et al.* 2011.

rural France of the nineteenth and early twentieth centuries CE, we have numerous examples of local coin production that was perceived as forgery by the central authorities but was entirely legitimate to a population who occasionally used fourth-century Late Roman bronze coins as small change. (On the legitimacy of forgeries for the users: Traimond 1994. On using Roman coins: the practice is reported for instance by famous French numismatists Jean-Baptiste Colbert de Beaulieu in Brittany and Jean Lafaurie in the southwest: Colbert de Beaulieu 1973: 330 note 660; Dumas 2008: 152.)

The physical production of coinage was therefore probably a much more mundane occupation than we tend to think. From what we know, this is also true for other forms of money. As mentioned previously, we know some of the commodities used as money from documents in Mesopotamia and Egypt: metals (gold, silver, copper and its alloys, but also lead), cloth, foodstuffs, and, in particular, cereals (barley being regularly mentioned) (Powell 1996; Menu

2001). If metal objects often had recognizable forms that probably indicated their monetary function (such as rings or special-shaped ingots), this barely required special craftsmanship. Even the metal objects that may have served as currency in the Bronze Age, whose alloy differed from that of everyday objects, were probably produced by the same craftsmen (Pare 2013). When it comes to foodstuffs, we generally have no indication of a special treatment. The *ostraca* from 'Ayn Manâwir do mention payments in "fine barley" but the meaning is unclear; it may be a special variety, but more probably it was just ordinary threshed barley (Agut-Labordère 2014).

Once currency was available to users, it still underwent manipulations as it was adapted to new monetary situations. The fractioning of coins, for instance, is commonly observed in the Roman period. There is the distinct possibility that the halving (less often quartering) of thick coins from the Republic and the Early Empire might have been official, for it is much harder than it seems (as a colleague who tried to halve a bronze *dupondius*, using a hammer and a chisel, knows from bitter experience!) although the common man certainly did have a go as well. It is not rare to find coins with chop-marks indicating a failed halving. Private initiative is certainly to be sought in the case of smaller coins, for instance the thin Late Antique bronzes. During the fifth and sixth centuries CE, all over the Roman Empire we find fourth-century bronze coins cut up to match the new weight standards (see, e.g., Asolati 2005: 19–22, with numerous examples from the Mediterranean; the phenomenon is also present in the northern provinces). At more or less the same time, other users found a somewhat easier way, although it required the possession of a fair number of old Roman coins from the Principate: on *c.* 150 pieces, mainly from Italy, new value marks corresponding to the Ostrogothic and Vandalic monetary systems were made with a chisel. Cécile Morrisson thinks that this practice started in the public sphere and was later taken up by private individuals. The choice of coins seems to have been dictated by sheer availability (see Asolati 2012: 113–34, with previous literature).

USING MONEY

Most people kept their money at home. Excavations in Pompeii give us some indication of how coins were kept in Roman houses. The hoard from the House of the Menander was in a big coffer (*arca*), stored in a cellar, with coins and jewels in a smaller box separate from the plate (Painter 2001). In a neighboring house, small clusters of coins were found in the sleeping rooms: each person apparently kept his/her purse under the bed. Because of the exceptional nature of the Vesuvian evidence, such details are difficult to obtain from other sites, but we can assume similar trends: valuable goods and big money were stored securely and sometimes hidden (this certainly accounts for an unknown number of hoards recovered in modern times), while small change was more readily at hand. Terracotta money boxes are relatively common throughout the period (Graeven 1901). Money could also be deposited at the bank (on Greek banks: Bogaert 1968; on Roman banks: Andreau 1987). In the Principate, this was common enough to appear in the *colloquia* of the *Hermeneumata Pseudodositheana* as a rather normal situation (*colloquia Monacensia* 4): One character withdraws 100 denarii from the bank to pay his lawyers. Dating from the Principate and intended for Greeks learning Latin, "*colloquia* are bilingual dialogues and narratives designed to be used at an early stage of language learning [and] many *colloquia* passages are vignettes about daily life in the Roman World" (Dickey 2016: 10). The texts have been recently reedited in Dickey (2012; 2015). Throughout Antiquity, including in Mesopotamia, temples could also receive deposits from private individuals (see below for further information on sanctuaries).

The way people keep and move their money tells us something about how they use it (on the transport of coins, see de Callataÿ and van Heesch 2006, notably the papers by François de Callataÿ and Reinhard Wolters). It is therefore interesting to see that purses seem to have been the most common method to carry coins around in both Greek and Roman times. This indicates that it was customary and useful to have some cash at hand and points to a rather widespread use of coinage. Few purses have survived, as they were made of perishable materials, but an impressively complete leather purse from the second century CE has been found in Barger-Compascuum in the Netherlands (Glasbergen *et al*. 1956). Several examples of a metal purse designed to be worn around the wrist are known from Roman times, some still containing coins, generally in bronze (see Figure 4.4). Bigger sums could also be carried in bags

FIGURE 4.4: A Roman bronze arm-purse from Mook (the Netherlands). Photograph National Museum of Antiquities, Leiden, inv. no. l 1939/5.1 (license CC-BY).

(the original meaning of the Latin word *follis* which eventually designated a coin) or in chests and boxes of various size. In some famous lines, Aristophanes wrote of Athenians carrying coins in their mouth (e.g., *Ecclesiazusae* 817–19). This was obviously very impractical and one of his characters swallows his small change (Aristophanes, *Aves* 503)!

The first use of money that comes to mind, and indeed one of its principle, if not main functions, was to pay for goods and services. Transactions could take place in a variety of places: shops, inns, private houses, and, of course, the marketplace. There appears to be some correlation between the density of coin finds in archaeological excavations and the intensity of coin use in Antiquity. For instance, Richard Hobbs (2013) has shown that in *insula* VI 1 of Pompeii, coins were more frequent along the street, around the small shops and at the shrine (see Figure 4.5). This is probably a general trend, as similar cases are found in both pre-Roman and Roman Gaul (Martin 2015).

The agoras in Sagalassos (Turkey) provide an interesting view of Late Antique urban marketplaces (Putzeys 2007; Lavan 2012; Stroobants and Poblome 2015). They present themselves as open courtyards surrounded by small built rooms. Positions for removable wooden stalls were indicated on the floor of the square. Numerous coins were found both in the rooms and on the central courtyards. These agoras were probably the setting for daily transactions similar to those described in some written sources. Once again, the *colloquia* of the

FIGURE 4.5: Pompeii, insula VI 1. Distribution map of coins found in the excavations of the Anglo–American Pompei Project. From Hobbs 2013: 102 fig. 18 (image courtesy of Richard Hobbs).

Hermeneumata Pseudodositheana offer some vivid depictions that supplement and lend credibility to what we find in Greco-Roman novels (*colloquia Monacensia* 8: going to the market with a servant; *colloquium Montepessulanum* 13: buying and bargaining over clothes; compare, e.g., with Apuleius, *Metamorphoses* 1.24). In Sagalassos, detailed analysis of the finds has made it possible to reconstruct the functions of the various rooms, most of which appear to have been retail stores, sometimes attached to workshops. In both agoras, weighing equipment was found with numerous coins in one of the rooms. These could have been the offices of moneychangers. Indeed, we know that moneychangers had an important role in everyday life, since for most of Antiquity coinage was never unified; users could be faced with a variety of coins (even during the Roman Empire various coinages circulated, particularly in the East). With the additional presence of forgeries, it was necessary to test coins frequently. Raymond Bogaert has gathered the evidence for Classical Antiquity (Bogaert 1976). The clearest text at our disposal is the so-called "Nikophon's Law" from 375/374 BCE (*Supplementum Epigraphicum Graecum* XXVI: 72): the city of Athens put in charge two approvers (*dokimastai*) to test coins in the market place, obviously on a daily basis. Testing appears to have been a craft in itself, involving not only touchstones, scales, and close visual examination, but also listening to the sound the coin made and even smelling it!

Games with money-prizes were of course already known in ancient times and engraved game-boards are often found in public squares (see Lanciani 1892 for an old but vivid account of ancient Rome). But Petronius in *Satyricon* (33.2) also mentions the use by Trimalchio of silver and gold coins as counters on a game-board: a convenient way to replace tokens that is likely to have happened in real life, although probably with coins of lesser value.

As testified by the graffiti from Pompeii, towns and marketplaces were witness to frequent money lending (e.g., CIL IV 4528) and pawning (e.g., CIL IV 8203), which could consist of very small sums. For instance, the person who pawned the earrings in CIL IV 8203 received thirty-one *asses*; according to some "shopping lists" inscribed on Pompeian walls, this would only support someone for a few days (see also *colloquia Monacensia* 5, for an impression of how a loan was conducted, and *colloquia Harleianum* 23, on how to be repaid). Although the transactions were indeed recorded, such pawning and money lending was certainly not the work of professionals. It is proof that the lower classes of the urban population needed cash for their everyday life. Although most of our documentation concerns towns, we should not underestimate the use of money in the countryside. The Egyptian papyri show that the traditional assumption of peasants accustomed to a "natural economy" is wrong. As always, it is difficult to find such precise documentation elsewhere, but it is worth mentioning a writing tablet dated to 29 CE. Found in the countryside in

Tolsum (the Netherlands) more than 100 km north of the Roman frontier, it is a loan-note for an unknown sum of money (Bowman, Tomlin, and Worp 2009). The location and the presence of a Batavian soldier as a witness make it likely that one of the contractees was a local.

Sanctuaries were also important loci for coin and money use (various contributions for the whole period in Chankowski 2005). Based on written documentation from Mesopotamia, Greece, and Rome, the sanctuaries' resources can be divided in three categories. First, objects belonging to the deity, normally inalienable. They could be transformed or sold in so far as it profited the gods (e.g., a new statue or repairs to the temple). Second, private deposits that could be retrieved by their owners. Indeed, it was not rare to deposit one's savings in a temple to benefit from the gods' protection. Finally came all the other resources from which the temple and its dependents made a living: fees for religious services and the sale of ex-votos or other artefacts, but also exploitation of landed property and financial operations such as loans. Thanks to progress in archaeological excavation, it is now possible to identity some of these practices in the material record. Much attention has been devoted recently to the use of coins in sanctuaries in Gaul, from the advent of coinage in the third century BCE to Late Antiquity, and there are some clear trends (see mainly Nouvel 2013). In the Iron Age, coins were probably deposited by the community in a public ceremony, in the form of precious hoards consisting mainly of high-value pieces. This changed from the mid-first century BCE onward, when low-value offerings became the norm: coins were deposited by individuals, sometimes thrown (*iactatio*), sometimes superficially buried into the ground. These coins were often mutilated to ensure they were withdrawn from circulation. In the sanctuary of the Martberg (Germany), David Wigg-Wolf (2005) could identify two phases: in the first (first century BCE), the defacement is uniform, pointing to some kind of control; on the contrary, in the early first century CE, each coin bears different marks, indicating that each worshipper now took care of his/her own offering. Because they were consecrated, coins could not leave the sanctuary, which explains why sanctuary finds are so common from *c*. 50 BCE to *c*. 50 CE. The sudden drop in coin finds from the end of the first century to the end of the third century CE marks a new management of the offerings and possibly a stronger control by the clergy. In Gaul, stone *thesauri* (collection boxes) date precisely to this period (there are others dated much earlier in Greece and Italy; see Kaminski 1991). These offerings were certainly reused according to their status, either to embellish the sanctuary or to make some profit. From the end of the third century to the early fifth century, small value coins are again found in great quantities. These offerings seemed to have been left on the floor, where they were thrown by visitors. The reason is unclear, but the very small value of each coin probably played a part. Finally, even when pagan sanctuaries were permanently closed in

c. 400 CE, objects belonging to the gods were not reused. This is demonstrated by a number of hoards from this period, which often mix coins with other artefacts (statuettes, vessels); they had probably been carefully buried, either definitively or with the hope of recovery in more favorable times.

An exceptional set of graffiti found in the first-century CE sanctuary of Châteauneuf (France) confirms that vows were expressed in monetary value, although it is unclear whether all of them were paid in actual coins (Mermet 1993; Rémy 1999; see Figure 4.1). Of course, not all coins found on a sanctuary site need to be offerings. Inside the sacred area of the sanctuary of Mandeure, "Champ des Fougères" (France), pottery kilns were unearthed dating to the second half of the first century BCE, a time when religious activities were clearly ongoing (Nouvel and Thivet 2011). It is tempting to interpret the kilns as a source of monetary income for the temple.

Another use of coins that has received considerable scholarly attention is the so-called "Charon's obol". This is still the favored interpretation for coins discovered in tombs, although it has become clear that funerary customs display strong chronological and geographical variation in the Ancient world. However useful, ancient texts propose too unified a picture. The meaning of funerary coin deposition must be asserted carefully for each region and period; important variation can be observed even in neighboring zones. For instance, coins are rarely found in Celtic Europe in the Late Iron Age, but they do appear in some spots, most notably in Northern Italy, some areas of Switzerland, and modern Luxembourg. A variety of practices can explain how the coin(s) arrived in the tomb. This is clear in the case of cremations: generally, only part of the offerings found in the tomb are burned, meaning that some were on the funeral pyre while others were deposited directly into the grave. A careful excavation and a close examination of the archaeological data are always desirable and worthwhile, but probably never more so than in the case of cemeteries; in funerary practices we can sense intentionality behind almost every gesture (see Stevens 1991 for a review of both literary and archaeological evidence; for the latter, many more data are now available).

We have so far distinguished between three main spheres of coin use: economic, ritual, and funerary. In real life, this distinction was, of course, not so clear cut. Moral and religious values could also impact the economic use of coins: Suetonius (*Tiberius* 58) writes that bringing a coin bearing Augustus' portrait to the latrines or a brothel was considered *lèse-majesté* under Tiberius; Epictetus (in Arrian, *Epicteti dissertationes* 4.5.15–18) relates that after Nero's downfall, a coin bearing his head could be rejected. Whether this actually happened is debatable, but they indicate that coins were not treated just as economic objects. However, coinage and other forms of money were used in sanctuaries or in tombs *because* they had an economic value. Monetary jewels are another case of coins with multiple values. These jewels are not at all uncommon and are known from the Hellenistic period onward (Vermeule 1975). They obviously acted as a store of value and certainly could have had a monetary use, but the coins they reuse are generally in good condition and their aesthetic quality certainly played a role as well. Conversely, coins can be melted down. Not just gold and silver; less-valuable coinage could also meet this fate: in some parts of nineteenth-century CE south-western France, for example, there was a shortage of copper coins because they were used to make cutlery and other utensils (Traimond 1994). But at least some of the objects made from coins would certainly have functioned as stores of value and maybe even as means of exchange, with the result that they did not totally lose their monetary function. The following examples aim to show some of the "non-monetary" functions assumed by coins, as well as illustrating how embedded coins were in everyday life.

The texts quoted in the previous paragraph indicate that people paid attention to coin designs and that coin collections already existed: when Suetonius (*Divus Augustus* 75) writes that the first emperor sometimes offered foreign or old coins, he implies that such items were available if one had the means. In Late Antiquity, the numismatic knowledge displayed by the author of the *Historia Augusta* probably indicates that he was himself a collector (Carlà 2007b). But attention to coin types was not confined to the educated aristocracy. In the Roman period we see respect for a coin's image of the emperor centuries after it was minted: the Late Antique value marks engraved on the obverse of coins from the Principate carefully avoid the portrait, although the emperors depicted had been dead for at least 250 years. Nina Crummy has published a group of Late Antique British infant burials where coins were obviously selected for their imagery: in numerous cases, the coins are older than the tombs by a century or more (Crummy 2010). Maybe we should take John Chrysostom (*Ad illuminados cathechesis* 2.5) literally when he writes, in the context of fourth-century CE Antioch (Turkey), "What should one say about those people, who use magic charms and amulets, and carry bronze coins of Alexander the Macedonian around their necks and on their feet?" Some scholars have doubted whether Alexander's coins were still available eight centuries after his death (Perassi 2011: 225–6), but in Merovingian Gaul, it is common to find graves with Celtic coins of comparable age along with more recent Roman coins (see Van Hoof 1991 for the situation in Belgium). Although it is hard to detect archaeologically, the ancient equivalent of modern collections of small change, for instance euro coins of various countries, surely existed, as did the odd foreign coin kept as a souvenir, which certainly accounts for a (very) minor part of the "exotic" coin finds one occasionally encounters.

Coin imagery appears to have been popular, as coins were reused, stamped, or copied on various media. Indeed, as coins were the most readily available images of circular shape, there seems to have been a connection between circular motifs and coins in the minds of the craftsmen and the public. A famous example is the third-century BCE black-glazed cups from Cales (Italy) reproducing the beautiful head of Arethusa engraved by Euainetos for Syracuse. The coin was impressed to obtain a matrix from which the central medallion was molded before being inserted in the cup. But this coin type was by no means the only one copied, and sometimes potters merely took inspiration from coinage (see for Richter 1959 other examples). For a later period, Marie-Christine Hellmann (1987) has devoted a short study to Roman lamps, highlighting their connections to numismatic imagery. One lamp type, itself a New Year's gift, depicted gifts, among them three coins (Hellmann 1987: pl. III no. 1; on this lamp type see Heres 1972). Other lamps drew inspiration from coins, one offering an imperial portrait obviously meant to look like a coin although it does not copy an actual type (Hellmann 1987: pl. IV no. 5). Similar examples can be found on metalwork (see, e.g., the sheet from Austria published in Haselgrove and Krmnicek 2016b: 10 fig. 1.4). Iconographic parallels also exist between coins and gems, which have other similarities: in addition to being small, both gems and coin dies had to be engraved in the negative (Guiraud 1996 provides a good introduction on gems).

In some contexts, coins seem to have carried enough authority to be used as seals (e.g., a fifth-century BCE case in Mesopotamia: Starr 1976 with reference to other occurrences). Similarly, some Roman glass containers have been stamped with a coin on the bottom. According to Luigi Taborelli, the practice is not decorative but linked to imperial involvement in glass production (Taborelli 1982; 1992). The author writes ambiguously "*conio monetale*": in Italian "*conio*" generally means "coin die" but sometimes designates the coin itself (in this case, it is clear that the impressions were made with coins). But sometimes coin impressions appear to have been purposeless, a mere game. A recent excavation in Oloron-Sainte-Marie, at the foot of the French Pyrenees, has yielded a late Roman broken tile (*tegula*) with at least thirteen coin impressions made before firing. Although various hypotheses can be made about the function of such an object, none is satisfactory. The best interpretation so far is that there was no particular reason (Callegarin and Geneviève 2007). This is not without recalling the recent reappraisal of Greek monetary lead objects by François de Callataÿ (2010). Against the current trend of interpreting all such leads as test pieces, he has interpreted most of them as "fantasies," artefacts reproducing pleasant or spectacular coin types in the cheapest of metals (for the value of lead, see Morrisson 1993: 79–84).

CONCLUSION: THE SOCIAL IMPACT OF MONEY

This chapter has tried to offer some insights on possible topics and ways to approach the uses of money in, and its influence on, the everyday. After its invention, coinage clearly became an important part of life. Coins were perceived by Greek and Roman authors as the main, if not the only, civilized form of money. They performed all functions traditionally assigned by economists to money and many more. Combined with the omnipresence of coins in the archaeological record, this has unsurprisingly introduced a bias against other forms of money and has also obscured the continued existence of "multiple money" after the invention of coinage. But Mesopotamian and Egyptian evidence clearly demonstrates that money use was widespread without coinage. However difficult it may prove, a better understanding of "multiple money" should be a priority. Bearing this in mind, a more complicated but much richer picture of how money enmeshed with everyday life will no doubt emerge.

As the forms and uses of money in different times and places become clearer, it will become possible to tackle the issue of the social impact of money. In her book *Money in Classical Antiquity*, Sitta von Reden dedicates her last chapter to the topic, remarking that "surprisingly, very little positive has been said about the social impact of money" (von Reden 2010: 186). Things have changed in the last decades, but her summary makes it clear that scholars (mainly Hellenists) have focused upon the symbolic value of money, underlining how Greek money and coinage must be understood within the framework of generalized exchange that characterized the *polis* (not only economic exchange, but also verbal and political; hence the importance of the *agora* and of discourse: Bresson 2016, chap XI).

Less attention has been given to the concrete impact of money on the living conditions of people. As early as 1970, Zvi Yavetz pointed out that the lower Roman *plebs* would have been most affected by monetary fluctuations. Citing studies on modern economies, David B. Hollander noted that "while monetization initially leads to an increase in the demand for money, as people become more financially sophisticated, their demand for money actually decreases" (Hollander 2007: 145). The point these scholars make is clear: the poorer you are, the fewer financial assets you have access to. If the rich of Antiquity had an easier access to "multiple money," the lower classes, particularly in towns, were highly dependent on the most commonly available and accepted form of money. The small-scale Pompeian loans mentioned above are a good example of this: people pawned their possessions to get the cash necessary for everyday transactions. Lack of documents makes it more difficult to gauge the situation in the countryside; "multiple money" was perhaps a more common situation, but we must be careful here not to exaggerate the discrepancy between rural and urban.

This social impact of money is not restricted to coinage, as recently shown by François Lerouxel (2015). In a very stimulating paper, he argues that, between the sixth and the fourth century BCE, Roman aristocrats used the *aes rude*, the weighed bronze used as money before the adoption of coinage, to force monetary loans with high interest rates onto plebeians. Because aristocrats probably controlled the production of *aes rude*, the loans were virtually unrepayable. Aristocrats thus aimed to put plebeians in debt bondage (*nexum*) to gain control over their workforce and use it on their own lands. *Nexum* was abolished in the late fourth century BCE, at about the same time the Roman state started the production of bronze currency, cast in weighty ingots (*aes grave*). This is probably not a coincidence and it dramatically reflects how money can affect one's life (interestingly, some of Lerouxel's remarks converge with David Graeber's observations in his book on debt: Graeber 2014). Whatever its form, the impact of money on everyday life goes far beyond the simple dichotomy between "swap or sale." The ways in which it influenced and structured the life of our ancestors, however, are still open for exploration.

ACKNOWLEDGMENTS

In preparing this chapter, I benefited from the help of various colleagues. I thank them warmly for their insights on various problems. I owe a great debt to Lydia Spielberg for considerably improving my English.

CHAPTER FIVE

Money, Art, and Representation

A Look at the Roman World

NATHAN T. ELKINS

First and foremost, ancient coins were monetary instruments and served an economic function. But an important secondary function of ancient coinage was as a purveyor of identity and/or political communication. When the first designs were impressed upon coins in Lydia in the seventh century BCE, they functioned to guard against forgeries and unofficial money. A coin with die-struck images or patterns on both sides is far more difficult to copy than a coin that is cast. But soon, images on coinage began to be more than guarantees of authority, authenticity, and value.

THE FUNCTION OF IMAGES

In Archaic and Classical Greece, the coinage most often referred to civic identity in some way. For example, Athena on the obverses, and her owl on the reverses, announced Athenian identity through the portrayal of the eponymous deity and her attribute on the coins struck at Athens. Local nymphs, as at Syracuse, and heroes or references to local myths, such as Pegasus on the reverses of coins at Corinth, also proclaimed the identity of the state that struck the coin. Commodities for which a city state was known were featured on the coinage as well, as a way of identifying the state that issued a particular coin, as with the

FIGURE 5.1: Silver *tetradrachm* of Cyrene, *c.* 435–375 BCE. Obverse: head of Zeus Ammon right; Reverse: Silphium plant (American Numismatic Society 1944.100.79444).

depiction of *kantharoi* and *amphorae* on coins of Boeotia, or grain on the coins of Metapontum, or *silphium* (the ancient abortion drug, ultimately cultivated to extinction in antiquity) on the coins of Cyrene (see Figure 5.1). Coins of other cities bore images or symbols that acted as a pun on a city's name, such as the rose (*rhodos*) on the coins of Rhodes or the sickle that represented Zancle (for further reading on Greek coin types see: Franke and Hirmer 1964; Kraay 1976; Carradice and Price 1988; Ritter 2002; de Callataÿ 2016).

Civic identity also played a major role in Roman provincial coinage. Although the coinage of the Late Roman Republic and of the Roman Empire struck at the central mints often referred to contemporary politics, especially those of the authorities in power, the base metal coinage struck in Greek cities under Roman rule, for the most part, trumpeted local identity (further reading on Roman provincial coin types: Harl 1987; Butcher 1988; Howgego, Heuchert, and Burnett 2005; Bennett 2014; Filges 2015). One way that provincial cities promoted their local identity, often in competition with neighboring cities, is by displaying the temples to the imperial cult that it possessed since the right to dedicate such temples was a privilege bestowed by the emperor (Burrell 2004).

COINS AND POLITICS

In the Hellenistic world, coinage began to depict the image of the monarch, often as a semi-divine figure, as state identity became intertwined with the king himself (on Hellenistic coinage and political identities, see: Howgego 1995: 63–7; Kroll 2007; de Callataÿ 2012b; Thonemann 2015). Roman Republican coins were heavily influenced by Classical Greek coinage early on, but their designs became politicized in the late second century BCE when they began to refer to the ancestry and prestige of the moneyer's family (generally, see Woytek

2012). It is widely accepted that the *lex Gabinia* of 139 BCE effected the sudden change in coin designs in the 130s BCE when images on the reverses of the *denarii* became less static than previous decades and began to display annual typological variety relating to the moneyer's family. The *lex Gabinia* is credited with these developments, as it allowed for a secret ballot in elections, thus giving moneyers (the office was a junior post in the *cursus honorum*) the ability to campaign for future office by advertising their familial prestige on the coinage they designed (Wiseman 1971: 148–9; Crawford 1974: 728). The impact of the *lex Gabinia* may be somewhat overstated, as Andrew Meadows and Jonathan Williams (2001: 39–49) have reminded us that Roman republican coins from the 130s BCE onward reflect the broader culture of the period that valued familial commemoration and monumentality, traceable in literature, public building, art, and coinage (cf. Cheung 1998–9). By the late Republic, moneyers deferred to strong men, as the designs on coins championed the policies and ideals of Sulla, Pompey, and Caesar. In the Roman Empire, coin iconography referred to the emperor, most often with his portrait on the obverse, and celebrated imperial policies, victories, familial piety, public building, or imperial ideals on the reverse (in general, see Burnett 1987). Attention to the imagery on ancient coinage can thus inform modern scholars about how ancient states, governments, and authorities perceived of themselves and their political outlooks. Study of imagery and iconography on Roman coinage is particularly fruitful for a number of reasons (Krmnicek and Elkins 2014: 11–12). First, there are well-organized type catalogs for the republican (Crawford 1974), imperial (*RIC*), and provincial series (*RPC* I, II, III, VII.1, IX, other volumes forthcoming) as well as the reliable and rather precise dates ascribed to most Roman coins, allowing them to be associated with immediate historical contexts. Second, there is a broad array of published hoards and archaeologically recovered finds that form the basis for circulation studies that can help inform the prominence of various images in antiquity and the audience at which certain types were directed. Finally, there is a tendency for images on Roman coins to be more varied and immediate in response to historical and political events than Greek or Hellenistic coins.

COINS AS A MEANS OF POLITICAL COMMUNICATION

While it has been rarely disputed that imagery on coins, especially on late Roman republican and imperial coins, communicated ideas about the moneyers' families, the Roman state or the emperor, the agency behind the construction of the imagery and its intent has been hotly debated. Many scholars have conceived of Roman coin iconography as an instrument of political propaganda. This modernizing interpretation of Roman coinage arose in the middle part of the twentieth century when the globe was embroiled in conflict and major players were concocting propaganda to maintain enthusiasm and support for war against the respective Allied or Axis powers. As Andrew Burnett (1987: 66–71) has pointed out, the debate over the understanding of Roman coin iconography as propaganda can be quite extreme. At one end of the debate was Arnold H.M. Jones (1956: 15–16), an economic historian, who compared Roman coin designs to modern postage stamps. Working on this assumption, Jones asserted that the images reflect the values and interests of the government and its mint workers and that there is no evidence or likelihood that average people paid them any attention. Other scholars take it for granted that coins communicated highly politicized messages to the viewer (e.g., Sutherland 1959 in response to Jones 1956). Indeed, there are scattered descriptions of coins in Roman literature that suggest people took note of the images, interpreted them, and sometimes emotionally responded to them (Burnett 1987b: 66–71). For example, Cassius Dio (47.25.3) describes the *denarius* of Brutus bearing the *pilleus*, the cap awarded to a freed slave and an attribute of Libertas, flanked by two daggers and the legend EID MAR (see Figure 5.2), and interprets the message to be that Brutus and Cassius had liberated the Roman people through their act of tyrannicide. Suetonius (*Nero* 25) evidently misinterpreted a coin of Nero that he describes as depicting Nero playing the lyre; it really depicts Apollo Citharoedus. Sometimes, reactions to coin iconography could be quite emotional. In his *Ecclesiastical History*, Socrates Scholasticus (3.17) described Julian's visit to Antioch. The Christians were angered by Julian's lowering of commodity prices, which they viewed as extortion, so they denounced the emperor and viewed the pagan bull on his coins (*RIC* VIII: (Antioch), nos. 216–18) as an indicator of the chaos caused by him (see Figure 5.3). Sometimes, we even have material evidence for individual responses to an emperor and his

FIGURE 5.2: Silver *denarius* of Brutus, struck in Greece, 43–42 BCE. Obverse: Head of Brutus right, BRVT IMP L PLAET CEST; Reverse: freedman's cap flanked by two daggers, EID MAR (American Numismatic Society 1944.100.4554).

FIGURE 5.3: Billon bronze coin of Julian II, struck at Antioch, 361–3 CE. Obverse: Pearl-diademed, draped, and cuirassed bust of Julian right, D N FL CL IVLIANVS P F AVG; Reverse: Bull, head facing, standing right, with two stars above, SECVRITAS REI PVB, ANTΔ in exergue (American Numismatic Society 1944.100.22355).

coinage, which most often manifests itself through defacement of the imperial portrait on the obverse. For instance, there are several examples of coins of Caligula with defaced portraits, presumably attacked by private individuals (Jucker 1982: 114–18; Varner 2004: 24–5). The portrait of Caligula on a framed *sestertius* in the Museum of Art and Archaeology at the University of Missouri bears witness to such an attack (see Figure 5.4). Another indication

FIGURE 5.4: Framed brass *sestertius* of Caligula, struck at Rome, 37–41 CE. Obverse: laureate head of Caligula left, with gouge marks on the portrait; Reverse: EX SC/OB CIVES/SERVATOS in three lines within an oak wreath (Museum of Art and Archaeology, University of Missouri, Gift of Mrs. Thomas O. Mabbot, 72.208).

that individuals paid attention to images on coins and ascribed meaning to them is the large body of evidence from coins in graves and tombs that indicate conscientious selection of coins according to their reverse iconography. For example, at Avenches, coins with images of Pax, Salus, Felicitas, and Roma were favored for deposition in inhumation graves and burial urns (Koenig 1999: 456–8 and his fig. 371). Roman graves around modern Cologne exhibit a preference for a deposition of coins with the deceased that in some way referred to the afterlife with reverse types such as HERCVLI IMMORTALI, MEMORIAE AETERNAE, and MEMORIA FELIX (Gorecki 1975: 271–6). In the city of Rome, in the Catacombs of Saints Peter and Marcellinus, coins for the young Divus Romulus were pressed into the seal around a Christian child's *loculus*. Evidently, the coins were chosen to adorn the burial owing to the child's likeness on the obverses of the coins (R.-Alföldi 1996).

While material and literary evidence suggests that the images were interpreted and reacted to by at least some people in the Roman Empire, is it appropriate to view coin images as instruments of propaganda? It is debatable whether Roman coin designs were constructed with the intent to convince or persuade the viewer of any specific viewpoint in the same way that propaganda functions. Instead, the images may have simply reinforced positive expectations of the prestigious republican families or the emperor that were already circulating in text, spoken word, art and architecture (e.g., Levick 1982; Wallace-Hadrill 1986: 67; Burnett 1987b: 69; Levick 1999a; Meadows and Williams 2001: 49). Carlos Noreña helpfully distinguishes between "agitation propaganda," the sort of propaganda we are primarily familiar with in twentieth-century history, and "integration propaganda." He summarizes:

> While agitation propaganda seeks to change attitudes, according to Ellul's definition, integration propaganda seeks to bolster them. The former is more visible and widespread, is often subversive, and bears 'the stamp of opposition,' while the latter aims instead at 'stabilizing the social body,' making it 'the preferred instrument of government.' This distinction is useful, and helps to explain why the imperial regime ever bothered to communicate a set of ideals and values associated with the reigning emperor. In general, there was not much in the way of agitation propaganda in the Roman imperial period. During the high empire in particular, there was little need to change attitudes and—even more important—the actual mechanics of imperial communications would have made it almost impossible to do so. That the regular, long-term dissemination of imperial ideals was instead intended, at least in part, to reinforce belief in the legitimacy of Roman imperial rule seems more plausible . . . But the official communication of imperial ideals by the central state necessarily entailed a positive valuation of imperial rule, which in turn entailed a degree of persuasion, even if only implicit. Moreover,

one of the media available to the imperial regime, the coinage, was particularly well suited to the slow, long-term diffusion of ideas upon which such integration propaganda depends. As a preliminary conclusion, then, we may see the central state in idealizing the figure of the emperor through a set of ideals and values associated with him, was motivated at least in part by the goal of reinforcing the legitimacy of Roman imperial rule.

—Noreña 2011a: 18

If numismatic scholars persist in using the word "propaganda," it is useful to theorize and thoroughly define that class of propaganda, as Noreña has done, to avoid confusion and misrepresentation of the function of images on coins. But arguably, the word "propaganda" has no place in the study of Roman art and coinage. The Roman Empire did not employ propaganda ministers, like Hitler's Joseph Goebbels, or devote government ministries to the formulation of propaganda that was anything akin to Goebbels's Reichsministerium für Volksaufklärung und Propaganda, and we know little or nothing about the mechanisms by which coin iconography was formulated. Historians and theoreticians of Roman art have already abandoned the term "propaganda" due to its implications of both a desired intent to "persuade" or "convince" a viewer of a certain political perspective and direct government agency, if not the direct involvement of the emperor himself (e.g., Zanker 1988: 3; Zanker 2010: 108–12; Stewart 2008: 112). Indeed, in the early and mid-twentieth century, numismatists assumed that the emperor chose the subjects and messages on imperial coinage (e.g., Sydenham 1920: 34; Mattingly 1962: 140). Even today, many numismatists perhaps too hastily ascribe, or even assume, imperial agency in the selection of coin types (e.g., Hekster 2003). But while any public state-sanctioned imagery or art must have been acceptable to the emperor, it is improbable that he was directly involved in the concoction of state-relief sculptures or imperial coin iconography as he had bigger affairs of state to occupy his energies.

For coinage, it is more probable that the imagery was formulated in the mint (e.g., Wolters 1999: 290–308; Cheung 1998–9: 58–60). In fact, a recent study of the transference of camp gate/city gate and baldachin iconography on Roman provincial coinage to the late imperial coinage suggests the agency of the mint in the formulation of imagery, as the local traditions of representation in provinces appeared first on imperial coins struck at mints in these regions (Elkins 2013). This indicates that die-cutters or mint officials accustomed to local iconographic traditions concocted and created the imagery. An earlier example, illustrating the initiative of the mint in the creation of coin iconography, is the Augustan coinage depicting the temple of Mars Ultor. In celebration of Augustus's Parthian settlement in 19 BCE, the Senate decreed a small temple on the Capitoline Hill to Mars Ultor, in a fashion similar to the Temple of Jupiter

Feretrius, to house the recovered military standards (Cassius Dio 54.8.3). Imperial branch mints in Spain and Pergamon immediately struck coins depicting what appears to be a small, round votive temple identifiable as a temple to Mars Ultor on account of the legends and the iconography (*RIC*² I: nos. 28, 39a–b, 64–9, 72–4, 103–6, 114–20, and 507). None the less this temple never appeared on the imperial coinage struck at Rome. The Temple of Mars Ultor, as we know it, was inaugurated in 2 BCE, along with the Forum of Augustus, in a larger and more monumental form and in a different location than the Senate had intended two decades before (on the association of this temple to Mars with the Parthian settlement from the outset, and not with the vengeance against Caesar's assassins, see Beckmann 2016). The Spanish and Asian coinages have caused scholars to assume that there was a temporary shrine on the Capitoline Hill until Augustus completed his more monumental temple in his forum or that there were two temples to Mars Ultor in Rome. A more pragmatic scenario is that Augustus rejected the Senate's decreed honor, as he intended to build a larger temple with his forum. This would explain the curious phenomenon whereby the branch imperial mints in Spain and Asia, for a short time, struck coins bearing images of the small temple in immediate response to the honorary decree, while the mint at Rome never had the opportunity to celebrate the honor bestowed on Augustus. The Spanish and Pergamene mints would have ceased striking coins as soon as news reached them that the emperor had not accepted the decree to build a temple to Mars Ultor on the Capitoline (Rich 1998: 86; Elkins 2015: 61–3, with further bibliography).

The term "propaganda" when applied to Roman art and coin iconography may also misrepresent the intent of the images themselves. It is useful to think of images on coins as we think about the construction of public buildings and monuments and their associated sculptural programs. Most Roman imperial monuments were not built and dedicated by the emperor but were instead initiated and dedicated by the Senate and Roman people *to* the emperor (Hölscher 1984; Zanker 2000; Mayer 2010; Hölscher 2014: 24–6). There is often a coherence in rhetoric and ideology communicated in public building, state-relief, coin iconography, and contemporary laudatory poetry and panegyric. Understanding Roman imperial coin iconography in this way has been best articulated by Barbara Levick (1982), who sees the emperor as the primary audience for images on coins, rather than the agent behind the selection of images (followed by Wallace-Hadrill 1986, among others).

The relationship between images on the coins and contemporary poetry and panegyric is a discernible in several periods of Roman imperial history. In Augustus's reign, images on coinage articulated the same ideas and rhetoric as conveyed through contemporary laudatory poetry and text; and the Parthian settlement is a key theme in coinage, art, and text (Zanker 1988; Lamp 2013: 80–108). A demonstrable relationship between texts and coin iconography appears again in the reign of Tiberius, when base-metal coinage celebrated several of Tiberius's imperial ideals: *moderatio, clementia, iustitia, pietas*, and *concordia*. As Velleius Paterculus and Valerius Maximus praise Tiberius's style of governance, the coinage visualizes the same adulatory rhetoric (Levick 1999b: 82–91). Valerius Maximus (5) ascribes the virtue of *clementia* to Tiberius (see, later, Tacitus, *Annales* 2.31.4; 3.50.3; 3.68.2; 6.25.4) while Tiberian *dupondii* depict a laureate bust on a shield accompanied by the legend CLEMENTIAE (*RIC*² I: no. 38). In honor of Tiberius and Sejanus, the Senate dedicated the Ara Clementiae in 28 CE (Tacitus, *Annales* 4.74). A similar design, but with a facing bust and the legend MODERATIONI (see Figure 5.5) occupies another group of *dupondii* (*RIC*² I: nos. 39–40) and is another quality attributed to Tiberius by contemporary authors (Velleius Paterculus 2.122.1; Valerius Maximus 4.1; and, later, Tacitus, *Annales* 1.7.6; 1.14.3; 2.36.2; 3.12.1; 3.50.2; 3.56.1,4; 3.69.8; 4.38.4; Suetonius, *Tiberius* 32.2). Some *dupondii* depict a bust of Iustitia, labelled thus (*RIC*² I: no. 46), and *iustitia* was also part of the contemporary rhetoric of the era in Valerius Maximus (6.5) and Velleius Paterculus (2.126.2). While Tiberius had rebuilt the Temple of Concord in the reign of Augustus, it was featured several decades later on his *sestertii* (*RIC*² I: nos. 74–6). As the coins do not reflect current building activity, they may instead refer to the rhetoric of *concordia* during Tiberius's reign and the public dedications made to Concordia after the failed conspiracy of Marcus Scribonius Libo Drusus (*CIL* VI 91–3, 904, 3674 (3075 = 30856); ILS 3783; Tacitus, *Annales* 2.32.2). Several coin types in Tiberius's reign honored the Deified Augustus and thus demonstrate the emperor's *pietas*. On account of his pious

FIGURE 5.5: Brass *dupondius* of Tiberius, struck at Rome, 16–22 CE. Obverse: laureate head of Tiberius left, TI CAESAR DIVI AVG F AVGVST IMP VIII; Reverse: Shield with facing bust, MODERATIONI (American Numismatic Society 1944.100.39284).

and dutiful qualities, Suetionius (*Tiberius* 17.2) claims that during Augustus's lifetime the *cognomen* "Pius" was offered to Tiberius, but Augustus would not allow it so that Tiberius could take his own *cognomen*. *Dupondii* of Tiberius also depict a veiled head of Pietas, with a descriptive legend (*RIC*² I: no. 43), suggesting again that *pietas* was part of the contemporary adulatory rhetoric aimed at the emperor.

Imperial coins referring to games can also illustrate a link between images and laudatory poetry. For example, Domitianic *quadrantes* dated to 83 CE or later, owing to the presence of GERM(ANIVCS) in the imperial titulature, display a rhinoceros (*RIC*² II.1: nos. 248–54). The contemporary poet Martial, in two epigrams, describes the unique and magnificent appearance of a rhinoceros in games at the Colosseum in praise of Caesar:

> The rhinoceros displayed all around the arena, Caesar, has delivered up combat that it did not promise. Launching itself headlong it flared up into such a terrible rage! What a great bull that was, for which a bull was but a toy!
> —Martial, *Spectacula* 11[9]

> While the trainers were nervously worrying a rhinoceros and the great beast's temper was taking a long time to gather strength, men began to give up hope of any battles ensuing in the conflict that they had been promised. But finally the rage that we had known earlier returned, for he picked up a heavy bear on his double horn like a bull tossing a load of dummies to the stars. [With how sure an aim does the sturdy hand of Carpophorus, still young, launch his Norican spears!] He scooped up a pair of bullocks on his pliable neck, the ferocious aurochs and the bison gave in to him; a lion trying to escape from him raced full tilt into the spears: go now spectators, and carp at sluggish days.
> —Martial, *Spectacula* 26 [22+23]

The identity of "Caesar" mentioned throughout the *Liber Spectaculorum* has long been assumed to be Titus, who inaugurated the Colosseum in 80 CE, but evidence suggests he could be Domitian instead or that the epigrams in the *Liber Spectaculorum* might have addressed both Titus and Domitian (Coleman 2006: xlv–lxiv; Buttrey 2007). Rhinoceroses were rare in Roman games due to their great size and mass, weighing up to three or four tons, making their transport difficult and expensive. The exceptionally wondrous display caused both the mint and Martial to praise the emperor.

A later example is the reverse of a coin depicting the barrier of the Circus Maximus bedecked with props to make it appear like the hull of a ship with the Augustan obelisk serving as its mast; it is surrounded by animals and accompanied by the legend LAETITIA TEMPORVM, "the happiness of the times," on

FIGURE 5.6: Silver *denarius* of Septimius Severus, struck at Rome, 202–10 CE. Obverse: Laureate bust of Septimius Severus right, SEVERVS PIVS AVG; Reverse: the barrier of the Circus Maximus staged as a ship surrounded by animals and charioteers, LAETITIA TEMPORVM (American Numismatic Society 1944.100.50203).

aurei and *denarii* of Septimius Severus (see Figure 5.6), Caracalla, and Geta from around 201 to 209 CE (*RIC* IV: nos. 274 [Severus], 133 and 157 [Caracalla], and 43 [Geta]). The coins refer to a spectacle during the games for the tenth anniversary of Septimius Severus's reign when the barrier of the Circus Maximus was dressed like a ship and rigged to collapse so that exotic beasts could emerge theatrically for a staged hunt. Cassius Dio, an eyewitness to the spectacle, recounts it in praise of the emperor (77.1.4–5). The description is similar to an honorary inscription dedicated to Septimius Severus, which reads "... *pro temporum Laetitia et felicitate sanctissimorum*," thus using the same language on the coinage (Carlson 1969; Rowan 2011: 51–2; on the inscription, see *CIL* VI 32326–32335, especially VI 32326). Even in the later Roman Empire there are sometimes clear correspondences between laudatory poetry and panegyric as in the reign of Maximian. The coinage of Maximian from 286 to 292 CE struck at the imperial mint at Lugdunum carries the same themes for which the emperor is praised at his court in Trier in contemporary panegyrics between 289 and 291 CE (Steinbock 2014).

Connections between laudatory rhetoric, poetry, and panegyric and images on coins may well indicate that the emperor was not the agent behind the selection of coin types. The coins would then be more similar to honorary monuments dedicated to the emperor or the laudatory poetry and panegyric that was similarly dedicated to him by other parties. If the emperor was not the agent behind the selection of imperial coin types, then who was?

AGENCY AND THE SELECTION OF IMPERIAL COIN TYPOLOGY

In the Roman Republic, the annually-appointed moneyers (*tresviri monetales*) were quite clearly the agents who formulated coin iconography. During the Roman Empire, we know that there were still *tresviri monetales* as late as the third century CE, although they are mostly anonymous, and little is known about them after the reign of Augustus. How exactly they functioned during the imperial period is unknown. A new office under the emperors was the *procurator monetae*, who was an equestrian who acted as a chief of the mint (Peachin 1986). There first-known *procurator monetae* is Lucius Vibius Lentulus, who served in this position from *c.* 98 to 102 CE during the reign of Trajan, although the post itself almost certainly existed before Trajan's reign (Pflaum 1960–1: 157–8; Peachin 1986: 95, n. 5). Before administering the mint, Lucius Vibius Lentulus was tribune of *Legio VII Geminae* from 88 to 89 CE and had thus served previously with Trajan. A likely scenario is that he came to know Trajan during this service and, after receiving the general's favor, began to be appointed to procuratorial positions when Trajan became emperor. After he was *procurator monetae*, he moved on to become *procurator* of Pannonia and Dalmatia and then, later, of Asia. His last career post was as *procurator a rationibus*, which is most analogous to a chief minister of finance; the *procurator monetae* was overseen by the *procurator a rationibus*. We cannot know for certain whether the *tresviri monetales*, the *procurator monetae* or the *procurator a rationibus* formulated the content of Roman imperial coin designs. But the case of Lucius Vibius Lentulus tells us he was an equestrian in the imperial service who had some relationship with the emperor. As a chief minister of finance late in his career, he would have been an essential member of Trajan's government and "cabinet." This suggests that those in charge of the mint directly, the *procuratores monetae*, or those overseeing the mint adminstrators, the *procuratores a rationibus*, were as close to the emperor as other prominent equestrians and senators who were the agents behind laudatory prose, poetry, and panegyric directed at the emperor (e.g., Statius, Martial, Pliny, Frontinus, and Tacitus). Pliny, for example, was consul with Trajan in 100 CE, Frontinus was the *curator aquarum* under both Nerva and Trajan and was appointed to important senatorial committees by Nerva; Tacitus was suffect consul under Nerva in 97 CE. As members of the emperor's "inner circle" or "cabinet," these figures in charge of the mint were thus aware of—and in a position to visualize—the adulatory rhetoric that was written and spoken by such poets and panegyrists (Burnett 1977 maintains a diarchy in the reign of Augustus whereby the *tresviri* acted on behalf of the Senate for base-metal coinage and a *procurator* acted on behalf of the emperor for silver and gold coinage).

COINS' IMAGERY AND AUDIENCE

The notion that coin iconography was formulated in the mint and is akin to contemporary poetry and panegyric (Levick 1982; Wallace-Hadrill 1986; Wolters 1999: 290–308; Cheung 1998–9) seems to be an appropriate way of understanding the character and agency of Roman imperial coin design. This does not mean, however, that the emperor was the *only* intended audience for designs on imperial coinage as this line of thinking can ultimately lead (e.g., Levick 1982; Wallace-Hadrill 1986).

Indeed, there are several examples that suggest that the government concerned itself with the end-users of coins. During the latter part of the first century CE and in the second century CE, there are dozens of coin types that relay populist messages to the urban plebs and illustrate the emperor's role in their well-being. For example, several emperors struck coins showing the *congiarium*, a distribution of cash to the privileged *plebs frumentaria*, which depict the emperor on a raised platform presiding over the distribution of cash (see Figure 5.7). These denotative images appear most often on bronze *sestertii*, which are not only broad coins that can easily host complex denotative designs but also base metal coins that would have been accessible to humble socioeconomic segments of Roman society. The more generic concept of *liberalitas* is, however, reserved for high-denomination gold and silver coinage (Metcalf 1993; see also Heckster 2003 on audience targeting by denominations, but who

FIGURE 5.7: Brass *sestertius* of Nero, struck at Rome, 64–8 CE. Obverse: Laureate head of Nero right, NERO CLAVDIVS CAESAR AVG GER P M TR P IMP P P; Reverse: Nero seated on raised platform accompanied by an attendant distributing money to a plebeian, statues of Minerva and Liberalitas are in the background, CONG I DAT POP (American Numismatic Society 1937.158.467).

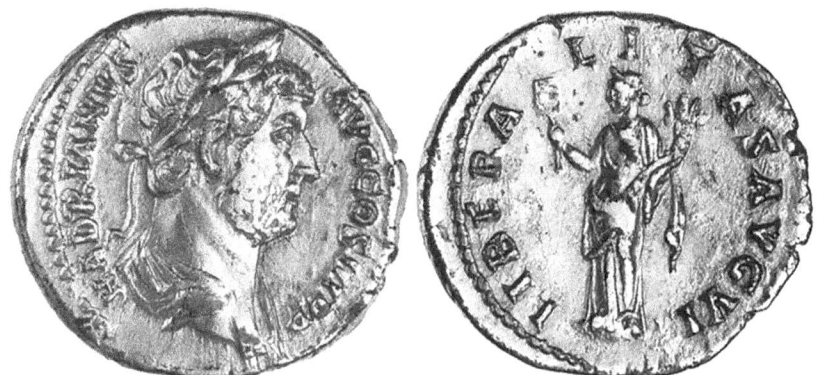

FIGURE 5.8: Silver *denarius* of Hadrian, struck at Rome, 134–8 CE. Obverse: Laureate bust of Hadrian right, HADRIANVS AVG COS III P P; Reverse: Liberalitas standing left, LIBERALITAS AVG VI (American Numismatic Society 0000.999.18933).

ascribes imperial agency throughout). On these coins, a personification of Liberalitas (see Figure 5.8) more generically refers to imperial generosity and benefaction, even though the word "*liberalitas*" came to replace "*congiarium*" in the second century CE. The differentiation in the types of designs that appear on certain denominations thus suggests that someone in the mint decided that the more specific and denotative depiction of the emperor distributing cash to the urban plebs should appear on the bigger, but lower-denomination, coins and that the personification of Liberalitas, referring more broadly to imperial generosity, should appear on the smaller, but higher-denomination, coins. In fact, the coinage of several emperors tends to depict populist messages on base metal coinage. In the reign of Nerva, for example, the *sestertii* refer to a *congiarium* (*RIC* II: nos. 56, 57, and 71), the remission of the burdens for the imperial post in Italy (*RIC* II: nos. 93 and 104), a distribution of grain (*RIC* II: nos. 89 and 103), and the Fortune of the Roman People (*RIC* II: nos. 62 and 85). His gold and silver coinage almost exclusively depicts, however, personifications of imperial ideals such as Libertas (*RIC* II: nos. 7, 19, 31, 36, 39, and 43), Aequitas (*RIC* II: nos. 1, 13, 25, and 44), Iustitia (*RIC* II: nos. 6, 18, and 30), and Fortuna (*RIC* II: nos. 4, 16, 28, 35, and 42). In the period from Nero to Trajan, buildings constructed for popular use also have a tendency to appear on bronze coinage, especially *sestertii* (Elkins 2015: 108–13). And the smallest of all Roman imperial coin denominations, the *quadrantes*, primarily circulated in Rome and the designs upon them typically referred to mundane aspects of day-to-day life rather than grander aspects of Roman imperial policy or ideology. For instance, Caligula's *quadrantes* referred to the remission of a ½ percent tax on auction sales, Claudius's *quadrantes* referred to a reform in weights and measures, and the *quadrantes* of Claudius, Nerva, and Hadrian depicted *modii* (grain measures) that related to the imperial provision of grain for the *plebs urbana*.

In addition to some apparent differences in the denominations and the varying themes that appear on them, empirical archaeological evidence indicates that the mint and/or treasury understood the potential for certain images to communicate ideas to different populations within the Roman Empire when it comes to bronze coinage, which was not as mobile as gold or silver (see Elkins 2009a: 42–6 for further discussion). Markus Peter's (1996) work on the circulation of second-century CE bronze coinage suggested some typological differentiation in the coin supply in the western provinces and presaged much work on the subject that has occurred over the last decade or so. Fleur Kemmers's study of the coin finds from the Flavian legionary fortress at Nijmegen has boldly indicated that the soldiers there were supplied with types bearing martial imagery as the concentrations of coins with such imagery there is markedly more prominent than in the finds from neighboring civilian settlements or from Rome (Kemmers 2006: 189–244, esp. 219–44). Additional research on typological differentiation on the coins supplied to the soldiers at other military sites has proven fruitful (Kemmers 2014). A study on the find spots of coins bearing architectural reverse types in Flavian and Trajanic periods suggests that denotative types celebrating public building in Rome are more prominent in finds from the city (Elkins 2011). The evidence is the strongest for coins referring to the construction of the Aqua Traiana (*RIC* II: nos. 463–4 and 606–9), which are significantly more common in finds from Rome than elsewhere (Elkins 2011: 652–3 and fig. 8). Without a doubt, further studies on typological differentiation of the bronze coinage must be conducted, but already what work has been done suggests that coins were supplied, in part, to some populations according to the relevance of the imagery they bore.

While more studies need to be conducted, a researcher must remember that coin types were first and foremost economic objects and that anomalies in the coin supply could also be caused by the movement of large groups of people, such as the imperial court, the foundation of colonies and legionary fortresses, and so on, and need not always indicate deliberate typological differentiation in the coin supply. For example, large quantities of *quadrantes*, which normally circulated in Rome and Italy, have been found along the Rhine. Their presence here is probably the result of need for small change in the region and the emperor's presence at Mainz at the outset of the war against the Chatti in 83 CE (Kemmers 2003). Similarly, the unusual presence of five very rare Flavian Colosseum *sestertii* of 80–1 CE in a few sites in Hessen and the Taunus-Wetterau *limes* system, which otherwise would be most relevant to an audience in Rome, also probably came to the region when the emperor and his retinue came to Mainz in 83 CE to oversee the invasion of the region (Elkins 2009b). We may speculate that designs such as these that would have resonated most with the urban audience of Rome would have meant little to people on the Roman frontier.

In addition to these finds-based methods to determine target audiences, scholars can also quantify the prominence of types relative to another according to hoards and excavated finds (on hoards, see primarily Noreña 2001; Noreña 2011a). This sort of work is particularly important, as some historians have overstated the importance of certain coin types, which are by comparison rare or even unique. For example, much is often made about the representation of buildings on Roman coins, one of the most beloved topics in the study of Roman coin iconography, although such coins made up a minuscule proportion of what was in circulation. During the Flavian and Trajanic periods, when architectural imagery was its most varied on the coinage, architectural types comprise 2.49 percent (12/482) of Vespasian's base-metal coins, 1.17 percent (13/1,109) of Domitian's coins, and 2.44 percent (14/573) of Trajan's coins. At Trier, architectural types made up 3.9 percent (10/256) of Vespasian's coins, 0.58 percent (2/353) of Domitian's coins, and 1.90 percent (8/240) of Trajan's coins (Elkins 2011: 654; Elkins 2015: 116). Quantification of types according to finds and hoards allows us to formulate an idea as to what images and messages people were encountering most often. As Noreña's work has already illustrated, images of personifications connoting imperial ideals were among the most common images encountered by viewers from the later first century CE through the early third century CE. Paradoxically, personifications are often ignored by modern scholars, who view them as repetitive and lacking the ability to carry potent messages as more complex "news types" celebrating public building, victory, *congiaria*, and so on (e.g., Duncan-Jones 2005, to be read with Beckmann 2009 as a retort). Modern scholars have generally preferred to study rarer denotative types referring to specific historical events. But this says more about our modern interests and outlooks rather than ancient reality. Monumental Roman art and relief sculptures are replete images of gods and personifications, as are private luxury arts, suggesting their relevance and intelligibility to a Roman audience. Additionally, Roman authors in the later first and second centuries CE have a tendency to judge Roman rulers by their qualities, as visualized by personifications on the imperial coinage, more than their specific actions suggesting again that personifications were intelligible as reflections of imperial ideals or qualities (e.g., Burnett 1987b: 78–9).

MONUMENTS IN MINIATURE

Roman coins served as "monuments in miniature," in that they were consistently immediate in terms of historical and political content and appear, in most cases, to have been directed in part at the emperor himself just as most public monuments were dedicated to the emperor and laudatory poetry and panegyric was aimed at pleasing him (Cheung 1998–9). The reverse designs on Roman coins cannot be treated as historical texts in the absence of other literature, as they have often been understood. Coins were a medium of state-sanctioned art and thus they operated independently of the biases of historical sources such as Tacitus, Suetonius, Cassius Dio, and always presented the emperor in a positive light. Although numismatics has often been an island among the historical disciplines, it clearly stands at the intersection of history, text and literature, epigraphy, art history, and archaeology. Coins were not created in a vacuum and were created in a living culture of art, monumentality, and literature, thus practitioners of coin iconography must attend to the multitudinous aspects of Roman society in their attempts to see the images as the Romans did.

CHAPTER SIX

Money and its Interpretation

Archaeological and Anthropological Perspectives

ALICIA JIMÉNEZ

This chapter investigates money as an object of scholarly interpretation as well as an archaeological artefact that provides evidence on ancient commodification, exchange, and consumption patterns. It briefly looks at evidence on how money was made, used, and lost in connection with recent debates about the ancient economy, the expression of identity through material culture, and colonialism. It concludes with some comments about the way we conceptualize coins in the present and the ethics of collecting cultural property, with no pretension of exhaustive coverage. I will focus on the Roman economy between the third century BCE and the second century CE and the relationship between Rome and the provinces, money, and imperialism, but I will also make punctual references to other geographical and chronological contexts to widen the discussion. The main aim of the following pages, mostly illustrated with examples from the ancient Roman world, is to make the point that the interpretation of money—and a particular kind of money: coins—needs to be part of ongoing debates in archaeology and cultural anthropology about the interpretation of material culture.

MONEY IS ONLY INFORMATION

Most scholars agree today that money is, foremost, a medium of exchange. It facilitates the exchange of objects or becomes itself the object to exchange; it also allows the store of wealth and it may be used as a unit of account (Aarts 2005: 2; Seaford 2004: 16–20; Harris 2006: 5). It is far less clear how money performs all these functions and how it should be interpreted. Keith Hart (2001: 234) claimed some time ago that money is a vehicle for the transmission of information, and an "act of remembering" to keep track of certain exchanges. This means that money is intrinsically linked, as a sign or symbol, with the complex philosophical problem of how (and if) material reality can represent an abstraction (Maurer 2005), and is caught in the paradox that, as an abstraction, money can be represented by virtually any object that a given society agrees in considering as such. Money is coinage. Money is bullion in Egypt and Mesopotamia in the third millennium BCE. Money is ingots in South East Asia between the seventeenth and the eleventh centuries CE, as well as paper money during the Song dynasty (960–1279 CE) in China, salt bars in nineteenth-century Ethiopia, copper axes in sixteenth-century Mexico, Tambu shells in New Britain (Papua New Guinea) in the nineteenth century, feathers in the Santa Cruz Islands (Solomon Islands) in the nineteenth century and cloth in the Congo during the seventeenth century CE (Eagleton and Williams 2007). The interpretation of money is therefore contingent upon our understanding of culturally constructed notions of production, consumption, and exchange as much as on the different ways each society makes sense of monetary exchanges in opposition to, or relative to, other spheres of exchange (Bloch and Parry 1989: 1). For this reason, any analysis of money based exclusively on economic transactions is irremediably obscured by the contextual and relational nature of money.

Money performs a series of complex operations related to its capacity to represent value. Money establishes equivalences between things that are not alike, assimilating them with respect to value and allowing comparisons between different commodities (Kopytoff 1986: 71). It involves a mysterious transubstantiation of matter into abstraction, reducing all differences of quality to a mere dissimilarity in quantity. Money dissolves the uniqueness of things into a common measurement system (Bloch and Parry 1989: 6). Money has been considered the root of both all good and all evil. Simmel (1900: 308–14) believed that the capacity of money to transform concrete things (coins, rods, salt, etc.) into an abstraction (value) was an advantage of this type of means of exchange, which increased human freedom and improved social integration. For example, serfs who were given the opportunity in medieval Europe to pay the lord of the manor in coin and not necessarily in beer, poultry, or cattle were free to produce what they wished as long as they could satisfy the payment, once they had obtained coins from the sale of their produce. Where barter requires a certain amount of trust between those involved in a transaction, for Simmel money allows extending that trust to anyone using the same kind of currency.

Others have considered money a source of misrepresentation. Marx analyzed the separation between producers that had no access to the means of production and the products of work that belonged to somebody else. Through the expression of monetary value, a relationship between people (the producer and the owner of the means of production) is disguised as a relationship among things (money and commodity). In this way, value is perceived as just another intrinsic characteristic of a commodity, a "natural attribute," which appears to be completely detached from the producer in the market (Ollman 1976: 195–6).

If money is a representation, where then does the value of money lie? As the different shapes money takes in various societies past and present show, its value does not lie in the precious metals it may be made of or the government's stamp that sometimes sanctions it, since there are societies where money is not metallic and does not need a government symbol to function as such. The abundance in different regions and periods of fiduciary coins is precisely a further example of the inadequacy between money's face and intrinsic value. As a representation of an abstraction, money is equally entangled with the inevitable failure of said representation that cannot exactly reproduce the real thing—it can be exchanged for many kinds of commodities, but it cannot fully stand for any of them. Bill Maurer has proposed experimenting with the idea of interpreting money not as yet another instance of failed representation or copy of an inapprehensible ideal form (in this case "value"), but as a means of exchange that mainly functions through homology and equivalence. For Maurer we need to consider whether the comparison between money and commodity, that is, equivalence and not intrinsic value, just as in other forms of barter, is what makes money's worth (2005: 142). Seaford (2004: 17–18) provides an interesting insight in connection to this. He points out that money ("x") provides a measure of value, and allows calculating how many units of "x" are necessary to meet the value of different commodities (e.g., "y" and "z"). This means that the exchange of commodities ("y" and "z") is possible even without the physical presence of money ("x") and that mere transfer of "x," "y" or "z" (rather than exchange) is possible because credit and debit can be recorded in terms of money ("x"). Since what constitutes "money" is culturally determined, sometimes what is considered barter from the point of view of one party is seen as a sale from the point of view of the other, who understands that he or she has paid with money in return for the goods provided by the other party (Einzig 1948: 327). In this respect barter and primitive money might be considered in some cases to be almost overlapping categories with very few elements of differentiation. We tend to give preeminence to money in our economic transactions because we live in a society where there are different types of all-purpose money, but the conceptual transaction can be reversed, if we realize that it is possible to "buy" coins in exchange for almost any kind of commodity, of course with a wide quantitative variation.

Money may allow further comparisons than other commodities, but, even more crucially, the process that makes possible establishing value equivalences between things that are not alike, allowing the exchange of, for example, yams and money, or in the case of barter yams and a pot, is, as anthropologists have shown, a cultural construction. Societies establish which things are considered to be conceptually equivalent with respect to value, arranging the world of natural things in a series of more or less independent spheres of exchange (Kopytoff 1986: 71–2). Most societies seem to impose a hierarchical order to the spheres of things that are cognitively similar based on their moral value and therefore belong to a category of interchangeable commodities (Bohannan 1955: 62; Kopytoff 1986: 69). Frequently, there is a group of things that cannot be purchased. These, in many cases, belong to the sphere of the sacred or are the monopoly of powerful groups who reinforce their status by their ability to possess them (Kopytoff 1986: 73). Other objects are restricted to a very narrow sphere and can be obtained only in exchange for other equally singular types of commodities, in contrast with the sphere of things that are exchanged frequently and are usually related with subsistence. To cite a classic case study, the Tiv, a people who live in the middle Benue Valley of northern Nigeria, had three main categories of exchange despite the absence of money prior to European colonialism, according to Paul Bohannan. The most visible consisted of foodstuffs, household utensils, and some tools. Women frequently sold yams for a pot. A second category was linked with prestige and involved the exchange of slaves, cattle, brass rods, and a type of large white cloth (*tugudu*). Interestingly, the price of a slave could be quoted in cows and brass rods, and that of cattle in both brass rods and *tugudu* cloths. Brass rods could be considered a general-purpose money *within* the prestige sphere but, unlike money, its functions in other exchange spheres were limited (Bohannan 1955: 67; Bohannan 1959: 498). The last category included one item only, which was considered to be the most singular and not exchangeable for anything outside its own sphere: rights in women and dependent human beings such as children (Bohannan 1955: 62–3). These divisions can be found in non-monetary and monetary societies alike. Even in highly monetized capitalist societies there are things that cannot be bought or are illegal or taboo to buy, such as people or political and academic favors (Kopytoff 1986: 77).

Despite the difficulties of scaping highly relativistic definitions of money when looked at in isolation—due to its cultural and contextually derived meaning—Bloch and Parry claimed that it is still possible to trace a common pattern among different cultures if we analyze the long and short reproduction cycles in which money, among other types of transactions, is involved. The short-term cycle is concerned with daily exchanges, commerce, wage-labor, and individual gains, while the long-term transactional order deals with the symbolic reproduction of social structure (Bloch and Parry 1989: 23–4; Aarts 2005: 17–27, for an application of the model to the Roman provinces). But probably the most interesting cross-cultural pattern is that even if the different spheres are nominally separated, the two cycles ultimately rely on each other, and it is not impossible to find various procedures to transfer short-term cycle commodities to the long-term cycle. Bloch and Parry (1989: 25) include among these transformations, for example, "the 'drinking' of cash in Fiji, the 'cooking' of money in Langkawi, and the 'digesting' of the pilgrims' gifts by the Brahmans of Benares."

From this perspective, the revolutionary role that has usually been assigned to money as one of the main agents of social transformation and the ultimate cause for the dissolution of the moral economy of traditional societies, is turned upside down. Money does not generate a specific worldview: a particular cultural matrix generates a certain definition of money. Transformations are mostly brought about by alterations in the exchange relations, not in the means of exchange (money) (Bloch and Parry 1989: 19). Money needs to be interpreted then in connection with all transactional systems, not only economic but also political and religious. This makes necessary a radical re-contextualization of money in archaeological and anthropological analyses as material culture involved in a process of becoming and ceasing to be a commodity, rather than a stable, clear-cut category. The limits for processes of commoditization that homogenize value among things that are not alike are the differences established by each society between different spheres of exchange (Kopytoff 1986: 73). Kopytoff (1986: 68) defines a commodity as "a thing that has use value and that can be exchanged in a discrete transaction for a counterpart" with an equivalent value in that context. Commoditized things continue to have an exchange value but may be "decommoditized" after a transaction or never exchanged again. The only point at which a thing is unequivocally a commodity is in the very moment it is exchanged directly, or indirectly using money (Kopytoff 1986: 68, 83). One crucial point here is the fluidity of spheres and categories. Another is that the exchange of money for a commodity can be part of a much more complex and not strictly economic transaction, such as the establishment of relations of patronage or the exchange of gifts at the beginning of marriage negotiations (Kopytoff 1986: 69). Commoditized things are open to individual redefinitions that singularize them among their own category and link them to the extra value that an individual may attach to an object because of personal or sentimental reasons, increasing its value or even withdrawing it from the sphere of exchange. Things can be singularized not only by individuals, but also by religious, professional, or ethnic groups who attach a particular value to certain kinds of things (Kopytoff 1986: 76). Consequently archaeologists need to acknowledge the fact that the only point at which the commodity status of a thing is completely out of question is the very moment in which it is exchanged, and the potential existence of contradictions in the spheres of exchange derived from the conflict among individual, group, and social perceptions of value, or even the interaction between different cultural constructions of commodities in colonial contexts (Kopytoff 1986: 88).

Commoditization, then, should be understood as a cultural process and not as part of the essence of any given object (Kopytoff 1986: 83) and considered as such in our interpretation of the archaeological record. Even commodities that function as a means of exchange such as coins may cease to be a commodity (e.g., when used for ritual purposes as in foundational or funerary rituals) or are taken out of circulation by an individual (e.g., to be transformed in jewelry) (Rowan 2011). Things have, in that sense, "biographies": they may belong to one sphere first and then to another, can be used in an economic transaction and cease to be commodity in a later phase, or have the capacity to function differently in another society. Kopytoff explains that the social identities of things and people are culturally dependent and constructed simultaneously in the same way. What a thing is, what a thing can do, the possibilities inherent in its "status," its "biography," are determined by cultural classifications that mark it as a particular kind of thing (Kopytoff 1986: 66, 90). This is the main reason why it is not possible to correctly interpret economic transactions without taking into account the moral economy and social practices in which they take place (Bohannan 1955: 64; Kopytoff 1986: 64), a path that some archaeologists and numismatists began to explore in the late 1970s (Nash 1978; Haselgrove 1987; Roymans 1990; Aarts 2005; Krmnicek 2009).

The consequence of interpreting money in the context of several spheres of exchange and the cultural construction of value are far reaching. This perspective challenges widespread views on the merely economic function of money. It shows that the division between the monetary and non-monetary functions of a particular class of object is problematic, since it is ultimately dependent on a fluid process of commodification and singularization and a series of possibilities integral to its status as a thing in a particular society that may or may not be realized in its "biography." This perspective takes into account the "fluidity of the categories through which coins can pass, from being media of exchange, to store of value, to functional items of adornment and display, or to objects signifying meaning in a ritual context" (Haselgrove and Krmnicek 2016a: 10). It also questions conventional views on the evolution of money and the rigid division between societies that use and those that do not use money, because it highlights the fact that the same society may use different kinds of money in different spheres of exchange or resort to barter in one sphere and to money in other. It highlights as well the importance of money in several "traditional" non-capitalist societies and the widespread commoditization in some of them (Kopytoff 1986: 79; Bloch and Parry 1989: 7).

BARTER, MONEY, COINAGE

Looking at money as a component of a complex system of different types of transactions brings new light to the interpretation of its history. Since the nineteenth century the prevailing discourse in scholarly literature has described a linear evolution in different stages: from barter, to money, and finally to coinage and other complex financial instruments that are not even backed by actual things in the present, such as derivatives (Maurer 2015: 140). The main difference between barter and money in this view is a conceptual one. Barter implies a one-time exchange of a certain amount of two things of a different kind, while in a monetary exchange money acts as intermediary, implying a previous agreement on an abstract unit of account. Yet general-purpose money is not the only way to calculate abstract value. As we have seen before, Paul Bohannan's studies, for example, showed that it was possible to do so before money was introduced in the exchange system of the Tiv society, by bartering things that were considered to be equivalent in kind (Bohannan 1959).

Even coins, a widespread type of general-purpose money, may, in some cases, function as special-purpose money. Benjamin P. Luley's analysis of the interactions between the Celtic-speaking settlement of Lattara and the Greek colony of Massalia in the southeast of France, from the end of the fourth century to the end of the second century BCE, is revealing. He suggested that the Greek coins circulating in the local center of Lattara belonged to a specific sphere of exchange in connection with trade with the Greek colony of Massalia (Luley 2008). Lattara was founded toward the end of the sixth century BCE, but its inhabitants did not begin to use Greek coins until the middle of the fourth century BCE, when they started to be hoarded, in most cases discarded or lost in domestic contexts and found by archaeologists together with other house artefacts, such as Massalian wine amphorae, cooking and eating ware (including local and imported black gloss Campanian A), and fragments of bronze jewelry and bronze or gold *fibulae* (Luley 2008: 180). Coins were found in houses with other objects that were the result of exchanges with Greek colonists, but they were not recovered by archaeologists in other areas linked to local productive activities (such as bronze workshops, bakeries, and flour mills) where exchange of goods might have taken place, until after the Roman conquest of the area in 121 BCE. Coins were never minted in Lattara, and even after the conquest the amount of Roman coins reaching the site was very limited. It is possible that Massalian coins at Lattara belonged to a foreign Greek value system and were not used to purchase locally produced goods, as the absence of silver objects—other than the coins introduced by the Greeks—in other Celtic-speaking settlements to the north seems to indicate (Luley 2008: 183). Perhaps, as Luley suggested, Massalian coinage was the mechanism, described in other colonial situations (Comaroff and Commaroff 2005), that rendered commensurate two different value systems: "tokens for designating the transactions of goods and for calculating credit" (Luley 2008: 184) that allowed exchanges between Greek merchants and the local Lattaran population. That is, in the local Lattaran value system in place before the Roman conquest,

Massalian silver coins might have been special purpose money used to purchase certain commodities.

A strictly linear evolution from barter to money first and from money to coins later seems to be contradicted by the evidence, not only because money is important in some of the so-called "traditional" societies, but also because barter and different types of money were never completely replaced by coinage in societies where the latter circulated widely. A few years ago, two studies by Harris (2006) and Hollander (2007) questioned the common assumption that all Roman money consisted only of coins and discussed the evidence in the Late Republic for the use of bullion (uncoined gold and silver), financial instruments, and other assets (such as grain, livestock, land, slaves, or labor) which reduced the demand for coinage when used as means of payment. In 1992, Christopher Howgego defended in a pioneer work the theory that "[p]atterns of money use may be defined not only in respect of exchange for goods, but also with reference to taxation, rents, wages, credit and the sophistication of finance" and suggested that the discussions about the Roman economy needed to "proceed beyond a simple description of the Roman economy as monetized" (Howgego 1992: 29). In fact, the same state in charge of producing a large number of coins during the Republic received taxes in different types of commodities such as gold and silver bullion (*aurum coronarium* or "crown gold") and paid in bullion and kind to cover expenses such as the *annona* (governmental distributions of grain to civilians) and the military and veteran pay (Howgego 1992: 9, 22–4; Hollander 2007: 93–4). Food and equipment were deducted, according to Polybius (6.39), from the soldiers' pay even though silver coins (*denarii*) were the unit of account of military wages (Roth 1999: 224). The Roman example makes it clear that a highly monetized economy has the effect of reducing the need for coinage and that its shortage should not be necessarily interpreted as an important deterrent of growth (Howgego 1992: 16; Harris 2006: 24; Hollander 2007: 57).

Even though coinage was still very important for most payments, the evidence gathered from some Roman sources indicates that payments of large amounts of money to purchase real-estate properties were sometimes made with credit, bonds, or even in instalments (Cicero, *De officiis* 3.59; Cicero, *Epistulae ad Atticum* 16.2.I; Harris 2006: 2–3). Bankers were able to make payments at a distance, presumably to other bankers who granted them credit (Harris 2006: 6, 11). Harris has suggested not only that credit was a form of money in Roman times, but also that in the second century CE there was a market for outstanding loans (*nomina*), which made it possible for individuals to make payments "by means of *nomina* that had originated not in loans they had made themselves, but in loans made by others which they had accepted as payment" (Harris 2006: 15; *contra* Howego 1992: 3; Andreau 1999: 132; von Reden 2002: 146). Romans made use of forms of money or near money with no intrinsic value, such as *partes* (shares in tax farming and commercial companies) and *syngraphae* (similar to promissory notes), or completely notional money in the case of *permutationes* (transfers of money over long distances) and *nomina,* although the information transmitted by the ancient sources (mostly in Cicero's texts for the Republic) does not entirely clarify their nature and how widespread they were during this period (Hollander 2007: 39).

To the previous observation that there are distinct spheres of exchange for which certain commodities are considered to be appropriate in a given society, Hollander's study of monetary zones adds a further nuance. In the daily sphere or the short-term cycle of commodities the use of money differed depending on the context, which also dictated which assets could replace money as means of payment, unit of account, and store of value. Hollander (2007: 88–9) defined four interconnected monetary zones during the Roman Republic: governmental (involving mainly taxes, public contracts, and the payment of soldiers), commercial (medium and long-distance trade by merchants), urban (private monetary activity of the town inhabitants), and rural (the economy of state managers as well as the agricultural and pastoral sector). While in the urban monetary zone the demand for money was likely high and the urban plebs paid mostly for food and shelter with coins acquired through wage labor, farmers had access to a series of assets to fulfil payments, including coins, which circulated in small amounts compared with the city.

MAKING MONEY, USING MONEY, LOSING MONEY

I turn now to a particular type of money—coins—and the complexities of its interpretation in a specific context: the late Roman Republic and the early Empire (roughly mid-third century BCE to second century CE). Although ancient Roman coins have often been seen as the raw material of catalog compilers, an important source of chronological information, and a form of evidence used to build an ancient history of elites, their contextual analysis portrays evidence about ancient commodification, exchange, and consumption patterns among the population in general, the expression of identity through material culture and Roman colonialism.

Two important questions about their interpretation are irremediably intertwined: their origins and their function. The matter is important because it links objects to practices; however, it also places the main emphasis in the agency of the producer, leaving out of the discussion the many uses a coin might have had before being lost or ceasing to be a commodity. It has often been said that money was invented in the eastern Mediterranean for financial reasons, to facilitate large state payments; this was the case during the Roman Republic as well, when the volume of struck coins fluctuated supposedly mostly in connection with the payment of the legions deployed in the newly conquered provinces (Crawford 1970: 46). Howgego (1990) suggested, citing evidence from ancient sources, that the reasons for coining were more complex. It is not possible to comprehend patterns of coin production without taking into account how bullion was obtained and how periods of abundance or shortage of gold and silver influenced the issue of coinage. Expenditure was not necessarily correlated with new coinage: we know of examples of both expenditure without new coinage and new coinage without expenditure. A direct link between new coinage and expenditure ignores the importance of other means of payment, such as bullion, old or foreign coin, and credit. Even if state payments were important, it is necessary to take into account other motivations, such as monetary reforms, which required re-striking old coins, the renewal of worn coins, political goals, or perhaps the punctual mining by the state on behalf of individuals for a fee during antiquity. Howgego (1990: 25) concludes that since it is not possible to be certain about what particular classes of coins were used by the state, the questions about the production of coins must focus on particular issues for which we have some evidence.

To understand the link between payments and new coinage it is necessary to establish whether the available evidence allows us to calculate ancient coin production and study its fluctuations over time. With no mint records surviving from the Roman world, Buttrey (1993; 1994) was adamant that we cannot quantify the quantity of coin produced during the Roman Republic or Empire, that it is impossible to know the rate of attrition of coins in circulation, and that we will never be able to determine the amount of Roman coin in circulation at any given time or place. The methodology employed by Crawford (1974), Hopkins (1980), and Duncan-Jones (1999) presupposed a correlation between the number of known obverse dies of a series of Roman silver coins issues (*denarii*) and the number of coins of each die occurring in the hoards known by numismatists up to that moment. The ratio coin : die was then extrapolated to calculate how many coins of a particular issue were struck.

There are several problems that impede reaching accurate estimations of coin production. Among them, Buttrey pointed out that the numbers obtained rely excessively on the hoards included in the study (which are biased toward periods of insecurity when treasures were not recovered), that the earlier issues were always under-represented (because they were less likely to appear in the hoards than contemporary coins), and that attrition due to hoarding, loss, or destruction was not properly taken into account when calculating the number of coins left, because the figure proposed by Hopkins (1980: 107), 2 percent, is just an educated guess and varies greatly depending on the period and the place as a result of loss, hoarding, export, melting of coins for jewelry and plate, and withdrawal by the government (Buttrey 1993: 336–8, 345).

It has been estimated, following some historical evidence and experiments reproducing ancient coinage methods, that the average number of coins produced by die for silver coinage during the Greco-Roman period was between 10,000 and 40,000 per obverse (de Callataÿ 2011b: 13). These numbers are just indicative, because the amount of coin output in any given mint is not stable even today and changes for reasons not exclusively related to the metallurgical quality of the set of dies (Buttrey 1993: 341–3). The very question of whether dies were produced mechanically in antiquity with a hub (a tool bearing the coin design in positive to sink a die), has caused disagreement among numismatists for almost a century. The use of hubs by official Greek and Roman mints would make it almost impossible to quantify emissions, since the technology would allow each die to be replicated a certain amount of times, rendering attempts to evaluate coin production from die numbers impossible. Recent reviews of the evidence claim that the engraving of small details in positive presented important technical challenges in classical antiquity and that there is no proof of the use of major-element piece punches in the ancient Mediterranean world (Stannard 2011: 67). It seems, however, that dies were mechanically reproduced in this period in small amounts, mostly by forgers who lacked the technical skills to cut a die and used different methods to impress and transfer the design of an official coin to produce plated coins, as well as by frontier communities in need of small official change, such as the iron-core, copper-plated coins that copied Roman bronzes in the distant provinces of Noricum and Pannonia or the mechanical reproduction of Roman coins by casting in Augusta Raurica in Germania Superior. The restricted amount of barbarian transfer die issues and the possibility of identifying plated forgeries somehow limit the problem that imitations create for the evaluation of monetary supply (Stannard 2011: 71–4). In any case, like in other predictive sciences, despite the impossibility of reaching exact numbers, other scholars have claimed that relative estimations of coin production, which they believe roughly fluctuate as Crawford and Hopkins advanced in their studies, are still useful for our interpretations of the production levels and money supply (de Callataÿ 1995: 305; Lockyear 1999; de Callataÿ 2011b; Hollander 2007: 50).

How much coinage was available for use depends, however, not only on the amount of new coin released by the mint, but also on the availability of other types of money (bullion, credit), the practices attached to coinage in a particular exchange sphere, the velocity of circulation (the number of transactions in which coins are involved), and how long they circulated until they were pulled out of circulation by official decree, wastage, or decommodification.

The similarities and dissimilarities in the distribution of imperial coin over the provinces have been interpreted as a sign of the integration of the Roman economy. According to Hopkins (1980) the broad similarity in the proportions of coins of different emperors in all provinces was a sign of the integration of the economy: the flow of coins from the provinces to Rome in taxes and rents and the outflow of money from Rome to the provinces through trade. Yet the study of a series of silver coin hoards by Duncan-Jones (1990: 30–47) showed that there were regional differences in coin circulation, and that the mixing of coins occurred predominantly in Rome, not in the provinces. Once the coins reached the provinces, they tended to remain within regional economies (Howgego 1994: 10, 20). Howgego concluded that archaeology and numismatics are unlikely to solve the question of the integration of the Roman economy, but are able to render evidence about both the highly centralized production of silver and gold in very few imperial mints (such as Rome and Lugdunum) in the Mediterranean and the fact that the movement of coin in certain areas did not eradicate local provincial differences. He also added to the previous picture the necessity of considering separately the circulation of silver and gold on the one hand, and that of imperial bronze (which seems to have been more regional once imported to the provinces) on the other.

It has also been commonly supposed that there is a correlation between how coins are used and how they are lost and found in archaeological sites. Even if there is a link between the number of transactions taking place in a certain place (such as commercial areas) and the index of coin loss, an analysis of the evidence also shows that finds today are not an accurate reflection of coin circulation in antiquity. Gold coins, for example, tended to be carried around only when they were required and were most likely carefully searched for whenever they were lost. Small-size coins seem to be lost slightly more often and there is also a strong correlation between the number of coins in circulation and the number of coins that are lost (Howgego 1992: 12; Newton 2006).

The findings at Pompeii and Herculaneum, the Roman cities destroyed by the Vesuvius eruption in 79 CE, offer important insights about the processes that create the archaeological record, and the influence of exceptional circumstances in it. They are not a frozen representation of daily coin circulation as much as the result of repeated selections: the coins that the inhabitants decided to use or kept during the first century CE, the coins left behind by those that fled the settlement before the volcano's eruption, the coins that were stored in a bank by the wealthy, and finally the coins that have been recovered by archaeologists (Andreau 2008: 210). Some of the coins or jewelry found near a cadaver (a single bronze coin, or two bronze coins and a silver coin), might be interpreted as being the things a person was carrying by chance that day. However, a woman found in room 10 of L. Carssius Tertius's villa in Oplontis (skeleton 7) carried a silver bracelet and 409 bronze, silver, and gold coins in a linen bag, including a mix of old coins that were the result of a process of hoarding during a certain time period and coins minted around 79 CE. People carried coins, but left silver and gold objects in their houses, which were more frequently found there than near human remains. It is not possible, in any case, to know if coin and plate found in houses represent the totality of the most precious belongings of their owner, or whether some of them had already been carried away by other members of the family. That might explain the small amount of coins (203 sesterces) found in some of the richest houses of Pompeii, such as the Casa del Fauno (Andreau 2008: 211–12, 216).

The Vesuvian cities also remind us that we need to take into account different types of Roman money when we interpret the record. Archaeologists have identified boxes or cupboards in the houses of rich individuals that contained their savings reserve, including not only coins but also silverware, goldware, silver and gold ingots, bricks and bars, whose value surpassed that of the stored coinage. In affluent houses there was a distinction too between, on the one hand, the manufactured gold and silver objects that fulfilled the function of store of wealth and were kept in a strong box and, on the other, the silverware used regularly. This seems to indicate that the same kind of object in a given context (even if with different quality levels) was either stored or used on a daily basis. However, important amounts of money have been occasionally found in modest houses and professional premises. Andreau (2008: 213) considers that these large groups of coins cannot be interpreted as savings, as is often suggested when they are found in wealthy houses; they probably correspond to coins that played an economic role in shops or were the result of the sale of a certain amount of agricultural produce, such as wine or olive oil.

Hoards are, for the same reason, part of a process of storage of value and do not necessarily reflect normal circulation in a given context, but patterns of personal selection of the available coin pool. In the case of the Roman Empire, for example, it has been pointed out that hoarders in the second half of the first century CE preferred old coins to new from Nero's reign onwards, because they knew that their silver content was higher (Harris 2006: 21). The bias of some hoards toward a single denomination and the clustering of hoards around certain dates during the Empire that do not coincide with outbreaks of war have been tentatively connected with imperial donations of coins to the army (Duncan-Jones 1994: 77–85).

Interpretative models of coin circulation and hoarding, which focus mainly on the place where coins were minted and not where they were found, have rightly been critiqued for ignoring the different practices attached to coinage in military, civilian, and ritual archaeological contexts (Kemmers 2009: 140). A contextual study of Severan's (193–235 CE) monetary policy in the north-western provinces shows interesting differences such as the intentional selection of small bronze denominations in ritual contexts or the fact that, contrary to the assumption that Severan bronzes did not circulate north of the Alps, these coins were indeed used in civilian and ritual sites, but for some reason did not enter circulation in Roman camps (Kemmers 2009: 146).

MONEY TALK

One of the most explored themes in Roman numismatics is coin iconography and legends and the discourses disseminated through them in Italy and the provinces. Considered mainly as an official document of local or imperial elites, most authors studying the Republican period have concentrated on the theme of power and the political role of the representation of divinities and the achievements of moneyers' ancestors. During the principate, the analysis has revolved around imperial portraits (with a very interesting small group of coin mints in free cities, such as Athens, Chios, Rhodes, and Tyre who chose not to depict Roman emperors), succession legitimation and the prevalence of representations of different personifications of the Emperor's virtues and ideals (Howgego 1995: 62–87; Howgego 2005: 15; Noreña 2011a; 2011b).

Questions of agency are clearer during the Republic, when the moneyers were three elected magistrates (*triumviri monetales*), than in the principate, when different officials were in charge of minting, and it is difficult to ascertain to what extent emperors themselves always selected the images to be struck in coins (Noreña 2011b: 250–1). If it seems clear that coins are means of communication, it has also been discussed whether the ubiquity of coins turned them into an ideal medium for the dissemination of political messages in Rome and the provinces and if it is possible to apply the concept of propaganda for these uses of coinage or should they better be included in a less anachronistic context of imperial imagery disseminated through different means (Burnett 1987b: 66–85; Levick 1999a; Wolters 2003a).

Ever since the sixteenth and seventeenth centuries, coin catalogs have looked with particular interest into the temples, theatres, amphitheatres, circuses, gates, bridges, and arches represented in coins in search of information about the monuments and the coins themselves. There is more to coin images than meets the eye. Like architectural representations in other media, these kinds of images make use of certain conventions that allow the viewer to see the interior and the exterior of some structures simultaneously from a bird's eye view (Bergmann 2008). Coins also let the provincial viewer contemplate monuments located far away in the metropolis, such as in the case of the representations of Rome's monuments by the mints of Alexandria and Lugdunum (Burnett 1999: 144; Hekster 2003: 33). Yet sometimes images on coins hinder our vision and make it difficult to see if we are looking at the representation of a rider or an equestrian statue, or to know whether the building depicted ever existed in the real world or took a different form to the one we see represented. Octavian's partisans, for example, used a gilded equestrian statue of their leader as a coin type before the statue itself was completed and unveiled beside the Speaker's platform in the Roman forum. In the case of the temple of Divus Iulius decreed in 42 BCE, the building was seen in Octavian's coins (36 BCE) years before it was dedicated in 29 BCE (Zanker 1988: 38; Burnett 1999: 139–42).

After studying the diverse images present in various denominations and contexts, some scholars have explored the possibility that the government targeted different population groups with different images (Metcalf 1993; Hekster 2003; Kemmers 2009); coins users also carefully selected specific coins for certain practices. This model gives some explanation as to why, for example, there is a higher occurrence of certain coin types offered by some users in specific contexts, such as *Mars* in military sites and *Sol* in ritual spaces during the Severan period in the northwestern provinces of the empire, or the coins and militaria most likely deposited by soldiers in the sanctuary of Hercules Magusanus in the Lower Rhine region. Most of all, it throws new light on the series of decisions taken not only by "senders" but also by "receivers" of coins (Roymans and Aarts 2005; Kemmers 2009: 151, 156). The powerful properties of some coin images were extended to the portrait of the emperor, as we see in the transfer of coin images to other materials, such as glass, metalwork, and ceramic (both pottery and tiles) by directly stamping a coin in some cases or imitating its shape in others. Not uncommonly, coins also became a new type of commodity by being transformed into a piece of jewellery or used to decorate vessels (Rowan 2011; Haselgrove and Krmnicek 2016a: 11).

The design and images of some coins were partially replicated in others. Roman bronze coins were copied in the provinces, such as Narbonensis in the south of France or what would become Tarraconensis in the northeast of Spain, and even in Italy with the intention to be seen as "official" Roman change (Crawford 1982: 140). But in the case of local provincial minting, the imitation processes in play are much more complex: the origins of the images seem to be multiple and they do not necessarily point to Rome. For instance, in Hispania, one of the first Roman provinces in the Mediterranean (the Roman conquest began in 218 BCE), what was found is an active selection and reinterpretation of iconographic types from the Mediterranean; not only from Rome, but also from Campania in the south of Italy and Sicily, and from other local coins from the Iberian Peninsula, including those with Punic roots (Chaves 1999). Mints may simultaneously imitate local traditional images and images borrowed from the colonizers' coinage. For example, in the Ebro valley in the northeast of the Iberian Peninsula, the mint of Turiaso reshaped the traditional representation of a horseman into an equestrian statue, quite possibly a representation of the first Roman emperor, Augustus. Not far away, in Iltirta, the depiction of a wolf that first appeared on local coins during the late Republic was made to resemble the Roman she-wolf in later issues minted in the early Empire (Trillmich 2003: 627–9).

In Pompeii the arrival, for reasons still unknown, of a substantial group of bronze coins (probably in the hundreds of thousands) with a representation of the Punic god Bes on the obverse and the reverse minted in Ebusus (modern Ibiza) about 140–130 BCE, triggered the production of local coins, not under Pompeii's name, but as copies of the Ebusan coins. "High quality" imitations coexisted with coins in which the figure of Bes was represented with a few abstract lines (Stannard 2013). These bronze imitations made up most of the circulating currency in Pompeii and were used in the settlement alongside

Roman silver coins (*denarii*) and small quantities of Roman bronze throughout the second century BCE. The process of imitation suggests complex questions about the interpretation of coins as mass produced objects and the transformative characteristics of mimesis. Despite the presence of Roman silver and bronze in most provinces and Italy, the coins from the metropolis were not always the model: images were also transferred between provincial territories and Italy. The symbols that make reference to local pasts and the imperial present simultaneously may be considered as "bilingual," as some of the legends present in the early provincial coinage (Chaves 1999: 305, 314).

In Hispania, coins often include a legend with the place-name of the mint in one of the different alphabets in use in the Iberian Peninsula during the second and first centuries BCE, such as Greek, Neo-Punic, southern Iberian, eastern Iberian, and Latin, although some engravers were not fluent in Latin, as the inaccuracies or the retrograde legends for the first series of Obulco, in the south of modern Spain, indicate (Chaves 1998: 151). In some of these cases the legend seems to have been "read" and reproduced as an "image," not as a series of letters. For example, some copies of Roman silver coins (*denarii*) in what is now Hungary which circulated into modern Poland, North Germany, and Scandinavia around 225–50 CE depicted a faithful copy of the bust of the emperor encircled by a legend that was gibberish. Stannard (2011: 73) has suggested interpreting these coins as "wealth objects in a premonetary society."

Two points are interesting. First, that even if the choice of languages is likely to reflect some kind of communal identity and the use of non-Latin alphabets was more frequent in some provinces after the conquest, it does not necessarily reflect the language spoken by the people living in the region where the coin was minted (Chaves 1999: 314; Howgego 2005: 12). Second, despite the fact that the coins evincing languages other than Greek and Latin disappear from the archaeological record of the provinces after Tiberius, the path toward Latin legends on coins is far from homogeneous. Coastal Phoenician colonies in the south of the Iberian Peninsula did not use Latin until very late in the reign of Augustus (Chaves 1998: 153); one of the oldest mints in the south, Iliberi, used Latin on the first coin issue, but later returned to the Iberian script, while other mints transitioned from local scripts to Latin, in the same way that Oscan and Umbrian were used in Italy on local coins during the Republic (Chaves 1998: 166).

Bilingual coins survived longer in the provinces than coins in local scripts and offer varied examples of code-switching: from simple translations and the recording of different names for the same place in different languages, to the specific use of different languages for different functions. For example, Sicilian mints sometimes included the toponym in Greek, while the name of magistrates is in Latin or Greek (Burnett 2002: 34).

CONCLUSION: THINGS MONEY CAN'T BUY

Roman coins have been traditionally studied by numismatists in relation to their chronology, typology, and distribution. Ancient historians have been mostly interested in analyzing Roman money in economic terms only. According to Aarts (2005: 1–2): "Although many historians seem to adopt the model of the embeddedness of the economy and take a substantivist view, the discussion seems to focus on money as an indicator for a monetary economy and the question of how this changed over time." The problem of monetization was traditionally framed in the context of nineteenth-century evolutionist perspectives, which described the transition between pre-monetary to monetary societies and, in the case of the Roman Empire, assimilated monetization with "Romanization." Despite the difficulties of interpretation, it is clear that it is not possible to tell if local coinages were inspired, let alone promoted, by Rome, and to what degree as symbols of collective self-definition they were intended to accommodate or replicate Roman practices (Howgego 2005: 1). The same coins were used by the same individuals differently depending on the context. For example, Batavian soldiers probably received coins as payment, which were hoarded and sometimes lost in rural areas and used for ritual purposes in ritual environments but brought back into circulation and exchange in markets of the *civitas* capital, forts, and the *vici* surrounding them (Aarts 2005: 11–12). Our studies of money in the Roman world need to bring back coins to their material context, analyzing different types of money not only in the context of the medium- and long-distance movement of goods (ceramic, agricultural produce such as wine and oil, marble, raw metals) and domestic and ritual practices in the Roman world, but also in relation to other exchange spheres beyond the economy (Howgego 1994: 5; Aarts 2005: 2). We should allow in our interpretations for the confluence and divergence of different regimens of value, the commodification and decommodification of a coin during its biography. We need to make space for different practices attached to different contexts and users inside Roman society and the co-presence of multiple types of currency in the Roman world. We must also include questions of material agency: not only what people do to coins, but also what coins do to the people using them (Kemmers and Myrberg 2009: 94–103). An archaeology of money opens new perspectives and invites us to rethink numismatics, exploring ethnographic similitudes, colonial contexts, and the function of coins (Kemmers and Myrberg 2009: 103–4; Haselgrove and Krmnicek 2012: 244–5).

In the present, ancient coins can be considered an example of the "individualization" of a certain commodity that has acquired a special value for specific social groups (Kopytoff 1986: 78). Coins are illegally obtained, exported, and sold on the internet, where they are fully commoditized. They are treated as part of the art market even if, in many cases, their esthetic value or even their monetary value is very low. However, in the past, the collections of important museums around the world have been acquired by methods that are not in accordance with modern heritage management standards. As Renfrew (2000: 36) put it, "[t]he underlying problem so far as antiquities are concerned is that the supply of legitimate antiquities is minimal. Very few countries currently have a system whereby antiquities of limited importance, once legitimately excavated and published, may be legally sold." Two ideas are in conflict: that heritage is not a commodity and should not enter the market; and the easy access to ancient coins by retrieving them from archaeological sites with metal detectors or by buying them online, from coin dealers and fairs. Of course, if all "orphans" (independently of the time when they were extracted from the ground) were made illegal, that would be the end of the coin market, since it is not possible legally to collect coins found in excavations. There are things that money cannot buy. Without archaeological context, the interpretation of ancient coins is severely reduced. Decontextualized coins still yield important information about typologies, dies, iconography, and legends, but when context is gone, we lose the opportunity to reconstruct the regimens of value under which commodities circulate, and to understand the "social history of a class object" (Appadurai 1986)—in this case Roman money with its many forms, related practices, and meanings.

CHAPTER SEVEN

Money and the Issues of the Age

Power, Contact, and Identity

CLARE ROWAN

For when they had come to supply themselves more from abroad by importing things in which they were deficient and exporting those of which they had a surplus, the employment of money necessarily came to be devised. For the natural necessities are not in every case readily portable; hence for the purpose of barter men made a mutual compact to give and accept some substance of such a sort as being itself a useful commodity, easy to handle in use for general life, iron for instance, silver and other metals, at the first stage defined merely by size and weight, but finally also by impressing on it a stamp (charaktēra) in order that this might relieve them of having to measure it; for the stamp was put on as a token (sēmeion) of the amount.

—Aristotle, *Pol.* 1257a

This passage is one of several texts about money attributed to Aristotle, located within his discussions of justice (*Nicomachaean Ethics*) and politics (*Politics*) (Finley 1970). Aristotle's thoughts on money reflect the views and anxieties of an educated wealthy Greek in the fourth century BCE, but significantly he attributes the invention of money to increasing overseas exchange, or transactions that went beyond localized groups. This tale of progression from "barter" to "money" has since been repeated in innumerable accounts of the "invention" of money, so much so that Aristotle's text here might seem almost clichéd. We should remember that as someone who had tutored Alexander the Great, and then lived to see his conquests, Aristotle was writing at a time of transformation and increasing connectivity with distant lands. Money loomed large in this period, funding Alexander's campaigns and facilitating the movement of large quantities of wealth that was suddenly mobilized. It is difficult to generalize about "the issues" of antiquity, but an overall theme can be found in increasing (cultural) connectivity and its consequences (conquest, trade networks, colonialism, war and conflict, cultural change). Connectivity, facilitated by money, and facilitating the adoption of money, thus forms the focus of this chapter.

CONNECTIVITY AND CULTURAL CONTACT

Herodotus records that the Lydians were the first ancient people to use coins of gold and silver (Herodotus 1.94). Archaeological evidence demonstrates that coinage did emerge in this region (modern-day Turkey), with weighed pieces of electrum (an alloy of gold and silver that naturally occurs in the area) found alongside stamped pieces of the same material. The earliest known context for these objects is a foundation deposit from the temple of Artemis at Ephesus, dated to the first half of the seventh century BCE (Thompson 2003: 68). But coinage was an evolution of earlier systems that had utilized other objects as money: increased urbanization in the Bronze Age and the resultant changes to material culture resulted in a greater demand for raw materials and a more developed trade network. Early exchanges relied on a common cultural "code" or agreement about what objects had value. Metals came to dominate these exchanges, since they were neither too rare nor too common, could circulate, and could be melted down and converted into objects appropriate to different local cultures. This development meant that participation within wider Mediterranean trade networks no longer relied on a common cultural code; rather, metals functioned as a form of "proto-currency" (Sherratt 1993). Scientific analysis of copper objects from the Bronze Age shows a common isotopic signature, suggesting a strong and dynamic series of inter-regional exchanges, with metal moving, being melted down and recycled repeatedly in different regions (Knapp 2000). The exchange of metals was both a product and a facilitator of increased connectivity. Metals took on set forms and weights. In the ancient Near East, linen-wrapped parcels of silver pieces have been found fastened with a seal as early as the twelfth century BCE. This has been seen as a development towards the invention of "coinage" proper, since a coin is essentially a pre-weighed piece of metal guaranteed with a stamp (Thompson 2003).

Further east other materials fulfilled an exchange role, but again we find remarkable connectivity. In China and India, cowrie shells may have functioned as a form of exchange along trade routes; indeed, one form of cowrie is called

Cypraea moneta in recognition of its monetary function (many Chinese characters to this day contain the pictograph for cowrie in words connected to value or money; Xinwei 1994: xxii). Like metals, cowrie shells had qualities that made them suitable as a form of exchange: they were durable, portable, and neither too rare nor too common. When cowrie shells acquired some of the functions of money within China remains a subject for debate (namely due to ongoing discussion about what the definition of "money" might be); but from the twelfth century BCE they are found in quantity, likely brought to the region from the Indian Ocean through Central Asia (Yang 2011). Bronze cowries and moulds for casting bronze cowries have been found in the region of the Chu state of the eastern Zhou period (*c.* 770–222 BCE); these bronze cowries carried inscriptions and clearly functioned as currency.

"Coinage" as we might recognize it appeared in Lydia in the seventh century BCE; by 480 BCE more than 100 Greek cities in Greece, Italy, Sicily, and Turkey were minting their own silver coinages (Osborne 2009: 239–41). Initially these coins circulated alongside bullion, suggesting that pre-weighed pieces of metal and coinage were interchangeable at this early stage. The speed with which silver coinage was adopted across the Mediterranean by Greek cities must reflect existing networks and connectivity, a suggestion furthered by the types of coinage adopted. Greek cities in the western Mediterranean frequently adopted coinage that initially weighed and/or looked similar to the issues of cities with whom they had connections in the eastern Mediterranean. The Greek colony of Massalia (Marseilles, France), for example, adopted denominations and designs that recalled the coinage of their "mother-city" Phocaea (located in western Anatolia). Existing cultural networks thus contributed to whether coinage was adopted and its form (Rowan 2013a: 112–13). That other factors were also at work in the adoption of coinage, however, is evident from the cities that encountered it but did not adopt the medium. Rome, for example, did not strike her own coinage until the third century BCE; instead she continued to use pieces of bronze (*aes rude*). Settlements, tribes, and peoples who were outside the connected Mediterranean (in Britain, Germany, interior Spain) were also slower to adopt coinage as a monetary form.

Cultural contact only increased from the fourth century BCE. The military campaigns of Alexander the Great and his successors brought Greek settlers, culture, and Greek silver coinage to India; the subsequent interactions between cultures resulted in coins of Indo-Greek kings in what is now Afghanistan and Pakistan, which carried Greek language on one side and Karosthi on the other (see Figure 7.1). A second-century BCE hoard from the Graeco-Bactrian settlement of Ai-Khanum contained Indian punch-marked silver coinage as well as coins in the name of the local Indo-Greek ruler Agathocles, demonstrating an intermingling of cultures and monetary systems. King Agathocles (*c.* 185–170 BCE) struck coinage on the Greek weight standard, with Greek legends and

FIGURE 7.1: Copper coin of the Indo-Greek Bactrian king Menander, c. 160–145 BCE, 2.44g. On the obverse is a helmeted bust and a Greek legend reading "King Menander, Saviour." The reverse shows the goddess Athena and a legend in Karosthi script naming Menander as King and Saviour. Yale University Art Gallery, 2001.87.14562.

images, including a "pedigree" series honoring previous Greek rulers of the area, but also issued currency on an Indian weight standard (square in shape) that carried imagery referring to Hindu deities and Buddhist beliefs with legends in Greek and Brahmi (Narain 1973; Hoover 2013: 25–31). Agathocles and other Bactrian kings were also the first to issue coinage in a copper-nickel alloy, otherwise only known in China at this time, and which would not be used again for coinage until the nineteenth century.

The date of the first Indian coins (square pieces of silver with punch marks) is extremely controversial (dates range from the seventh to the fifth century BCE); archaeological evidence suggests, however, that Indian proto-coinage (bent silver bars) may have been influenced by Greek coinage via Achaemenid Persia (Cribb 2005a: 8–19). Indian Kushan gold coinage was inspired by the arrival of Roman gold issues, with designs at times imitating their Roman predecessors (Cribb 2005a: 10). Again, the connectivity between cultures arises as an overall theme in the adoption of monetary forms. Alexander the Great's silver coinage, characterized by designs showing the head of Hercules and a seated Zeus, was influenced by the coinage of Persian satraps he encountered as he moved east through Cilicia (modern Çukurova in Turkey) (de Callataÿ 2012b: 178). Roman expansion and the resultant Roman Empire only intensified the connectivity in those regions that fell under Roman control (Versluys 2014), resulting in an increased adoption of money and monetization. That money may have carried more than value with it is indicative in the adoption of coinage in Britain: the issues struck by Iron Age kings in the first century BCE, for example, are the earliest evidence for the adoption of writing in the region (Williams 2001).

DEMOCRACY AND IMPERIALISM

Money was also key in the formation of different governmental systems in antiquity, be they the democracy of classical Athens or the Empires of China and Rome. Athens had used pieces of silver (described as *Hacksilber* by modern archaeologists) as money before the adoption of coinage under the tyranny of Peisistratus in the sixth century BCE (van Alfen 2012: 88–9). After a period of varying numismatic designs (*Wappenmünzen*), Athens adopted a standard imagery for its money: the head of the city's patron goddess Athena on the obverse, and an owl (an animal associated with Athena) and an olive sprig on the reverse, accompanied by a legend naming the coin as a product of Athens: ΑΘΕ (see Figure 7.2). Money enabled a citizen democracy like Athens to function by allowing the city to compensate its citizens for participation in assemblies, jury courts, and for acting as magistrates, among other activities. Aristotle records that before the introduction of payment, attendance at the assembly had been poor (*Athenaion politeia* 41.3). Money also enabled cultural development in the city by allowing government officials to pay poets and offer prizes for music and literary festivals, a development which has been linked to the rise of Greek tragedy (Seaford 2008).

Athenian silver coinage continued to be produced until the first century BCE, becoming a symbol of Athens and Athenian democracy (the latter the prerogative of elite citizen males). In this sense money acted as a medium of exchange and payment, but also as a medium of identity that one might "think with." The imagery on Athenian coinage provided a material focal point for Athenian identity, but so too did the quality of the metal (silver): the purity of Athenian silver coinage became equated with the purity of Athenian citizens. Indeed, Athens resisted striking the convenient, bronze small change that gradually appeared in other Greek cities, suggesting that the ideological role of Athenian

FIGURE 7.2: Athenian silver *tetradrachm*, fifth century BCE, 16.71g. Yale University Art Gallery, 2007.182.271.

coinage at times overrode its functionality. The connection between Athens's silver coinage and its democracy is clearest when both came under threat during the Peloponnesian War (431–404 BCE). In 406/405 BCE, having been cut off from their silver mines by the Spartans, the Athenians issued two emergency coinages: bronze coinage plated with silver, and small coins made with gold that came from the Nike statues on the Athenian acropolis (van Alfen 2012: 95). The contemporary playwright Aristophanes equated this corruption of the coinage with the corruption of Athens itself, now witness to an influx of foreigners:

> We often thought that the same thing has happened
> to the city, in respect of the good and fine men among its citizens,
> as happened with the old coinage and the new gold.
> We do not make use of these coins, not counterfeit
> but the fairest, as it seems, of all, and only the ones
> struck well and ringing true among the Greeks
> and the barbarians everywhere, but (we use)
> these wicked little bronzes, struck yesterday
> and the day before with the worst possible striking.
> And those of the citizens whom we know to be noble and
> respectable, just and good and fine, reared in (the traditions of)
> the wrestling ground, the dance and music,
> we treat outrageously, and we make use of the bronze ones
> for every purpose, foreigners, red-heads, villains from evil stock, recent arrivals
> whom the city in the past would not have used
> even in the most random way as scapegoats.
> —Aristophanes, *Ranae* 718–33 (= Melville Jones 1993 no. 86)

Aristophanes here equates what he considers to be "true" Athenians with the well-struck, high-quality silver coins of the city; the influx of foreigners is equivalent to the city's use of poorly struck bronze issues. We see the connection again in language: officials named *dokimastēs* tested Athenian coinage for forgeries, while the process of *dokimasia* tested the authenticity of a citizen; both words come ultimately from the Greek verb "to test" or "to evaluate" (δοκιμάζω). The Greek word for "stamp" or "die" was *charaktēr*, from which we derive our word "character" and which in antiquity could also mean a characteristic or character of a particular person. The play between the two meanings of the word is found in Greek texts throughout antiquity. The philosopher Epictectus, for example, stated that one should reject a coin of the emperor Nero in favor of one issued by Trajan, since Nero's coinage is "rotten." A person who was gentle, generous, patient, and affectionate would be accepted by Epictectus and made a citizen, "only see that he does not have the *charaktēra* of Nero" (Arrian, *Epicteti dissertationes* 4.5.16–18). Epictetus demonstrates how coinage provided a metaphor for thought within ancient philosophy; Seaford has gone so far as to argue that the adoption of coinage within Athens (a homogenous, impersonal, universal medium that is both abstract as a unit of value and concrete as a physical object) was a precondition of pre-Socratic metaphysics, "in which universal power belongs to an abstract substance which is, like money, transformed into and from everything else," as well as other philosophical thought (Seaford 2004).

At the height of her power Athens produced such a quantity of coinage that the phrase "sending owls to Athens" became a proverb to describe a pointless action (the equivalent of "sending coals to Newcastle" in English, although the phrase survives in its original in German: *Eule nach Athen tragen* (Melville Jones 1993 no. 56). The sheer volume of coinage produced by Athens, and its purity, meant that Athenian coinage transformed into what might be described as an "international" currency, accepted in numerous regions in the eastern and (at times) western Mediterranean, and even minted by others. This last development meant that the Athenians had to introduce a law in 375/374 BCE detailing which "Athenian" coins would be acceptable in the city: coins of Athenian type and pure silver were acceptable (regardless of the mint), plated or otherwise forged coins were removed from circulation (Melville Jones 1993 no. 91; van Alfen 2005).

As Athenian influence and coinage increased, other Greek cities reduced or ceased production. It remains debated whether this was due to the ready supply of Athenian issues or was the result of an Athenian insistence that her allies use only her currency (van Alfen 2005: 94). A decree of the second half of the fifth century BCE (the "Standards" or "Coinage" decree, preserved on various stone fragments found in different regions) records that allied cities, who paid tribute to Athens each year, were to use Athenian coinage, weights and measures; silver could be brought to Athens to be converted into the appropriate currency for a fee (Melville Jones 1993 no. 78). Although much remains controversial, it is evident that at the height of her power Athens demanded payment from her allies in her own currency. Money played a role in visualizing democracy, but it also came to shape the Athenian empire. A parallel might be found in the Zhou coinage of China: the inscriptions on these coins refer to a variety of locations, although they are only ever found within the region controlled by the Zhou dynasty. The likely explanation is that the inscriptions refer to the source of the tribute that funded the coinage (Cribb 2005b: 434).

Money, and in particular coinage, also played a role in the formation of the Roman Empire. The northern boundaries of the Roman Empire roughly correspond to the areas that had been monetized in the Iron Age, suggesting that societies with money were easier to conquer (Howgego 2013). Money acts as a medium of commensuration that renders different value and cultural systems equivalent; it thus plays a key role in contact, conquest, and colonial situations (Comaroff and Comaroff 2006). Whether the existence of money meant that differing regimes of value could more easily merge, and/or the use of coinage reflected an elite social hierarchy that made conquest easier, or because the adoption of coinage was also frequently followed by the adoption of other parts of Roman culture like imagery and writing (as in Britain), the geographical alignment between the use of coinage and Roman expansion indicates the connection between money and imperialism (Howgego 2013).

The Greek historian Polybius, who lived during an intensive period of Roman expansion in the second century BCE, also appears to have realized the connection. In his *Histories*, Polybius compares the constitutions of Rome and Sparta. The Spartans were slow to adopt coinage, a point that Polybius notes caused a problem in terms of growing Spartan power. He argued that while the Spartans conquered their neighbors, iron currency rods and goods-exchange were sufficient, but once they sought to expand beyond the Peloponnese, their exchange systems proved insufficient, "since these enterprises demanded a currency in universal circulation and supplies drawn from abroad" (Polybius 6.49.8–10). Polybius wrote as the Roman silver coin, the *denarius*, was becoming just such a "universal" currency. The *denarius* was introduced in *c.* 211 BCE during the Second Punic War, at a time when Rome emerged as a serious Mediterranean power. Roman *denarii* were initially produced by melting down other precious metal currencies, an imperialist act that ensured that the regions under her control (Sicily, Italy, and Spain at this stage) utilized only the precious metal coinage of Rome, and the messages it carried (Burnett 1995).

The unification of China under the Qin dynasty in 221 BCE also brought with it a standardized currency (see Figure 7.3). Bronze *qin ban liang* (round coins with a square hole in the center) circulated as accepted currency until the end of imperial China (Yang 2011: 9), initially with gold bullion also acting as a form of money (Scheidel 2008). Other types of currency that existed in China

FIGURE 7.3: *Ban Liang Qian*, 400–100 BCE. Yale University Art Gallery, 2001.87.45339.

(e.g., cowrie shells, bronze cowrie shells, and utensil-shaped money) were repressed (Scheidel 2008). The control of monetary forms that frequently accompanied the formation of Empires in antiquity is also found in Ptolemaic Egypt. Evidence suggests that a "closed currency" system was introduced, in which incoming currency had to be exchanged for lighter Ptolemaic coins; the government gained 3g of silver and 1.5g of gold for each gold or silver coin exchanged, as well as the fee charged for the conversion (von Reden 2010: 43–7). Under Ptolemy II a monetary poll tax was introduced, frequently paid in bronze coinage, which ensured monetization throughout the Egyptian countryside.

Money was thus used to form and consolidate governmental systems, but it also played a role in rebellions against established hierarchies. Indeed, the particular ideological emphasis given to coinage by the Romans (who treated coinage as a "monument in miniature") meant money played a symbolic role among the differing groups who opposed Roman power. As an object connected to the government and, in the Roman Empire, the person of the emperor, money attracted expressions of discontent. During the rebellion of Rome's Italian allies in the Social War of 91–88 BCE, Italians struck their own coinage with imagery communicating their own ideologies and carrying the local Oscan language (Campana 1987; the coins also possessed some "Roman" characteristics, like a Roman weight standard). One of the most poignant designs from this series was a silver *denarius* that had as its reverse a bull (representative of Italy) goring a wolf (representative of Rome) (Rutter 2001: no. 427).

The successive Jewish revolts against Roman control in 66–70 CE and 132–5 CE also witnessed the issuing of coinage that declared independence from Roman hegemony. During the First Jewish War silver shekels and half shekels were struck depicting the *omer* cup on one side and pomegranates on the other, accompanied by legends in Paleo-Hebrew script reading "Sheqel of Israel" and "Holy Jeruslaem." A new dating system was placed on the currency (Meshorer 2001: 115–34; bronze coinage was also struck). The weight standard, writing (an intentionally archaic script no longer in use), and imagery were all statements of independent identity. During the Second Jewish War a form of local currency was again released, this time created by overstriking the Roman currency that was in circulation. This had the effect of proclaiming and fostering a sense of Jewish identity and independence while at the same time destroying the imagery of the government they were opposing (Gitler 2012: 491). When the Romans recaptured Jersualem after the Second Jewish War, they melted down and re-struck the coinage of the rebels (see Figure 7.4) and cut the bronze coins to prevent their continued use. Roman reaction is seen in the Jerusalem Talmud, which records that coins issued by rebels were not accepted (Meshorer 2001: 161–2).

FIGURE 7.4: Silver *denarius* of the second Jewish revolt, 134/5 CE, 3.3g, overstruck on a *denarius* of the emperor Vespasian. Legend in Paleo-Hebrew on both sides and a palm branch on the reverse; the remnants of the Latin legend from Vespasianic coin visible on both sides. Yale University Art Gallery, 2002.121.42.

Local civic coinages in the Roman Empire also occasionally show the removal or defacement of the portraits of emperors who attracted posthumous condemnation (labeled *damnatio memoriae* in scholarship). At times, this looks like the concerted actions of a local government, but other cases might have been isolated acts by individuals (Harl 1987: 35). Roman coins found at the battlefield site of Kalkriese in Germany displayed signs of defacement (cuts and piercings); these were originally interpreted as expressions of disillusionment made by Roman soldiers serving in the area, but they might equally be the actions of the victorious Germans who might have "dismembered" these objects of the Roman government after their victory (Kemmers and Myrberg 2011: 98). These instances demonstrate the ideological role of coinage, and its connection to the person (and portrait) of the emperor.

WAR AND CRISIS

Money revolutionized warfare in the ancient Mediterranean. The conquests of Alexander the Great were facilitated by the professionalization of the Macedonian army by his father Philip II, a revolution funded by the acquisition of the rich mines of Mount Pangaion. With the coinage produced from these mines, Philip II was able to hire mercenaries and other Greeks, creating a highly trained professional army that could wage warfare all year round, a significant departure from the largely citizen-based military forces of classical Greece (Diodorus Siculus 16.7.6). Philip struck the first "Greek" gold coins (Greeks previously used Persian gold coinage, the "daric"), which were called *philippeioi* after their issuer (the word later came to mean gold coinage more broadly, de Callataÿ 2012b: 176–7). Philip II also struck silver coins in greater quantity than any previous Macedonian king. The quantities and wide circulation of both these issues must have been a factor in the imitation of these coins by Celtic tribes in northern Europe.

Money also facilitated purchases and developments in military hardware, most noticeably with the acquisition of navies by Athens and other states (Herodotus 7.144; Trundle 2010: 237). The use of money to hire mercenaries meant that warfare increased in scale, but so too did the mobility of individuals, as soldiers became detached from their homelands. The movement of mercenaries became a key issue in the Mediterranean from the fourth century BCE (Trundle 2010: 229). A telling example is that of Entella in Sicily: Campanian mercenaries, who had been serving in Sicily and were discharged, travelled to the city. They were initially admitted as fellow citizens, but then the mercenaries slew all the men young enough to serve in the military, married the women of the city and claimed it as their own, overstriking what was likely their pay with a new coin design "of the Campanians" (Diodorus Siculus 14.8–9; Lee 2000).

If money assisted in creating larger professional armies, then the existence of these forces in turn necessitated the continued issuing of coinage to pay them; a cycle that we see continuing throughout Mediterranean antiquity. The payment of military expenses would have formed, for example, a significant part of the expenditure of Rome, although coinage would also have been struck for other expenses. Funds would have arrived through rents, fines, taxes, as well as mines, but also through war indemnities and booty—indeed, the need to pay an army likely resulted in greater ferocity and looting in warfare (Rowan 2013b). The incoming wealth from war is responsible for a cultural revolution in the Roman world, funding, among other things, building projects in Rome that transformed the city (Wallace-Hadrill 2008: 356). But war was not always successful or profitable. The ongoing and seemingly ever-present cost of maintaining an army is likely one contributing reason to the continuing debasement of Roman silver coinage throughout the third century CE; intensive periods of warfare, and Roman military defeats in this period, as well as a decrease in productivity of the Roman mines, meant that lead was increasingly added to silver coinage with the fineness eventually falling to about five percent (Estiot 2012: 543). The economic effects of this debasement need further research, but the economic stress of the Roman Empire at this time is evident in the repeated reforms of the Roman monetary system. Eventually a system was created that relied not on silver, but upon a pure gold coinage, the *solidus*, which remained in use until the tenth century CE.

War also affected credit in the Roman world. When the Pontic king Mithridates VI invaded Asia in 88 BCE and instigated a massacre of Romans and

Italians in the region, the resulting economic loss caused a collapse of credit in Rome. Cicero wrote that the monetary system that operated within the forum at Rome was linked with Asia: "the loss of one inevitably undermines the other and causes its collapse" (Cicero, *De imperio Cn. Pompeii* 19; Kay 2014: 245). Similarly, Julius Caesar's crossing of the Rubicon in 49 BCE, his seizure of the Roman treasury, and the ensuing civil wars created such unease that lenders called in their debts. The resulting economic crisis required several official measures to counteract it (Cassius Dio 41.37.2; Verboven 2003).

The disruptive effects of war are also evident in China, particularly in the Chu–Han war (206–202 BCE). The conflict resulted in millions of casualties and disrupted agricultural production. The solution to the lack of goods seemed simple: produce more coins so that more people would be able to buy things (Xinwei 1994: 148). The Han dynasty reduced the weight of their gold and bronze currency in implementing this plan, not realizing that this would cause inflation (indeed, the rise in prices was blamed on merchants hoarding goods). Evidence of credit in China is harder to find, although the *Rituals of Zhou* record that governmental coin offices would make loans, whose size and duration were determined by the loan's purpose (Xinwei 1994: 98). Money thus both affected, and was affected by, the intense periods of military conflict in antiquity.

IDENTITY AND COLONIALISM

A recurring feature of ethnographic descriptions in classical antiquity is mention of whether a particular people made use of money, and what type of money they used. The *Geography* of Strabo (64/63 BCE–24 CE), for example, contains numerous passages on the topic: the Persians use coined money but gold and silver is channelled more toward objects than coinage (15.21), some on the Iberian peninsula use barter rather than money, or *Hacksilber* (3.7), those in Albania do not use coined money, nor accurate weights or measures, and do not plan "war or government or farming" (11.4). That a coinage or form of money might come to characterize a particular people is also evident in the repeated mention of Spartan money: the legendary Lycurgus allegedly banned the use of gold and silver coinage in the city, instead preferring to use the "ancestral" currency of iron spits (*obols*). Lycurgus also reputedly made the currency so worthless that "ten mina's worth required a large store in a house and a yoke of animals to transport it" (Plutarch, *Vitae Parallelae Lycurgus* 9.1-4). Thus, say our ancient sources, illegality and wickedness were prevented in the city, since the allure of money had been averted, for who would attempt to steal or take something that "could not be hidden, envied if possessed, or even cut into pieces with any benefit?"

This connection between money, identity, and character is more marked in the classical world than elsewhere in antiquity. Ancient Chinese coins, although they had varying shapes, carried only texts, not images. The peculiar direction taken by money in the classical world might be explained by the very beginnings of coinage. One of the earliest known coins is an electrum piece decorated with a stag and a Greek legend that reads "I am the badge/sign (*sēma*) of Phanes" (British Museum, museum no. BNK,G.950). Electrum was an alloy with variable gold:silver ratios, which made the intrinsic value of each piece of metal variable. Scholars believe this problem led to the expedient of "stamping" electrum; the value of the piece was thus guaranteed by the state (or in the case above, by Phanes), rather than by the metal content of the object (Wallace 1987; Kroll 2012). Although electrum was quickly replaced by coinage of gold and silver, the practical uses of the "badge" or "stamp" had already been demonstrated; the practice persisted throughout the classical world. It is this twist of materiality, perhaps, that led to the association between money and the identity of the issuer in the classical world, placing it on a different monetary trajectory.

Coinage and its designs not only reflected particular identities in classical antiquity, they also actively assisted in forming them. Just as politicians of the nineteenth century saw currency design as a medium that might foster collective traditions and identities (Helleiner 2003), so too did emergent cities and settlements in the ancient Mediterranean often strike coinage with deliberately chosen types. An engaging case study can be found in the Greek settlements of southern Italy and Sicily. Although ancient literature, and subsequently scholarship of the modern colonial period, characterized these settlements as "colonies" of a particular Greek "mother-city," the archaeology of these towns reveals them to be more diverse than initially believed. None the less the ideology of these settlers was that they were connected to mainland Greece and Asia Minor (Osborne 1998; Malkin 2003).

A unique, but none the less Hellenic "Achaean" statement can be found on the coinage of Greek settlements of southern Italy (known as "Magna Grecia"). In the seventh century BCE a series of Greek cities were founded in the region, and in the sixth century several of these cities adopted coinage. The fabric of these issues was unique, although shared by several of the cities in the region: the reverse of the coin was an incuse imitation of the obverse. The overall effect gave the illusion of the design having been impressed onto the coin in repoussé style, although the coin was struck from both an obverse and reverse die (see Figure 7.5). The skill and labor involved in this type of coinage was significant. Scholars disagree over why this particular design was adopted, but its use in several Greek cities in the region must have contributed to a sense of regional identity. Find evidence suggests that although the coinage did not circulate outside Magna Grecia, coins of differing cities could be hoarded together (and thus presumably circulated together), at least before 480 BCE (Holloway 2000: 480). The designs adopted for these first coinages in the region reflected the

FIGURE 7.5: Silver *stater* of Kroton, Southern Italy, 500–480 BCE, 7.98g. The repoussé effect can be seen with the tripod, in relief on the obverse, and incuse on the reverse. Yale University Art Gallery, 2001.87.2344.

traditional stores of value that had existed in archaic Greece before the advent of coinage (e.g., a bull on coins of Sybaris, a tripod on coinage of Kroton, grain on the money of Metapontum). These images thus contributed to the idea that these cities were connected to a "motherland" and a Greek heroic age, fostering a sense of "being Achaean" (Papadopoulos 2002). The persistent representation of objects that had acted as stores of value before money can also be seen in ancient China, with the use of small spade-coins, knife-coins, and ring-coins (Xinwei 1994: xxiii).

Coinages of other Greek cities in southern Italy and Sicily focus on local landscapes, with rivers and springs appearing with frequency. Modern studies of colonization have demonstrated the importance of local landscapes in shaping new communities, and, in the case of rivers, how they mark the connectivity of one settlement with another (Frisone 2012). Rivers, represented as a man-faced bull, appeared on coins struck by Neapolis (Naples) and ancient Gela in Sicily, amongst others. The issuing of money at the beginning of a colony allowed the expression of what vision the (presumably elite) settlers had for their city. When the Romans began creating colonies outside of Italy in the first century BCE, part of the foundation often included the striking of a "local" coinage (sometimes the *only* time local coinage was issued), whose imagery reflected the "idea" of a colony and its identity. The use of this money must have contributed to a sense of common heritage among an otherwise mixed group of settlers (Rowan 2014). Both local landscapes and coinage provided a means of self-definition for settlers in a foreign land.

That, as in the modern world, these "colonial currencies" may have reflected the conqueror's gaze, or vision of an area, rather than any reality, might be seen in the coinage struck by for the veteran settlement of Emerita (Mérida) in Spain.

The colony was founded in *c.* 25 BCE with veterans from the tenth and fifth legions (Cassius Dio 53.26.1). Silver coinage was struck carrying the portrait of the emperor on the obverse, with the city walls of Emerita on the reverse (Sutherland 1984: no. 9). The city itself was under construction for decades after its foundation, but the image of a "final" or "complete" city on currency must have aided settlers in visualizing and identifying with their new home. The earliest bronze coinage struck in the name of Emerita showed the Roman city foundation ritual (contributing to the idea that Emerita, like other colonies, was a "mini-Rome"), representations of the local river (shown as a female goddess spitting water out of her mouth), and legionary standards (Burnett, Amandry, and Ripolles 1992: 5–11). The use of these coins, and their images, would have contributed to a cohesive identity for the new town. The connection between coinage and civic identity can be traced throughout the first 300 years of the Roman Empire, particularly in the eastern Mediterranean (Howgego, Heuchert, and Burnett 2005).

There is also a strong connection between money and personal identity. Graeber has pointed out the strange parallel between objects of personal adornment and objects that serve as currency in cultures across the ages: beads, shells, precious metals, and other objects could be worn as jewelry as well as used as money (Graeber 1996). Jewelry, after all, serves as a store of value. Personal decorative objects, however, cannot be defined as all-purpose money, although at times they might have had a particular monetary function. For example, some metal torques (neck rings) within Celtic Germany weigh exactly the same amount as 100 coins of local weight, suggesting some connection between the two. Torques were also deposited, at times in identifiable religious contexts, suggesting that this object, which communicated personal prestige, might also have a secondary function (Hunter 2015: 103–5). Graeber connects personal adornment with monetary materials to the potential power this material holds for action—a public display of (purchasing) capacity. The same might be said of the personal display of money itself. As precious metal coinage travelled beyond the northern borders of the Roman Empire to Barbaricum in Late Antiquity, gold coins and medallions were converted into jewelry. This was frequently designed so that the portrait of the Roman emperor was on display (Bursche 2001; Eremić 2014). In a society which had no tradition of portraiture, the image of the emperor may have held as much power and prestige as the gold itself.

The imperial portrait certainly held power within the Roman Empire, imbuing the currency with the power of the monarch: the fifth century CE legal text, the *Theodosian code*, records that all *solidi* (gold coins) on which the imperial portrait appears are of equal worth; the law was evidently formulated in response to people valuing coins carrying "larger" portraits as being worth more than coins with "smaller" portraits (*Codex Theodosianus* 9.22.1). We should not take the surviving textual evidence at face value, but since Roman imperial coinage bore the face of the emperor, reports survive that it was illegal to carry coins into brothels, toilets, or other places that might disgrace the imperial visage. Evidently the power of money was coupled with the power of the emperor (Wolters 1999: 308–18). The power or "charisma" of the portrait is also the likely explanation behind the appearance of Roman coins, as well as imitation Roman coins, as pendants in Southeast Asia. The coins likely arrived via India with other goods and again the portrait appears to have been the important aspect of the object (Borrell 2014). The appearance of (imitative) Roman imperial portraiture in this region of the world again demonstrates the connectivity of antiquity.

RELIGION

America's banknotes carry the phrase "In god we trust," a motto of the nation that also, in this context, inadvertently references the role of trust in fiduciary money. Similarly, many Greek coinages from the classical world carried imagery of deities, and one must wonder whether this imagery contributed to the trust placed in its value. It was only after Alexander the Great, when powerful kings came to be worshipped like gods, that living rulers began to appear on coinage in the Mediterranean (kings more so than queens, but women did appear. It was the rediscovery of Roman coinage in the Renaissance that led to the revival of portraiture on money, a tradition that has persisted until the present day; Stahl 2013). Dies, flans, and other minting materials have been found in temples in several classical cities (e.g., Himera in Sicily, Argos and Sounion in Greece), although we cannot always tell whether this meant minting operations took place in these spaces or if the objects were simply deposited there after use (Cutroni Tusa 1982; Kalligas 1997).

The deposition of mint materials in temples has a parallel in the removal of temple holdings to be used as money. The most celebrated example is perhaps that of Athens, mentioned above. The gold coinage struck during the Peloponnesian War was made from the gold of the statues of Nike in the Parthenon. The dies used to make these coins were then deposited in the temple of Athena as an offering (Melville Jones 1993: no. 170). Some temples also invested or loaned money, capitalizing on the fact that, after the invention of coinage, offerings could now take the form of (or could be converted into) coin, which might then be used as a commodity to increase the temple's wealth. This investment could not occur when religious offerings consisted of grain, meat, or other goods; metallic, all-purpose money was transformative here. This change was not universal, but the invention of coinage collapsed any boundaries that might have existed between cult, government administration, and warfare in classical Greece. Davies has demonstrated that many of the cities that made use of their temple assets were cities that relied on expensive naval power, which perhaps made them more pragmatic towards their cultic wealth (Davies 2001).

Given the strong connection between money, identity, and government it is not surprising that religion shaped the decoration (and at times the use) of money throughout antiquity. The currencies of the Jewish rebellions against Roman rule have already been mentioned; the Hasmonean dynasty (semi-autonomous rulers of Judea from c. 140–16 BCE) also largely refrained from reproducing human figures on their coinage in accordance with the commandment against graven images (Gitler 2012). The silver currency of the Sasanian Persian kings, who ruled Iran from 224 CE until the Islamic invasion of 651 CE, was also dominated by religious iconography, with many issues carrying representations of the Zoroastrian fire altar (Schindel 2005). This religious imagery might have contributed to the "trust" of the currency as much as it underlined the religious right of the Persian "king of kings" (*shahanshah*) to rule.

The rise of Christianity, by contrast, was slow to have a marked effect on money, probably because it remained a "private," rather than a governmental, religion for quite some time. The city of Apamaea in Phrygia placed an image from the story of Noah on its local coinage in the third century CE, since the local Ararat Mountain was identified as the biblical "mountains of Ararat" where Noah's ark came to rest. This tradition likely arose out of, and was connected to, a local Phrygian legend about a flood (Spoerri Butcher 2006: 250–60). Constantine's conversion did not result in a monetary revolution: overt Christian symbols were restricted to the chi-rho symbol and *labarum* (a military standard with the chi-rho symbol upon it; Abdy 2012). Although overt Christian imagery was slow and subtle in its appearance, Christian inhabitants of the Roman Empire saw Christian imagery even where it may not have existed. The Christian author Eusebius interpreted Constantine's numismatic portrait, shown gazing upwards in the style of Alexander the Great, as the emperor with his eyes uplifted in prayer (Eusebius, *Vita Constantini* 4.15). Whether this was the intended interpretation (and it is more likely Constantine was aligning himself to Alexander), it was evidently important to Eusebius that money, as an object guaranteed by the emperor and associated with him, should reflect his own religious world view.

Money, and its design, did not escape the tension that existed between "pagans" and Christians in late antiquity. When coins of the "pagan" emperor Julian (361–3 CE) were released showing a bull on the reverse (see Figure 7.6), the design became a point of contention (inadvertently revealing just how much the inhabitants of the Roman Empire held the emperor responsible for the coinage struck in his name). The church historian Socrates (3.17.4-5) wrote that the Christian citizens of Antioch said that the bull "which was impressed

FIGURE 7.6: Argentiferous bronze *nummus* of Julian II, 361–3 CE, 8.45g. Julian II is shown diademed and bearded on the obverse, while the reverse shows a bull and carries a legend referring to the security of the empire (*res publica*). Yale University Art Gallery, 2001.87.17834.

upon his coin, was a symbol of his having desolated the world" and was connected to Julian's "pagan" practice of animal sacrifice. Another church historian, Sozomen (5.19.2), records that the context behind these insults was that war preparations in Antioch had resulted in a rise in prices. When Julian attempted to reduce prices, merchants allegedly fled the city, and scarcity ensued; the emperor's beard and coin design became the focus of frustrations. Julian retaliated with a satirical work, *Misopogon* ("Beard-Hater"), directed at the citizens of Antioch, which referred to the fact that he had been insulted not only on account of his beard, but also for the designs of his coins (355D). In the *Hymns against Julian*, Ephrem the Syrian identifies the bull as the golden calf of the Jews: "The bull of paganism engraved on his heart [Julian] imprinted on that image for the People who love it" (1.16–20). Numismatic imagery thus might evoke a variety of interpretations according to culture and context.

PSEUDO-, PRIVATE, AND ALTERNATIVE CURRENCIES

Keith Hart has observed that the two sides of a coin, "heads" and "tails," reflect the dual nature of money itself. Money (and its value) is simultaneously the product of a social organization that is "top down" ("heads") and "bottom up" ("tails") (Hart 1986). Although money may be underwritten by the state, at its heart it is also a commodity whose value is agreed upon by two or more individuals. Although this chapter has focused on governmental currencies, money also existed beyond the state in antiquity, creating exchanges and relationships at a local level. In both imperial Rome and imperial China, much currency production remained local—either through the production of provincial coinage, small change struck by individual cities in the Roman Empire or through the local production of coinage by individuals in China—the western Han dynasty, for example, allowed the private minting of coins (Xinwei 1994: 151).

The decision of the emperor Wen to allow private minting, a policy of non-interference that conformed to the emperor's Confucian outlook, did cause concern among officials. Jia Yi's "Memorial admonishing against letting people have private coinage" was one of China's earliest monographs on monetary problems, and observed that people were abandoning the land to take up coin production instead (Xinwei 1994: 175–6). In 175 BC Jia Shan wrote:

> Money is a useless commodity, but it may be exchanged for items of great value. These items of great value are that over which the ruler exercises authority. To allow people to make coins is to have the ruler share his authority with them. This cannot be done for long.
> —*Han History*, "Biography of Jia Shin," in Xinwei 1994: 177

The anxieties about currency produced "beyond" the government here echoes the modern anxieties surrounding alternative currencies in the current age. At times, the private production of currencies in China was restricted or banned. The *Han Shu* records that if an individual produced poor-quality coinage their face was to be tattooed in black ink (24B, 3b in Swan 1950: 234). Production of coinage by individuals outside the government is also known in the classical Mediterranean, although here the evidence is archaeological.

In the Roman world we find privately produced coins that imitate governmental currency (whose "legality" or "acceptance" remains a topic of discussion), as well as locally produced currencies that imitate the coinage of other cities, intended for local use. The best studied of these are the coins produced within central Italy in the first century BCE in workshops that have been labelled "pseudo-mints" (Stannard and Frey-Kupper 2008). One "pseudo-mint" was probably located in Pompeii and produced coinage, without any legend, that carried imagery adopted from the coinage of the cities of Ebusus (Ibiza) in Spain and Massalia (Marseilles) in France. Excavations at Pompeii have revealed that a significant portion of the small change in the city consisted of these "pseudo" currencies (e.g., 45 percent of the coin assemblage from the recent American excavations consisted of these types (Hobbs 2013: 32)). Another "pseudo-mint" was likely located at ancient Minturnae (Minturno, Italy) and produced coins with designs adopted from Paestum and elsewhere; these issues are found in Italy and Sicily (Stannard and Frey-Kupper 2008). The production of these "unofficial imitations" and "pseudo" issues has been connected to the increased monetization of Italy in the first century BCE, and hence an increased need for small change.

This demand was not met by the Roman authorities who, for reasons unknown, ceased to produce small coinage between 82 and 46 BCE (Hollander 2007: 24; Stannard and Frey-Kupper 2008: 376–8). It is evident, though, that for this region at this time, unofficial or pseudo-currencies played a key role in facilitating daily transactions and, through their imagery, undoubtedly contributed to shaping local identities and communities.

These roles can also be identified in the lead "token currencies" that appeared in quantity in parts of ancient Egypt during the third century CE. The production of these alternative currencies again occurred in a vacuum of "officially" produced small change: the government mint at Alexandria ceased to produce bronze coinage in any quantity (Milne 1971: xvii). Instead, lead tokens were produced for use by different cities (Milne 1930). That these token currencies may have reflected and shaped local identities can be seen in the differences between cities: Memphite tokens carried images of the Nile and Egyptian deities (Isis-Hekate, Apis), while those of Oxyrhynchus were more Greek in design, with images of Athena, Zeus, and Nike (Milne 1971: nos. 5276–319). Excavations at Oxyrhynchus uncovered thirty-seven different types of tokens, with 184 carrying one of twelve local Oxyrhynchite designs (Milne 1930: 301). These objects thus likely facilitated local, everyday transactions within the region, and might be seen as historical precursors to community currencies like the Brixton pound.

Monetary objects whose value was constructed within a very local setting can also be found in the use of old or obsolete currencies. The bronze coinage of Rome's rival Carthage, for example, remained in circulation in Roman Africa for more than 100 years after Carthage's destruction (Burnett 1987: 179). Ptolemaic coinage also continued to circulate for hundreds of years after the Roman conquest in 30 BCE (some issues have been found in archaeological strata as late as the third century CE; Buttrey 1987: 165). In India, the fourth-century BCE coinage of the Mauryan kings continued to circulate until the third century CE (Hoover 2013: lxiii). These locally agreed-upon monetary forms (notably, for the Roman imperial period, confined to small change) could be also resuscitated: Roman coinage was used in Africa for small change in the nineteenth century CE (Greenhalgh 2014: 89). This demonstrates the diversity of monetary objects that might have existed within antiquity, as well as their contribution to more recent monetary practice. Although this contribution has traced what this author (admittedly a Greco-Roman specialist) identifies as key issues of the age, the diversity of antiquity and monetary practice cannot hope to be fully captured within one book chapter. Money reveals connectivity in this period, but it also reveals diversity.

BIBLIOGRAPHY

Aarts, Joris (2005), "Coins, Money and Exchange in the Roman World. A Cultural–Economic Perspective," *Archaeological Dialogues* 12(1): 1–44.
Abdy, Richard (2012), "Earliest Christian Symbols on Roman Coins," in William E. Metcalf (ed.), *The Oxford Handbook of Greek and Roman Coinage*, Oxford: Oxford University Press, 663–6.
Agut-Labordère, Damien (2014), "L'orge et l'argent. Les usages monétaires à 'Ayn Manâwir à l'époque perse," *Annales. Histoire, Sciences Sociales* 69(1): 75–90.
Alföldy-Gazdac, Agnes and Cristian Gazdac (2013), "Who pays the Ferryman? The Testimony of Ancient Sources on the Myth of Charon," *Klio* 95(2): 285–314.
Allason-Jones, Lindsay and Bruce McKay (1985), *Coventina's Well*. The Trustees of the Clayton Collection. Oxford: Chester Museum.
Amandry, Michel (1993), "Manipulations, innovations monétaires et techniques financières dans le monde grec," in Tony Hackens and Ghislane Moucharte (eds.), *Actes du XIe Congrès International de Numismatique*, Louvain-la-Neuve: Séminaire de Numismatique M. Hoc, 1–7.
Andreau, Jean (1987), *La vie financière dans le monde romain. Les métiers de manieurs d'argent (IVe siècle av. J.–C.–IIIe siècle ap. J.–C.)*, Rome: École française de Rome.
Andreau, Jean (1999), *Banking and Business in the Roman World*, Cambridge: Cambridge University Press.
Andreau, Jean (2008), "The Use and Survival of Coins and of Gold and Silver in the Vesuvian Cities," in William V. Harris (ed.), *The Monetary Systems of the Greeks and Romans*. Oxford: Oxford University Press, 208–25.
Antonaccio, Carla (2005), "Dedications and the Character of Cult," in Robin Hägg and Brita Alroth (eds.), *Greek Sacrificial Ritual, Olympian and Chthonian. Proceedings of the Sixth International Seminar on Ancient Greek Cult. Organized by the Department of Classical Archaeology and Ancient History. Göteborg University. April 25–27, 1997*, Acta Instituti Atheniensis Regni Sueciae 18. Stockholm: Svenska Institutet i Athen, 99–112.
Appadurai, Arjun (1986), "Introduction: Commodities and the Politics of Value," in Arjun Appadurai (ed.), *The Social Life of Things*, Cambridge: Cambridge University Press, 3–63.

Arnold-Biucchi, Carmen and Caccamo Caltabiano, Maria, eds. (2015), *Survey of Numismatic Research 2008–2013*, International Association of Professional Numismatists Special Publication 16. Rome: Arbor Sapientiae.

Asolati, Michele (2005), *Il tesoro di* Falerii Novi. *Nuovi contributi sulla monetazione italica in bronzo degli anni di Ricimero, 457–472 d. C.* Padova: Esedra.

Asolati, Michele (2012), *Praestantia nummorum. Temi e note di numismatica tardo antica e alto medievale*. Padova: Esedra.

Aubert, Jean-Jacques (2014), "For Swap or Sale? The Roman Law of Barter," in Catherine Apicella, Marie-Laurence Haack, and François Lerouxel (eds.), *Les affaires de Monsieur Andreau. Économie et société du monde romain*. Bordeaux: Ausonius, 109–21.

Baldus, Hans Roland (1969), *Mon(eta) urb(is)—Antioxia: Rom und Antiochia als Prägestätten syrischer Tetradrachmen des Philippus Arabs*. Frankfurt: Dr. Busso Peus.

Beckmann, Martin (2009), "The Significance of Roman Imperial Coin Types," *Klio* 91: 144–61.

Beckmann, Martin (2016), "Trajan's Column and Mars Ultor," *Journal of Roman Studies* 106: 124–46.

Beilke-Voigt, Ines (2007), *Das "Opfer" im archäologischen Befund. Studien zu den sog. Bauopfern, kultischen Niederlegungen und Bestattungen in ur- und frühgeschichtlichen Siedlungen Norddeutschlands und Dänemarks*. Berliner Archäologische Forschungen 4. Rahden/Westf.: Leidorf.

Bell, Harold W. (1916), *Coins, Part 1: 1910–1914*. Sardis 11. Leiden: Brill.

Bennett, Robert (2014), *Local Elites and Local Coinage: Elite Self-Representation on the Provincial Coinage of Asia, 31 BC to AD 275*. Royal Numismatic Society Special Publication 51. London: Royal Numismatic Society.

Bérard, François, Denis Feissel, Nicolas Laubry, Pierre Auteur Petitmengin, Denis Rousset and Michel Sève (2010), *Guide de l'épigraphiste. Bibliographie choisie des épigraphies antiques et médiévales*. 4th edn, Paris: Éditions Rue d'Ulm.

Bergmann, Bettina (2008), "Pictorial Narratives of the Roman Circus," in Jocelyne Nelis-Clément and Jean-Michel Roddaz (eds.), *Le cirque romain et son image*. Bordeaux: Ausonius, 359–89.

Bernholz, Peter and Roland Vaubel, eds. (2014), *Explaining Monetary and Financial Innovation. A Historical Analysis*. Cham: Springer.

Berthold, Angela (2013), *Entwurf und Ausführung in den artes minores: Münz- und Gemmenkünstler des 6.–4. Jahrhunderts v. Chr.* Schriftenreihe Antiquitates 61. Hamburg: Verlag Dr. Kovac.

Bland, Roger (2013), "Hoarding in Britain: An Overview," *British Numismatic Journal* 83: 214–38.

Bloch, Marc (1939), "Économie-nature ou économie-argent: Un pseudo-dilemme," *Annales d'histoire sociale* 1(1): 7–16.

Bloch, Marc (1967), *Land and Work in Medieval Europe. Selected Papers*. Translated by J. E. Anderson. London: Routledge.

Bloch, Maurice and Jonathan Parry (1989), "Introduction: Money and the Morality of Exchange," in Jonathan Parry and Maurice Bloch (eds.), *Money and the Morality of Exchange*. Cambridge and New York: Cambridge University Press, 1–32.

Bodenstedt, Friedrich (1981), *Die Elektronmünzen von Phokaia und Mytilene*. Tübingen: Wasmuth.

Bogaert, Raymond (1968), *Banques et banquiers dans les cités grecques*. Leiden: A.W. Sijthoff.

Bogaert, Raymond (1976), "L'essai des monnaies dans l'Antiquité," *Revue Belge de Numismatique et de Sigillographie* 122: 5–34.

Bohannan, Paul (1955), "Some Principles of Exchange and Investment among the Tiv," *American Anthropologist. New Series* 57(1): 60–70.

Bohannan, Paul (1959), "The Impact of Money on an African Subsistence Economy," *Journal of Economic History* 19(4): 491–503.

Bolin, Sture (1958), *State and Currency in the Roman Empire to 300 AD*. Stockholm: Almquist & Wiksell.

Borrell, Brigitte (2014), "The Power of Images—Coin Portraits of Roman Emperors on Jewellery Pendants in Early Southeast Asia," *Zeitschrift für Archäologie außereuropäischer Kulturen* 6: 7–44.

Bowes, Kimberly (2015), "At Home," in Rubina Raja and Jörg Rüpke (eds.), *A Companion to the Archaeology of Religion in the Ancient World*. Malden, MA: Wiley-Blackwell, 209–19.

Bowman, Alan K., J. David Thomas, and Roger S. O. Tomlin (2010), "The Vindolanda Writing-Tablets (*Tabulae Vindolandenses* IV, Part 1)," *Britannia* 41: 187–224.

Bowman, Alan K., J. David Thomas, and Roger S. O. Tomlin (2011), "The Vindolanda Writing-Tablets (*Tabulae Vindolandenses* IV, Part 2)," *Britannia* 42: 113–44.

Bradley, Richard (2003), "A Life Less Ordinary: The Ritualization of the Domestic Sphere in Later Prehistoric Europe," *Cambridge Archaeological Journal* 13(1): 5–23.

Bradley, Richard (2005), *Ritual and Domestic Life in Prehistoric Europe*. London: Routledge.

Bresson, Alain (2005), "Coinage and Money Supply in the Hellenistic Age," in Zofia H. Archibald, John K. Davies, and Vincent Gabrielsen (eds.), *Making, Moving and Managing: The New World of Ancient Economies, 323–31 BC*. Oxford: Oxbow Books, 44–72.

Bresson, Alain (2016), *The Making of the Ancient Greek Economy. Institutions, Markets, and Growth in the City-States*. Translated by Steven Rendall. Princeton: Princeton University Press.

Bringmann, Klaus (2011), *Kleine Kulturgeschichte der Antike*. Munich: Verlag C.H. Beck.

Burgon, Thomas (1837), "An Inquiry into the Motives which Influenced the Ancients, in their Choice of the Various Representations which we Find Stamped on Their Money," *The Numismatic Journal* 1: 97–131.

Burnett, Andrew (1977), "The Authority to Coin in the Late Republic and Early Empire," *Numismatic Chronicle* 137: 37–63.

Burnett, Andrew (1987a), "Africa," in Andrew Burnett and Michael Crawford (eds.), *The Coinage of the Roman World in the Late Republic*. Oxford: British Archaeological Reports, 175–85.

Burnett, Andrew (1987b), *Coinage in the Roman World*. London: Seaby.

Burnett, Andrew (1995), "The Unification of the Monetary Systems of the Roman West: Accident or Design?" in Judith Swaddling, Susan Walker, and Paul Roberts (eds.), *Italy in Europe: Economic Relations 700 BC–AD 50*. London: The British Museum, 313–20.

Burnett, Andrew (1999), "Buildings and Monuments on Roman Coins," in George M. Paul and Michael Ierardi (eds.), *Roman Coins and Public Life under the Empire*. Ann Arbor: The University of Michigan Press, 137–64.

Burnett, Andrew (2001), "The Invisibility of Roman Imperial Mints," in Rina La Guardia (ed.), *I luoghi della moneta. Le sedi delle zecche dall'antichità all'età moderna. Atti del convegno internazionale, ottobre 22–23 (1999)*, Milan: Comune di Milano, 41–8.

Burnett, Andrew (2002), "Latin on Coins of the Western Empire," in Alison Cooley (ed.), *Becoming Roman, Writing Latin? Literacy and Epigraphy in the Roman West*. Porstmouth, RI: Journal of Roman Archaeology, 33–40.

Burnett, Andrew (2012), "Early Roman Coinage and its Italian Context," in William E. Metcalf (ed.), *The Oxford Handbook of Greek and Roman Coinage*. Oxford: Oxford University Press, 297–314.

Burnett, Andrew and Michel Amandry, eds. (1992–), *Roman Provincial Coinage*. Vols. 1–3, 9. London and Paris: The British Museum and the Bibliothèque Nationale de France.

Burnett, Andrew, Michel Amandry, and Pere Pau Ripolles (1992), *Roman Provincial Coinage Vol 1*. London: British Museum Press.

Burrell, Barbara (2004), *Neokoroi: Greek Cities and Roman Emperors*. Leiden: Brill.

Bursche, Alexander (2001), "Roman Gold Medallions as Power Symbols of the Germanic Élite," in Bente Magnus (ed.), *Roman Gold and the Development of the Early Germanic Kingdoms*. Stockholm: Kungl. Vitterhets, historie och antikvitets akademien, 83–102.

Butcher, Kevin (1988), *Roman Provincial Coins: An Introduction to the Greek Imperials*. London: Seaby.

Butcher, Kevin (2003), *Small Change in Ancient Beirut. Coins from BEY 006 and 045*. Beirut: American University.

Butcher, Kevin (2004), *Coinage in Roman Syria: Northern Syria, 64 BC–AD 253*. Royal Numismatic Society Special Publication 34. London: Royal Numismatic Society.

Butcher, Kevin and Matthew Ponting (2014), *The Metallurgy of Roman Silver Coinage: From the Reform of Nero to the Reform of Trajan*. Cambridge: Cambridge University Press.

Butler, Howard C. (1911), "Second Preliminary Report on the American Excavations at Sardes in Asia Minor," *American Journal of Archaeology* 15: 445–58.

Butler, Howard C. (1922), *The Excavations, Part 1: 1910–1914*. Sardis 1. Leiden: Brill.

Buttrey, Theodore V. (1987), "Crete and Cyrenaica," in Andrew Burnett and Michael Crawford (eds.), *The Coinage of the Roman World in the Late Republic*. Oxford: British Archaeological Reports, 165–74.

Buttrey, Theodore V. (1993), "Calculating Ancient Coin Production: Facts and Fantasies," *Numismatic Chronicle* 153: 335–51.

Buttrey, Theodore V. (1994), "Calculating Ancient Coin Production: Why It Cannot be Done," *Numismatic Chronicle* 154: 341–52.

Buttrey, Theodore V. (2007), "Domitian, the Rhinoceros, and the Date of Martial's 'Liber de Spectaculis'," *Journal of Roman Studies* 97: 101–12.

Buttrey, Theodore V. and Samuel E. Buttrey (1997), "Review Article: Calculating Ancient Coin Production, Again," *American Journal of Numismatics* 9, 113–35.

Buttrey, Theodore V., Kenan T. Erim, Thomas D. Groves, and R. Ross Holoway (1989), *Morgantina Studies II. The Coins*. Princeton, NJ: Princeton University Press.

Callegarin, Laurent and Vincent Geneviève (2007), "Une *tegula* portant des empreintes monétaires du IVe siècle découverte à *Iluro*—Oloron-Sainte-Marie (Pyrénées-Atlantiques, France)," *Aquitania* 23: 137–50.

Camp, John McKesson and John H. Kroll (2001), "The Agora Mint and Athenian Bronze Coinage," *Hesperia* 70(2): 127–62.

Campana, Alberto (1987), *La monetazione degli insorti italici durante la guerra sociale*. Soliera: Apparuti Edizioni.

Carlà, Filippo (2007a), "Il sistema monetario in età tardoantica: spunti per una revisione," *Annali. Istituto Italiano di Numismatica* 53: 155–218.

Carlà, Filippo (2007b), "Usi ed abusi della terminologia monetale nell'*Historia Augusta*," *Hormos. Ricerche di Storia Antica* 9: 399–424.

Carlà, Filippo (2010), "The End of Roman Gold Coinage and the Disintegration of a Monetary Area," *Annali. Istituto Italiano di Numismatica* 56: 103–72.

Carlson, Carl W.A. (1969), "The 'Laetitia Temporum' Reverses of the Severan Dynasty," *Journal of the Society for Ancient Numismatics* 3: 9–11.

Carradice, Ian and Martin J. Price (1988), *Coinage in the Greek World*. London: Seaby.

Carter, Giles F. (1983), "A Simplified Method for Calculating the Original Number of Dies from Die Link Statistics," *American Numismatic Society Museum Notes* 28, 195–206.

Chankowski, Véronique (2001), "Divine Financiers: Cults as Consumers and Generators of Value," in Zozia H. Archibald, John K. Davies, and Vincent Gabrielsen (eds.), *The Economies of Hellenistic Societies, Third to First Centuries BC*. Oxford: Oxford University Press, 142–65.

Chankowski, Véronique (ed.) (2005), "Les dieux manieurs d'argent: activités bancaires et formes de gestion dans les sanctuaires," *Topoi. Orient–Occident* 12–13(1): 9–132.

Chankowski, Véronique (2013), "Richesse et patrimoine dans les cités grecques: de la thésaurisation à la croissance," in Catherine Baroin and Cécile Michel (eds.), *Richesses et sociétés*. Paris: De Boccard, 66–83.

Chaves, Francisca (1998), "The Iberian and Early Roman Coinage of Hispania Ulterior Baetica," in Simon Keay (ed.), *The Archaeology of Early Roman Baetica*. Portsmouth, RI: Journal of Roman Archaeology, 145–70.

Chaves, Francisca (1999), "El papel de los 'itálicos' en la amonedación hispana," *Gerión* 17: 295–315.

Cheung, Ada (1998–9), "The Political Significance of Roman Imperial Coin Types," *Schweizer Münzblätter* 48–9: 53–61.

CIL = *Corpus Inscriptionum Latinarum*. Multiple vols.

Čižmár, Miloš, Eva Kolníková, and Hans-Christoph Noeske (2008), "Němčice-Víceměřice, ein neues Handels- und Industriezentrum der Latènezeit in Mähren," *Germania* 86: 655–700.

Coarelli, Filippo (1994), "Moneta. Le officine della zecca di Roma tra Repubblica e Impero," *Annali dell'Istituto Italiano di Numismatica* 38–41, 23–66.

Cohen, Ed E. (1992), *Athenian Economy and Society: A Banking Perspective*. Princeton: Princeton University Press.

Cohen, Ed E. (2008), "The Elasticity of the Money Supply at Athens," in William V. Harris (ed.), *The Monetary Systems of the Greeks and Romans*. Oxford: Oxford University Press, 112–36.

Colbert de Beaulieu, Jean-Baptiste (1973), *Traité de numismatique celtique I. Méthodologie des ensembles*. Paris: Les Belles Lettres.

Coleman, Kathleen M. (2006), *Martial: Liber Spectaculorum*. Oxford and New York: Oxford University Press.

Comaroff, Jean and John Comaroff (2005), "Beasts, Banknotes and the Colour of Money in Colonial South Africa," *Archaeological Dialogues* 12: 107–32.

Condominas, Georges (1972), "Aspects of Economics among the Mnong Gar of Vietnam: Multiple Money and the Middleman," *Ethnology* 11(3): 202–19.

Condominas, Georges (1989), "De la monnaie multiple," *Communications* 50: 95–119.
Conophagos, Constantin. E (1980), *Le Laurium antique et la technique grecque de la production de l'argent*, Athens: Ekdotike Hellados.
Conzett, Jürg (2005), "Einleitung," in Urusla Kampmann (ed.), *Geld und Macht in der Antike*. Zürich: Sunflower Foundation, 7–13.
Cook, John Manuel and William Hugh Plommer (eds.), (1966), *The Sanctuary of Hemithea at Kastabos*. Cambridge: Cambridge University Press.
Corpus Inscriptionum Latinarum. Available online at: http://arachne.uni-koeln.de/drupal/node/291 (accessed March 30, 2016).
Crawford, Michael H. (1968), "Plated Coins—False Coins," *Numismatic Chronicle* 8, 55–9.
Crawford, Michael H. (1970), "Money and Exchange in the Roman World," *Journal of Roman Studies* 60, 40–8.
Crawford, Michael H. (1971), "Le problème des liquidités dans l'Antiquité classique," *Annales. Économies, Sociétés, Civilisations* 26: 1228–33.
Crawford, Michael H. (1974), *Roman Republican Coinage*. 2 volumes. Cambridge: Cambridge University Press.
Crawford, Michael H. (1982), "Unofficial Imitations and Small Change under the Roman Republic," *Annali dell'Istituto Italiano di Numismatica* 29, 139–64.
Crawford, Michael H. (1985), "Review Hasler," *Journal of Roman Studies* 75, 320–1
Crawford, Michael H. (2003), "Thesauri, Hoards and Votive Deposits," in Olivier De Cazanove and John Scheid (eds.), *Sancutuaires et sources dans l'antiquité. Les sources documentaires et leurs limites dans la description des lieux de culte. Actes de la table ronde organisée par le Collège de France, l'UMR 8585 Centre Gustave-Glotz, l'Ecole française de Rome et le Centre Jean Bérand*. Naples: Publications du Centre Jean Bérard, 69–84.
Creighton, John (2000), *Coins and Power in Late Iron Age Britain*. Cambridge: Cambridge University Press.
Cribb, Joe (2005a), "The President's Address: Money as Metaphor," *Numismatic Chronicle* 165: 417–38.
Cribb, Joe (2005b), *The Indian Coinage Tradition: Origins, Continuity and Change*. Anjaneri, India: IIRNS Publications.
Crummy, Nina (2010), "Bears and Coins: The Iconography of Protection in Late Roman Infant Burials," *Britannia* 41: 37–93.
Cunliffe, Barry, ed. (1988), *The Temple of Sulis Minerva at Bath, 2. The Finds From the Sacred Spring*. Oxford: Oxford University Committee for Archaeology.
Cunliffe, Barry and Cynthia Poole (2008), *The Danebury Environs Roman Programme. A Wessex Landscape during the Roman Era. Vol. 2—Part 7. Dunkirt Barn, Abbotts Ann, Hants, 2005 and (2006)*, Oxford University School of Archaeology Monograph 71. Oxford: University of Oxford School of Archaeology.
Curteis, Mark (2005), "Ritual Coin Deposition on Iron Age Settlements in the South Midlands," in Colin Haselgrove and David Wigg-Wolf (eds.), *Iron Age Coinage and Ritual Practices*. Studien zu Fundmünzen der Antike 20. Mainz: Zabern, 207–25.
Curtius, Ernst (1870), "On the Religious Character of Greek Coins," *Numismatic Chronicle* n. Ser. 10: 91–111.
Cutroni Tusa, Aldina (1982), "Una officina monetale a Himera? Il problemo cronologico," *Secondo Quaderno Imerese* 3: 167–74.
Dahmen, Karsten (2007), *The Legend of Alexander the Great on Greek and Roman Coins*. New York: Routledge.

Davies, John K. (2001), "Temples, Credit and the Circulation of Money," in Andrew Meadows and Kirsty Shipton (eds.), *Money and its Uses in the Ancient Greek World*. Oxford: Oxford University Press, 117–28.

Debord, Jean (1989), "L'atelier monétaire gaulois de Villeneuve-Saint-Germain (Aisne) et sa Production," *Revue Numismatique* 6 (31): 7–24.

de Callataÿ, François (1989), "Les trésors achéménides et les monnayages d'Alexandre: espèces immobilisées et espèces circulantes?" *Revue des Etudes Anciennes* 91(1–2): 259–76.

de Callataÿ, François (1995), "Calculating Ancient Coin Production: Seeking Balance," *Numismatic Chronicle* 145: 289–312.

de Callataÿ, François (1997a), *Les monnaies grecques et l'orientation des axes, Glaux*. Collana di Studi e Ricerche di Numismatica 12, Milan: Ennerre.

de Callataÿ, François (1997b), *L'histoire des guerres mithridatiques vue par les monnaies*. Louvain-la-Neuve: Numismatica Lovaniensia.

de Callataÿ, François (1997c), *Recueil quantitatif des émissions monétaires hellénistiques*. Wetteren: Ed. Numismatique Romaine.

de Callataÿ, François (1999a), "Fiscalité et monnayage dans l'œuvre de Georges Le Rider," in Michel Amandry and Silvia Hurter (eds.), *Travaux de numismatique grecque offerts à Georges Le Rider*. London: Spink, 109–21.

de Callataÿ, François (1999b), "Guerres et monnayages à l'époque hellénistique," *Dossiers d'Archéologie* 248: 28–35.

de Callataÿ, François (2000a), "Guerre et monnayage à l'époque hellénistique. Essai de mise en perspective suivi d'une annexe sur le monnayage de Mithridate VI Eupator," in Jean Andreau, Pierre Briant, and Raymond Descat (eds.), *Économie antique. La guerre dans les économies antiques*. Entretiens d'Archéologie et d'Histoire 5. Saint-Bertrand-de-Comminges: Conseil général de Haute Garonne, 337–64.

de Callataÿ, François (2000b), "Le taux de survie des émissions monétaires antiques, médiévales et modernes. Essai de mise en perspective et conséquences quant à la productivité des coins dans l'Antiquité," *Revue Numismatique* 155: 87–109.

de Callataÿ, François (2003), *Recueil quantitatif des émissions monétaires archaïques et classiques*. Wetteren: Ed. Numismatique Romaine.

de Callataÿ, Francois (2005), "A Quantitative Survey of Hellenistic Coinages. Recent Achievements," in Zofia H. Archibald, John K. Davies, and Vincent Gabrielsen (eds.), *Making, Moving and Managing: The New World of Ancient Economies, 323–31 BC*. Oxford: Oxbow Books, 73–91.

de Callataÿ, François (2006a) "Les applications restreintes de la « loi de Gresham » au monde hellénistique," in Michele Asolati and Giovanni Gorini (eds.), *I ritrovamenti monetali e la legge di Gresham. Atti del III Congresso Internzionale di Numismatica e di Storia Monetaria, Padova, ottobre 28–29 (2005)*, Padova: Esedra editrice, 21–33.

de Callataÿ, François (2006b), *Quantifications et numismatique antique: Choix d'articles (1984–2004)*. Collection Moneta 52. Wetteren: Moneta.

de Callataÿ, François (2006c), "Le transport des monnaies dans le monde grec," *Revue belge de Numismatique et Sigillographie* 152, 5–14.

de Callataÿ, François (2006d), "Réflexions quantitatives sur l'or et l'argent non monnayés à l'époque hellénistique (pompes, triomphes, réquisitions, fortunes des temples, orfèvrerie et masses métalliques disponibles)," in Raymond Descat (ed.), *Approches de l'économie hellénistique*. Entretiens d'Archéologie et d'Histoire 7. Saint-Bertrand-de-Comminges. Conseil général de Haute Garonne, 37–84.

de Callataÿ, François (2009), "Armies Poorly Paid in Coins (the Anabasis of the Ten-Thousands) and Coins for Soldiers Poorly Transformed by the Markets (the Hellenistic Thasian-Type Tetradrachms) in Ancient Greece," *Revue belge de Numismatique* 155: 51–70.

de Callataÿ, François (2010), "Les plombs à types monétaires en Grèce ancienne: monnaies (officielles, votives ou contrefaites), jetons, sceaux, poids, épreuves ou fantaisies?" *Revue numismatique* 166: 219–55.

de Callataÿ, François, ed. (2011a), *Quantifying Monetary Supplies in Greco–Roman Times*. Pragmateiai 19. Bari: Edipuglia.

de Callataÿ, François (2011b), "Quantifying Monetary Production in Greco–Roman Times: A General Frame," in François de Callataÿ (ed.), *Quantifying Monetary Supplies in Greco–Roman Times*. Bari: Edipuglia, 7–29.

de Callataÿ, François (2011c), "More than it Would Seem: The Use of Coinage by the Romans in Late Hellenistic Asia Minor (133–63 BC)," *American Journal of Numismatics* 23: 55–86.

de Callataÿ, François (2012a), "Control Marks on Hellenistic Royal Coinages: Use, and Evolution Towards Simplification?" *Revue Belge de Numismatique et de Sigillographie* 158, 39–62.

de Callataÿ, François (2012b), "Royal Hellenistic Coinages: From Alexander to Mithradates," in William E. Metcalf (ed.), *The Oxford Handbook of Greek and Roman Coinage*. Oxford: Oxford University Press, 175–90.

de Callataÿ, François (2014), "Revisiting a Numismatic Corpus. The Case of Eupator, Last King of Pontus," in Kayan Dörtlük, Oğuz Tekin, and Remziye Boyraz Seyhan (eds.), *Proceedings of the First International Congress of the Anatolian Monetary History and Numismatics, February 25–28, 2013 Antalya*. Antalya: Suna & Inan Kiraç Research Institute: 117–37.

de Callataÿ, François (2015), "Comedies of Plautus and Terence: An Unusual Opportunity to Look into the Use of Money in Hellenistic Time," *Revue belge de Numismatique* 161: 17–53.

de Callataÿ, François (2016a), "Greek Coin Types in Context: A Short State of the Art," *Pharos* 21(2). Forthcoming.

de Callataÿ, François (2016b), "The Coinages Struck for the Romans in Hellenistic Greece: A Quantified Overview (Mid 2nd–Mid 1st c. BCE)," in Florian Haymann and Wilhelm Hollstein (eds.), *New Research in Roman Republican Coinage*. Bonn: Habelt Verlag.

de Callataÿ, François (2016c), "Apparition, utilisation et disparition de l'or monnayé au nom d'Alexandre le Grand: une monétisation massive sans croissance économique?" in Sofia Kremydi and Marie-Christine Marcellesi (eds.), *Les alexandres après Alexandre: histoire d'une monnaie commune*. Athens: Meletemata (forthcoming).

de Callataÿ, François, Georges Depeyrot, and Leandre Villaronga (1993), *L'argent monnayé d'Alexandre le Grand à Auguste*. Bruxelles: Cercle d'Etudes Numismatiques.

de Callataÿ, François and Johan van Heesch, eds. (2006), "The Transport of Coins through the Ages," *Revue Belge de Numismatique et de Sigillographie* 152: 1–94.

Deichmann, Friedrich Wilhelm and Arnold Tschira (1957), "Das Mausoleum der Kaiserin Helena und die Basilika der heiligen Marcellinus und Petrus an der Via Labicana vor Rom," *Jahrbuch des Deutschen Archäologischen Instituts* 72: 44–110.

de Jersey, Philip (2005), "Deliberate Defacement of British Iron Age Coinage," in Colin Haselgrove and David Wigg-Wolf (eds.), *Iron Age Coinage and Ritual Practices*. Studien zu Fundmünzen der Antike 20. Mainz: Zabern, 85–113.

Delamare, François (1994), *Le frai et ses lois ou de l'évolution des espèces*. Paris: Centre national de la recherche scientifique.

Dembski, Günther, Heinz Winter, and Bernhard Woytek (2007), "Regalianus und Dryantilla. Historischer Hintergrund, numismatische Evidenz, Forschungsgeschichte (Moneta imperii Romani 43—Neubearbeitung)," in Michael Alram and Franziska Schmidt-Dick (eds.), *Numismata Carnuntina. Forschungen und Material. Die Fundmünzen der römischen Zeit in Österreich III/2*. Vienna: Verlag der Österreichischen Akademie der Wissenschaften, 523–96.

Dickey, Eleanor (2012), *The colloquia of the Hermeneumata Pseudodositheana, volume I. Colloquia Monacensia-Einsidlensia, Leidense-Stephani, and Stephani*. Cambridge: Cambridge University Press.

Dickey, Eleanor (2015), *The colloquia of the Hermeneumata Pseudodositheana, volume II. Colloquium Harleianum, colloquium Montepessulanum, colloquium Celtis, and fragments*. Cambridge: Cambridge University Press.

Dickey, Eleanor (2016), *Learning Latin the Ancient Way. Latin Textbooks from the Ancient World*. Cambridge: Cambridge University Press.

Donderer, Michael (1984), "Münzen als Bauopfer in römischen Privathäusern," *Bonner Jahrbücher* 184: 177–88.

Doppler, Hugo (2007), "Die Münzfunde aus der Quelle 'Grosser Heisser Stein' in Baden AG," *Schweizerische Numismatische Rundschau* 86: 91–115.

Down, Alec (1979), *Chichester Excavations IV*. Chichester: Phillimore.

Ducros, Hippolyte (1908), "Étude sur les balances égyptiennes," *Annales des Services de l'Antiquité de l'Égypte* 9: 32–53.

Dumas, Françoise (2008), "Nécrologie de Jean Lafaurie," *Bulletin de la Société française de numismatique* 63(5): 152–4.

Duncan-Jones, Richard (1990), *Structure and Scale in the Roman Economy*. Cambridge and New York: Cambridge University Press.

Duncan-Jones, Richard (1994), *Money and Government in the Roman Empire*. Cambridge: Cambridge University Press.

Duncan-Jones, Richard (1999), "Die Productivity and Wastage in Roman Republican Coinage," *Numismatic Chronicle* 159: 245–54.

Duncan-Jones, Richard (2005), "Implications of Roman Coinage: Debates and Differences," *Klio* 87: 459–87.

Eagleton, Catherine and Jonathan Williams (2007), *Money: A History*. London: British Museum.

Edlund-Berry, Ingrid (2006), "Hot, Cold, or Smelly: The Power of Sacred Water in Roman Religion, 400–100 BCE," in Celia Schultz and Paul Harvey Jr (eds.), *Religion in Republican Italy*. Cambridge: Cambridge University Press, 162–80.

Egger, Rudolf (1961), *Die Stadt auf dem Magdalensberg. Ein Großhandelsplatz*. Denkschriften der Österreichischen Akademie der Wissenschaften, philosophisch-historische Klasse 79. Wien: Verlag der Österreichischen Akademie der Wissenschaften.

Ehling, Kay (2005/6), "'Wer wird jetzt noch an Schicksalserforschung und Horoskop glauben?' (Ephraim d. Syrer 4, 26). Bemerkungen zu Julians Stiermünzen und dem Geburtsdatum des Kaisers," *Jahrbuch für Numismatik und Geldgeschichte* 55–56, 111–32.

Einzig, Paul (1948), *Primitive Money and its Ethnological, Historical and Economic Aspects*. London: Eyre and Spottiswoode.

Elkins, Nathan T. (2009a), "Coins, Contexts, and an Iconographic Approach for the 21st Century," in Hans-Markus von Kaenel and Fleur Kemmers (eds.), *Coins in*

Context I: New Perspectives for the Interpretation of Coin Finds. Studien zu Fundmünzen der Antike 23. Mainz: Verlag Philipp von Zabern, 25–46.

Elkins, Nathan T. (2009b), "What are They Doing Here? Flavian Colosseum *Sestertii* from Archaeological Contexts in Hessen and the Taunus–Wetterau *Limes* (with an Addendum to NC 2006)," *Numismatic Chronicle* 169: 199–204.

Elkins, Nathan T. (2011), "Monuments on the Move: Architectural Coin Types and Audience Targeting in the Flavian and Trajanic Periods," in Nicholas Holmes (ed.), *Proceedings of the XIVth International Numismatic Congress, Glasgow (2009)*, Glasgow 2011: The University of Glasgow. 645–55.

Elkins, Nathan T. (2013), "A Note on Late Roman Art: The Provincial Origins of Camp Gate and Baldachin Iconography on the Late Imperial Coinage," *American Journal of Numismatics* 25, Second Series: 283–302.

Elkins, Nathan T. (2015), *Monuments in Miniature: Architecture on Roman Coinage*. Numismatic Studies 29. New York: American Numismatic Society.

Erdman, Katherine (2014), "Votives and Values: Communicating with the Supernatural," in Annabel Bokern and Clare Rowan (eds.), *Embodying Value? The Transformation of Objects in and from the Ancient World*, British Archaeological Reports International Series 2592. Oxford: Archaeopress, 89–99.

Eremić, Dragana (2014), "Coin Finds Beyond the Danube: Functions of Fourth Century Gold Coins within Barbarian Societies," in Annabel Bokern and Clare Rowan (eds.), *Embodying Value? The Transformation of Objects in and from the Roman World*. Oxford: British Archaeological Reports, 121–30.

Estiot, Sylviane (2012), "The Later Third Century," in William E. Metcalf (ed.), *The Oxford Handbook of Greek and Roman Coinage*. Oxford: Oxford University Press, 538–60.

Esty, Warren W. (1986), "Estimation of the Size of a Coinage: A Survey and Comparison of Methods," *Numismatic Chronicle* 146, 185–215.

Facchinetti, Grazia (2003), "Iactae stipes. L'offerta di monete nelle acque nella penisola italiana," *Rivista Italiana di Numismatica* 104: 13–55.

Facchinetti, Grazia (2010), "Offrire nelle acque: bacini e altre strutture artificiali," in Helga Di Giuseppe and Mirella Serlorenzi (eds.), *I riti del costruire nelle acque violate. Atti del convegno, Roma, 12–14 giugno (2008)*, Rome: Scienze e Lettere, 43–67.

Faucher, Thomas and Bérengère Redon (2014), "Le prix de l'entrée au bain en Égypte hellénistique et romaine d'après les données textuelles et numismatiques," in Marie-Françoise Boussac, Sylvie Denoix, Thibaud Fournet, and Bérengère Redon (eds.), *25 siècles de bains collectifs en Orient. Actes du colloque de Damas, (2009)*, Cairo: Institut français d'archéologie orientale du Caire, 835–56.

Faucher, Thomas, Laurent Coulon, Elsa Frangin, Cyril Giorgio, Soline Delcros, and Laurent Vallières (2011), "Un atelier monétaire à Karnak au IIe s. av. J.–C," *Bulletin de l'Institut Français d'Archéologie Orientale* 111: 143–66.

Filges, Axel (2015), *Münzbild und Gemeinschaft. Die Prägungen der römischen Kolonien in Kleinasien*. Frankfurter Archäologische Schriften 29. Bonn: Habelt Verlag.

Finley, Moses I (1970), "Aristotle and Economic Analysis," *Past and Present* 47: 3–25.

Finley, Moses I (1985), *The Ancient Economy*, 2nd edn, London: Hogarth.

Fischer, Thomas, ed. (2012), *Die Krise des 3. Jahrhunderts n. Chr. und das Gallische Sonderreich. Akten des Interdisziplinären Kolloquiums Xanten 26. bis 28. Februar (2009)*, Wiesbaden: Reichert Verlag.

Fischer-Bossert, Wolfgang (1999), *Chronologie der Didrachmenprägung von Tarent, 510–280 v. Chr*. Antike Münzen und geschnittene Steine 14. Berlin: de Gruyter.

Fischer-Bossert, Wolfgang (2012), "The Coinage of Sicily," in William E. Metcalf (ed.), *The Oxford Handbook of Greek and Roman Coinage*. Oxford: Oxford University Press, 142–56.

Fischer-Bossert, Wolfgang (2015), "Kyzikener Falzschrötlinge," *Mitteilungen der Österreichischen Numismatischen Gesellschaft* 55(2), 79–92.

Flament, Christophe (2007), *Le monnayage en argent d'Athènes. De l'époque archaïque à l'époque hellénistique, c. 550–c. 40 av. J.-C.* Etudes numismatiques 1. Louvain-la-Neuve: Association Numismatique Hoc.

FMRD = *Fundmünzen der römischen Zeit in Deutschland*. Multiple vols.

Fogelin, Lars (2007), "The Archaeology of Religious Ritual," *Annual Review of Anthropology* 36: 55–71.

Foraboschi, Daniele (2006), "Free Coinage e scarsezza di moneta," in Elio Lo Cascio (ed.), *Credito e moneta nel mondo romano. Atti degli Incontri capresi di storia dell'economia antica (Capri ottobre 12–14 2000)*. Bari: Edipuglia, 231–44.

Franke, Peter R. and Max Hirmer (1964), *Die griechische Münze*. Munich: Hirmer Verlag.

Frascone, Daniel (2013), *Zeugma IV. Les monnaies*. Lyon: Maison de l'Orient et de la Méditerranée-Jean Pouilloux.

Frey-Kupper, Suzanne (2013), "*Die antiken Fundmünzen vom Monte Iato 1971–(1990). Ein Beitrag zur Geldgeschichte Westsiziliens.*" 2 vols. Lausanne: Éditions du Zèbre.

Frey-Kupper, Susanne and Clive Stannard (forthcoming). "Evidence for the Importation and Monetary Use of Blocks of Foreign and Obsolete Bronze Coins in the Ancient World," in Bernhard Woytek (ed.), *Infrastructure and Distribution in Ancient Economies. The Flow of Money, Goods and Services. Proceedings of an International Conference held at the Austrian Academy of Sciences, October 28–31, 2014*, Vienna.

Frisone, Flavia (2012), "Rivers, Land Organization, and Identity in Greek Western *apoikiai*," *Mediterranean Historical Review* 27: 87–115.

Furtwängler, Andreas (1982), "Griechische Vieltypenprägung und Münzbeamte," *Schweizerische Numismatische Rundschau* 61, 5–25.

Gabrielsen, Vincent (1986), "*Phanera* and *Aphanes Ousia* in Classical Athens," *Classica et Mediaevalia* 36: 99–114.

Gilles, Karl-Josef (2001), "Zeit im Strom. Römerzeitliche und nachrömerzeitliche Funde von der Römerbrücke in Trier," in Hans-Peter Kuhnen (ed.), *Abgetaucht, aufgetaucht. Flussfundstücke*. Trier: Rheinisches Landesmuseum, 87–92.

Gilliard, Frank D. (1964), "Notes on the Coinage of Julian the Apostate," *Journal of Roman Studies* 54, 135–41.

Gitler, Haim (2012), "Roman Coinages of Palestine," in William E. Metcalf (ed.), *The Oxford Handbook of Greek and Roman Coinage*. Oxford: Oxford University Press, 485–98.

Glasbergen, Willem, Karl Schlabow, Annie N. Zadoks-Josephus Jitta, and Wilhem van Zeist. (1956), "Der römische Münzschatz von Bargercompascuum (Drenthe)," *Palaeohistoria* 5: 77–99.

Göbl, Robert (1967), "Der Bericht des Religionsstifters Mani über die Münzherstellung. Versuch einer Analyse," *Anzeiger philosophisch–historischen Klasse der Österreichischen Akademie der Wissenschaften* 104, no. 17, 113–32.

Göbl, Robert (1978), *Antike Numismatik*. München: Battenberg.

Gorecki, Joachim (1975), "Studien zur Sitte der Münzbeigabe in römerzeitlichen Körpergräbern zwischen Rhein, Mosel und Somme," *Bericht der Römisch–Germanischen Kommission* 56: 179–467.

Gorini, Giovanni (2011), "L'offerta della moneta agli dei: forma di religiosità privata nel mondo antico," in Maddalena Bassani and Francesca Ghedini (eds.), *Religionem significare. Aspetti storico–religiosi, strutturali, iconografici e materiali dei sacra privata, Atti dell'incontro di studi Padova 8–9 giugno (2009)*, Rome: Edizioni Quasar, 245–56.

Görlich, Walter (1950), "Das Felsheiligtum," in Rudolf Egger (ed.), *Die Ausgrabungen auf dem Magdalensberg 1949*. Magdalensberg–Grabungsbericht 2. Klagenfurt: Verlag des Landesmuseums Klagenfurt, 451–6.

Gozalbes, Manuel and Pere Pau Ripollès (2002), "La fabricacion de moneda en la antigüedad," in Antonio Beltrán Martínez (ed.), *Actas del XI Congreso Nacional de Numismática: [16 a 19 de octubre de 2002 (Zaragoza)]*. Madrid: Real Casa de la Moneda y Timbre, 11–33.

Graeber, David (1996), "Beads and Money: Notes toward a Theory of Wealth and Power," *American Ethnologist* 23: 4–24.

Graeber, David (2014), *Debt: The first 5,000 years*. 2nd edn [1st edn: 2011]. Brooklyn: Melville House.

Graeven, Hans (1901), "Die thönerne Sparbüchse im Altertum," *Jahrbuch des Kaiserlichen Deutschen Archäologischen Instituts* 16: 169–89.

Greenhalgh, Michael (2014), *The Military and Colonial Destruction of the Roman Landscape of North Africa*, 1830–1900. Leiden: Brill.

Grierson, Philip (1956), "The Roman Law of Counterfeiting," in Robert A.G. Carson and Carol Humphrey Vivian Sutherland (eds.), *Essays in Roman Coinage Presented to Harold Mattingly*. Oxford: Oxford University Press, 240–61.

Gruel, Katherine, ed. (1995), "Les potins gaulois : typologie, diffusion, chronologie. État de la question à partir de plusieurs contributions," *Gallia* 52: 1–144.

Grüner, Andreas (2014), "Antike Reproduktionsmedien. Münze, Siegel und Stempel zwischen Serialität und Authentizität," in Walter Cupperi (ed.), *Multiples in Pre-Modern Art*. Zürich: Diphanes, 59–93.

Guest, Peter (2005), "The Clipping of Siliquae in Late Roman Britain," in Peter Guest (ed.), *The Late Roman Gold and Silver Coins from the Hoxne Hoard*. London: British Museum: 110–15.

Guide de l'épigraphiste. Supplements available online at: http://129.199.13.51/ressources/publications–aux–p–e–n–s/guide–de–l–epigraphiste/article/overview (accessed April 30, 2016).

Guidobaldi, Federico (1992), *San Clemente. Gli edifici romani, la basilica paleocristiana e le fasi altomedievali*. Rome: Collegio San Clemente.

Guiraud, Hélène (1996), *Intailles et camées romains*. Paris: Picard.

Hackens, Tony (1970), "Les monnaies," in Philippe Bruneau Claude Vatin, Ulpiano Bezerra de Meneses, and Guy Donnay (eds.), *L'îlot de la Maison des Comédiens*. Exploration archéologique de Délos Vol. 27. Paris: E. De Boccard, 387–419.

Hanfmann, George M.A. and Barbara Burell (1981), "Notes on Some Archaeological Contexts," in Theodore Buttrey (ed.), *Greek, Roman and Islamic Coins from Sardis*. Archaeological Exploration of Sardis Monograph 7. Cambridge, MA: Harvard University Press, xx–xxiv.

Hanfmann, George M.A. and Kenneth J. Frazer (1975), "The Temple of Artemis: New Soundings," in George M.A. Hanfmann and Jane C. Waldbaum (eds.), *A Survey of Sardis and the Major Monuments Outside the City Walls*. Archaeological Exploration of Sardis 1. Cambridge, MA: Harvard University Press, 74–87.

Hänsel, Alix and Bernhard Hänsel, eds. (1997), *Gaben an die Götter. Schätze der Bronzezeit Europas. Ausstellung der Freien Universität Berlin in Verbindung mit dem*

Museum für Vor- und Frühgeschichte, Staatliche Museen zu Berlin—Preußischer Kulturbesitz. Berlin: Staatl. Museen zu Berlin.
Harl, Kenneth W. (1987), *Civic Coins and Civic Politics in the Roman East* AD *180–275.* Berkeley: University of California Press.
Harris, William V. (2006), "A Revisionist View of Roman Money," *Journal of Roman Studies* 96: 1–24.
Harris, William V. (2010), "Introduction," in William V. Harris (ed.), *The Monetary Systems of the Greeks and Romans.* Oxford: Oxford University Press: 1–11.
Hart, Keith (1986), "Heads or Tails? Two Sides of a Coin," *Man* 21: 637–56.
Hart, Keith (2001), *Money in an Unequal World.* London: Textere.
Haselgrove, Colin (2005), "A new approach to analysing the circulation of Iron Age coinage," *Numismatic Chronicle* 165: 1–45.
Haselgrove, Colin and Stefan Krmnicek (2012), "Archaeology of Money," *Annual Review of Anthropology* 41: 235–50.
Haselgrove, Colin and Stefan Krmnicek (2016a), "Archaeology of Money: From Electrum Rings to Mobile Money," in Colin Haselgrove and Stefan Krmnicek (eds.), *The Archaeology of Money. Proceedings of the Workshop 'Archaeology of Money', University of Tübingen, October (2013),* Leicester: School of Archaeology and Ancient History, 1–18.
Haselgrove, Colin and Stefan Krmnicek, eds. (2016b), *The Archaeology of Money. Proceedings of the Workshop 'Archaeology of Money', University of Tübingen, October (2013),* Leicester Archaeology Monograph 24. Leicester: School of Archaeology and Ancient History.
Haselgrove, Colin and Leo Webley (2016), "Lost Purses and Loose Change? Coin Deposition on Settlements in Iron Age Europe," in Colin Haselgrove and Stefan Krmnicek (eds.), *The Archaeology of Money. Proceedings of the Workshop 'Archaeology of Money', University of Tübingen, October (2013),* Leicester Archaeology Monograph 24. Leicester: School of Archaeology and Ancient History, 85–113.
Haselgrove, Colin and David Wigg-Wolf, eds. (2005), *Iron Age Coinage and Ritual Practices.* Studien zu Fundmünzen der Antike 20. Mainz: Philipp von Zabern.
Hekster, Olivier (2003), "Coins and Messages. Audience Targeting on Coins of Different Denominations?" in Lukas de Blois, Paul Erdkamp, Olivier Hekster, Gerda de Kleijn, and Stephan Mols (eds.), *The Representation and Perception of Roman Imperial Power.* Amsterdam: J.C. Gieben, 20–35.
Held, Winfried (2015), "Hemithea von Kastabos. Eine karische Heilgöttin, ihr Kultbild und ihre Schwestern," in Barabara Beck–Brandt, Sabine Ladstätter, and Banu Yener–Marksteiner (eds.), *Turm und Tor. Siedlungsstrukturen in Lykien und benachbarten Kulturlandschaften, Akten des Gedenkkolloquiums für Thomas Marksteiner, Wien (2012),* Forschungen in Limyra 7. Vienna: Österreichisches Archäologisches Institut, 179–94.
Helleiner, Eric (2003), *The Making of National Money. Territorial Currencies in Historical Perspective.* Ithaca: Cornell University Press.
Hellmann, Marie-Christine (1987), "Monnaies et lampes romaines: de l'intérêt des études comparatives," *Revue numismatique* 6ème série (29): 25–37.
Hensler, Martin (2014), "Der Wert des Kupfers—Über die Entstehung und den Wandel von Wert vor 4000 Jahren," in Annabel Bokern and Clare Rowan (eds.), *Embodying Value? The Transformation of Objects in and from the Ancient World.* British Archaeological Reports International Series 2592. Oxford: Archaeopress, 53–64.

Heres, Gerald (1972), "Römische Neujahrsgeschenke," *Forschungen und Berichte* 14: 182–93.
Herz, Peter (2003), "Die Arbeitsweise der staatlichen Finanzverwaltung in der Kaiserzeit," in Gianpaolo Russo (ed.), *Moneta mercanti banchieri. I precedenti greci e romani dell'Euro. Atti del convegno internazionale Cividale del Friuli, 26–28 settembre 2002*, Pisa: Edizioni ETS, 167–86.
Heseltine, Michael (1956), *Petronius. With an English Translation by Michael Heseltine.* Cambridge, MA: Harvard University Press.
Higginson, Thomas Wentworth (1890), *The Works of Epictetus: His Discourses, in Four Books, the Enchiridion, and Fragments. Translated from the Greek by Thomas Wentworth Higginson.* New York: Thomas Nelson and Sons.
Hill, George F. (1906), *Historical Greek Coins.* London: Archibald Constable.
Hill, George F. (1922), "Ancient Methods of Coining," *Numismatic Chronicle* 2, 1–42.
Hingley, Richard (2011), "Rome: Imperial and Local Religions," in Timothy Insoll (ed.), *The Oxford Handbook of the Archaeology of Ritual and Religion.* Oxford: Oxford University Press, 745–57.
Hingley, Richard and Steven Willis, eds. (2007), *Roman Finds: Context and Theory.* Oxford: Oxbow.
Hobbs, Richard (2006), *Late Roman Precious Metal Deposits.* Oxford: British Archaeological Reports.
Hobbs, Richard (2013), *Currency and Exchange in Ancient Pompeii. Coins from the AAPP Excavations at Regio VI, Insula I.* London: Institute of Classical Studies.
Hollander, David B. (2007), *Money in the Late Roman Republic.* Leiden: Brill.
Hollander, David B. (2008), "The Demand for Money in the late Roman Republic," in William V. Harris (ed.), *The Monetary Systems of the Greeks and Romans.* Oxford: Oxford University Press, 112–36.
Holloway, Robert Ross (2000), "Remarks on the Taranto Hoard of 1911," *Revue Belge de Numismatique* 146: 1–8.
Hölscher, Tonio (1984), *Staatsdenkmal und Publikum. Vom Untergang der Republik bis zur Festigung des Kaisertums in Rom.* Konstanz: Universitätsverlag Konstanz.
Hölscher, Tonio (2014), "Historical Representations of the Roman Republic: The Repertory of Coinage in Comparison with Other Art Media," in Nathan T. Elkins and Stefan Krmnicek (eds.), *"Art in the Round": New Approaches to Ancient Coin Iconography.* Tübinger Archäologische Forschungen 16. Rahden: Verlag Marie Leidorf, 23–37.
Hommel, Hildebrecht (1965), "Ein antiker Bericht über die Arbeitsgänge der Münzherstellung," *Schweizer Münzblätter* 59, 111–21.
Hommel, Hildbrecht (1966), "Der Religionsstifter Mani über die Arbeitsgänge der Münzherstellung: eine Nachlese," *Schweizer Münzblätter* 61, 33–8.
Hoover, Oliver D. (2013), *Handbook of the Coins of Bactria and Ancient India.* London: Classical Numismatic Group.
Hopkins, Keith (1980), "Taxes and Trade in the Roman Empire, 200 BC–AD 400," *Journal of Roman Studies* 70: 101–25.
Horsnaes, Helle W. (2011), "Coinages of Indigenous Communities in Archaic Southern Italy—The Mint as a means of Promoting Identity?" in Margarita Gleba and Helle W. Horsnaes (eds.), *Communicating Identity in Italic Iron Age Communities.* Oxford: Oxbow Books, 197–209.
Howgego, Christopher (1990), "Why did Ancient States Strike Coins?" *Numismatic Chronicle* 150: 1–25.

Howgego, Christopher (1992), "The Supply and Use of Money in the Roman World 200 B.C. to A.D. 300," *Journal of Roman Studies* 82: 1–31.
Howgego, Christopher (1994), "Coin Circulation and the Integration of the Roman Economy," *Journal of Roman Archaeology* 7: 5–21.
Howgego, Christopher (1995), *Ancient History from Coins*. London and New York: Routledge.
Howgego, Christopher (2005), "Coinage and Identity in the Roman Provinces," in Christopher Howgego, Volker Heuchert, and Andrew Burnett (eds.), *Coinage and Identity in the Roman Provinces*. Oxford and New York: Oxford University Press, 1–17.
Howgego, Christopher (2013), "The Monetization of Temperate Europe," *Journal of Roman Studies* 103: 16–45.
Howgego, Christopher (2014), "Questions of Coin Circulation in the Roman World," in Kayhan Dörtlük, Oğuz Tekin, and Remziye Boyraz Seyhan (eds.), *First International Congress of the Anatolian Monetary History and Numismatics— Proceedings*. Vienna: Phoibos Verlag, 307–17.
Howgego, Christopher, Volker Heuchert, and Andrew Burnett, eds. (2005), *Coinage and Identity in the Roman Provinces*. Oxford: Oxford University Press.
Hultgård, Anders (2003), "Religion," in Heinrich Beck, Dieter Geuenich, and Heiko Steuer (eds.), *Reallexikon der Germanischen Altertumskunde* 24. Berlin: de Gruyter, 429–57.
Hunt, Arthur Surridge and Campbell Cowan Edgar (1933), *Select Papyri II. Non-literary Papyri. Public Documents*. London: Heinemann.
Hunter, Fraser (2015), "Powerful Objects: The Uses of Art in the Iron Age," in Julia Farley and Fraser Hunter (eds.), *Celts: Art and Identity*. London: The British Museum, 81–107.
IG = *Inscriptiones Graecae*. Multiple vols.
ILS = *Inscriptiones Latinae Selectae*. Multiple vols.
Insoll, Timothy (2005), "Archaeology of Cult and Religion," in Colin Renfrew and Paul Bahn (eds.), *Archaeology. Key Concepts*. London: Routledge, 45–9.
Insoll, Timothy (2011), "Introduction: Ritual and Religion in Archaeological Perspective," in Timothy Insoll (ed.), *The Oxford Handbook of the Archaeology of Ritual and Religion*. Oxford: Oxford University Press, 1–5.
Instinsky, Hans Ulrich (1962), *Die Siegel des Kaisers Augustus. Ein Kapitel zur Geschichte und Symbolik des antiken Herrschersiegels*. Baden-Baden: Verlag für Kunst und Wissenschaft.
IOSPE = *Inscriptiones Orae Septentrionalis Ponti Euxini Graecae et Latinae*. Multiple vols.
Jenkins, Kenneth (1970), *The Coinage of Gela*. Antike Münzen und geschnittene Steine 2. Berlin: de Gruyter.
Jones, Arnold H.M. (1956), "Numismatics and History," in Robert A.G. Carson and Carol Humphrey Vivian Sutherland (eds.), *Essays in Roman Coinage Presented to Harold Mattingly*. Oxford: Oxford University Press, 13–33.
Jones, William Henry Samuel and Henry Ardene Omerod (1933), *Pausanias. Description of Greece. Vol. 3*. Translated by W. H. S. Jones and H. A. Omerod. Cambridge, MA: Harvard University Press.
Jucker, Hans (1982), "Die Bildnistrafen gegen den toten Caligula," in Bettina von Freytag gen. Löringhoff, Dietrich Mannsperger, and Friedhelm Prayon (eds.), *Praestant Interna. Festschrift für Ulrich Hausmann*. Tübingen: Verlag Ernst Wasmuth, 110–18.

Kalligas, Peter G. (1997), "A Bronze Die from Sounion," in Kenneth A. Sheedy and Charikleia Papageorgiadou-Banis (eds.), *Numismatic Archaeology, Archaeological Numismatics*. Oxford: Oxbow Books, 141–7.

Kaminski, G. (1991), "Thesauros. Untersuchungen zum Antiken Opferstock," *Jahrbuch des Deutschen Archäologischen Instituts* 106: 63–181.

Kay, Philip (2014), *Rome's Economic Revolution*. Oxford: Oxford University Press.

Kemmers, Fleur (2003), "Quadrantes from Nijmegen: Small Change in a Frontier Province," *Schweizerische Numismatische Rundschau* 82, 17–35.

Kemmers, Fleur (2006), *Coins for a Legion: An Analysis of the Coin Finds from Augustan Legionary Fortress and Flavian canabae legionis at Nijmegen*. Studien zu Fundmünzen der Antike 21. Mainz: von Zabern.

Kemmers, Fleur (2009), "Sender or Receiver? Contexts of Coin Supply and Coin Use," in Hans-Markus von Kaenel and Fleur Kemmers (eds.), *Coins in Context 1. New Perspectives for the Interpretation of Coin Finds*. Studien zu Fundmünzen der Antike 23. Mainz: Philipp von Zabern, 137–56.

Kemmers, Fleur (2014), "Buying Loyalty: Targeted Iconography and the Distribution of Cash to the Legions," in Michel Redde (ed.), *De l'or pour les braves! Soldes, armées et circulation monétaire dans le monde romain. Actes de la table ronde INHA Paris, septembre (2013)*, Scripta Antiqua 69. Bordeaux: Éditions Ausonius, 229–41.

Kemmers, Fleur and Nanouschka Myrberg (2011), "Rethinking Numismatics. The Archaeology of Coins," *Archaeological Dialogues* 18: 87–108.

Kerschner, Michael (2015), "Der Ursprung des Artemisions von Ephesos als Naturheiligtum: Naturmale als kultische Bezugspunkte in den grossen Heiligtümern Ioniens," in Katja Sporn, Sabine Ladstätter, and Michael Kerschner (eds.), *Natur, Kult, Raum: Akten des internationalen Kolloquiums Paris–Lodron–Universität Salzburg, 20.–22. Jänner*. Vienna: Österreichisches Archäologisches Institut, 187–243.

Kerschner, Michael and Koray Konuk (forthcoming), "Electrum Coins Found and Their Archaeological Context. The Case of the Artemision of Ephesus," in Haim Gitler, Koray Konuk, and Ute Wartenberg (eds.), *White Gold. Proceedings of the International Congress at The Israel Museum, Jerusalem*. New York: American Numismatic Society.

Kerschner, Michael and Walter Prochaska (2011), "Die Tempel und Altäre der Artemis und ihre Baumaterialien," *Jahreshefte des Österreichischen Archäologischen Institutes* 80: 73–153.

Kiernan, Philip (2001), "The Ritual Mutilation of Coins on Romano–British Sites," *British Numismatic Journal* 71:18–33.

Kim, Henry (2001), "Archaic Coinage as Evidence for the Use of Money," in Andrew Meadows and Kirsty Shipton (eds.), *Money and its Uses in the Ancient Greek World*. Oxford: Oxford University Press, 7–22.

Kinns, Philip (1983), "The Amphictionic Coinage Reconsidered," *Numismatic Chronicle* 143, 1–22.

Knapp, A. Bernard (2000), "Archaeology, Science-Based Archaeology and the Mediterranean Bronze Age Metals Trade," *European Journal of Archaeology* 3: 31–56.

Knapp, Georg Friedrich (1905), *Die staatliche Theorie des Geldes*. Leipzig: Duncker & Humblot.

Koenig, Franz E. (1999), "Les monnaies," in Daniel Castella, Chantal Martin Pruvot, Heidi Amrein, Anika Duvanchelle, and Frabz E. Koenig (eds.), *La nécropole gallo-romaine d'Avenches "En Chaplix," Fouilles 1987– (1992)*, Volume 2. Étude du *mobilier*. Lausanne: Cahiers d'archéologie romande de la Bibliothèque Historique Vaudoise, 427–62.

Konuk, Koray (2012), "Asia Minor to the Ionian Revolt," in William E. Metcalf (ed.), *The Oxford Handbook of Greek and Roman Coinage*. Oxford: Oxford University Press, 43–60

Kopytoff, Igor (1986), "The Cultural Biography of Things. Commoditization as Process," in Arjun Appadurai (ed.), *The Social Life of Things*. Cambridge: Cambridge University Press, 64–91.

Kortüm, Klaus (2014), "Topographie und Stadtentwicklung von Neuenstadt am Kocher," in Marcus Reuter (ed.), *Ein Traum von Rom*. Darmstadt: Wissenschaftliche Buchgesellschaft, 257–71.

Kortüm, Klaus and Andrea Neth (2004), "Markt und Mithras—Neues vom römischen vicus in Güglingen, Kreis Heilbronn," *Archäologische Ausgrabungen in Baden-Württemberg* 2003: 113–7.

Kos, Peter and David G. Wigg (2002), "Keltisches Münzwesen," *Reallexikon der Altertumskunde* 20: 364–72.

Kraay, Colin M. (1976), *Archaic and Classical Greek Coins*. Berkeley: University of California Press.

Kraay, Colin M. (1985), "Greek Coinage at War," in Waldemar Heckel and Richard Sullivan (eds.), *Ancient Coins of the Graeco–Roman World. The Nickle Numismatic Papers*. Waterloo: Nickle Museum: 3–18.

Krist, Pam (2015), *A Fountain for Memory: The Trevi Flow of Power and Transcultural Performance*. Ph.D thesis, Royal Holloway, University of London. Available at: https://pure.royalholloway.ac.uk/portal/files/24383674/2015kristpphd.pdf (accessed May 11, 2016).

Krmnicek, Stefan (2009), "Das Konzept der Objektbiographie in der antiken Numismatik," in Hans-Markus von Kaenel and Fleur Kemmers (eds.), *Coins in Context I. New Perspectives for the Interpretation of Coin Finds*. Mainz: Philipp von Zabern, 47–59.

Krmnicek, Stefan (2010), *Münze und Geld im frührömischen Ostalpenraum: Studien zum Münzumlauf und zur Funktion von Münzgeld anhand der Funde und Befunde vom Magdalensberg*. Klagenfurt: Verlag des Landesmuseums Kärnten.

Krmnicek, Stefan and Nathan T. Elkins (2014), "Dinosaurs, Cocks, and Coins: An Introduction to 'Art in the Round'," in Nathan T. Elkins and Stefan Krmnicek (eds.), *"Art in the Round": New Approaches to Ancient Coin Iconography*. Tübinger Archäologische Forschungen 16. Rahden: Verlag Marie Leidorf, 7–22.

Krmnicek, Stefan and Klaus Kortüm (2016), "Der numismatische Fingerabdruck. Fallstudien und Vorüberlegungen zum obergermanisch-rätischen Limes," *Uppsala University Coin Cabinet Working Papers* 19: 1–53. Available online at: urn:nbn:se:uu:diva-278018 (accessed July 11, 2016)

Kroll, John H. (1993), *The Greek Coins*. The Athenian Agora Vol. 26. Princeton: Princeton University Press.

Kroll, John H. (2007), "The Emergence of Ruler Portraiture on Early Hellenistic Coins," in Peter Schultz and Ralf von den Hoff (eds.), *Early Hellenistic Portraiture: Image, Style, Context*. Cambridge: Cambridge University Press, 113–22.

Kroll, John H. (2008), "The Monetary Uses of Weighted Bullion in Archaic Greece," in William V. Harris (ed.), *The Monetary Systems of the Greeks and Romans*. Oxford: Oxford University Press, 12–37.

Kroll, John H. (2011), "The Reminting of Athenian Silver Coinage, 353 B.C," *Hesperia* 80, 229–59.

Kroll, John H. (2012), "The Monetary Background of Early Coinage," in William E. Metcalf (ed.), *The Oxford Handbook of Greek and Roman Coinage*. Oxford: Oxford University Press, 33–42.

Kroll, John H. (2013), "Hacksilber," in Roger S. Bagnall, Kai Brodersen, Craige B. Champion, Andrew Erskine, and Sabine R. Huebner (eds.), *The Encyclopedia of Ancient History* Vol. 6. Chichester: Wiley-Blackwell, 3016–7.

Lamp, Kathleen S. (2013), *A City of Marble: The Rhetoric of Augustan Rome*. Columbia, SC: University of South Carolina.

Lanciani, Rodolfo (1892), "Gambling and Cheating in Ancient Rome," *The North American Review* 155 (428): 97–105.

Lang, Mabel (1976), *The Athenian Agora XXI. Graffiti and Dipinti*. Princeton: The American School of Classical Studies at Athens.

Lavan, Luke (2012), "The Agorai of Sagalassos in Late Antiquity: An Interpretive Study," in Luke Lavan and Michael Mulryan (eds.), *Field Methods and Post-Excavation Techniques in Late Antique Archaeology*. Leiden: Brill, 289–353.

Le Rider, Georges (1965), *Suse sous les Séleucides et les Parthes. Les trouvailles monétaires et l'histoire de la ville*. Mémoires de la mission archéologique en Iran Vol. 38. Paris: P. Geuthner.

Le Rider, Georges (1998), *Séleucie du Tigre. Les monnaies séleucides et parthes*. Firenze: Le Lettere.

Le Rider, Georges (2001), *La naissance de la monnaie. Pratiques monétaires de l'Orient ancien*. Paris: Presses Universitaires de France.

Le Rider, Georges and François de Callataÿ (2006), *Les Séleucides et les Ptolémées. L'héritage monétaire et financier d'Alexandre*. Paris: Ed. du Rocher.

Lee, Ian (2000), "Entella: The Silver Coinage of the Campanian Mercenaries and the Site of the First Carthaginian Mint 410–409 BC," *Numismatic Chronicle* 160: 1–66.

Lerouxel, François (2012), "Le marché du crédit privé, la bibliothèque des acquêts et les tâches publiques en Égypte romaine," *Annales. Histoire, Sciences sociales* 67(4): 943–76.

Lerouxel, François (2015), "Bronze pesé, dette et travail contraint (*nexum*) dans la Rome archaïque (VIe s.–IVe s. a. C.)," in Julien Zurbach (ed.), *La main-d'oeuvre agricole en Méditerranée archaïque. Statuts et dynamiques économiques*. Bordeaux: Ausonius/École française d'Athènes, 109–52.

Lerouxel, François (2016), *Le marché du crédit privé dans le monde romain (Égypte et Campanie)*. Rome: Bibliothèque des Écoles françaises d'Athènes et de Rome.

Levick, Barbara (1982), "Propaganda and Imperial Coinage," *Antichthon* 16: 104–16.

Levick, Barbara (1999a), "Messages on the Roman Coinage: Types and Inscriptions," In George M. Paul and Michael Ierardi (eds.), *Roman Coins and Public Life under the Empire*. Ann Arbor: The University of Michigan Press, 41–60.

Levick, Barbara (1999b), *Tiberius the Politician* (Revised Edition). London: Routledge.

Lichtenberger, Achim, Katharina Martin, H.-Helge Nieswandt, and Dieter Salzmann, eds. (2014), BildWert. *Nominalspezifische Kommunikationsstrategien in der Münzprägung hellenistischer Herrscher*. Bonn: Rudolf Habelt.

Liver, Alfred and Jürg Rageth (2001), "Neue Beiträge zur spätrömischen Kulthöhle von Zillis. Die Grabungen von 1994/95," *Zeitschrift für schweizerische Archäologie und Kunstgeschichte* 58: 111–26.

Lo Cascio, Elio (1981), "State and Coinage in the Late Republic and Early Empire," *Journal of Roman Studies* 71: 76–86.

Lo Cascio, Elio (1996), "How Did the Romans View their Coinage and its Function," in Cathy E. King and David G. Wigg (eds.), *Coin Finds and Coin Use in the Roman*

World. The Thirteenth Oxford Symposium on Coinage and Monetary History March 25–27 (1993), Studien zu Fundmünzen der Antike 10. Berlin: Gebr. Mann, 273–87.

Lo Cascio, Elio (2011), "La quantificazione dell'offerta di moneta a Roma: il ruolo del credito," in François de Callataÿ (ed.), *Quantifying Monetary Supplies in Greco-Roman Times*. Bari: Edipuglia, 31–42.

Lockyear, Kris (1999), "Hoard Structure and Coin Production in Antiquity—an Empirical Investigation," *The Numismatic Chronicle* 159: 215–43.

Luley, Benjamin P. (2008), "Coinage at Lattara. Using Archaeological Context to Understand Ancient Coins," *Archaeological Dialogues* 15(2): 174–95.

Luzón, José María (1982), "Bericht über zwei kürzlich bei Italica ausgegrabene Wohnhäuser," in Dietrich Papenfuss and Volker Michael Strocka (eds.), *Palast und Hütte: Beiträge zum Bauen und Wohnen im Altertum von Archäologen, Vor- und Frühgeschichtlern*. Mainz: Zabern, 447–59.

Malkin, Irad (2003), "Networks and the Emergence of Greek Identity," *Mediterranean Historical Review* 18: 56–74.

Malkmus, William (2007), "Ancient and Medieval Coin Dies: Catalogue and Notes," in Lucia Travaini and Alessia Bolis (eds.), *Conii e scene di coniazione*. Rome: Edizioni Quasar, 75–240.

Marchetti, Patrick (1999), "Autour de la frappe du nouvel Amphictionique," *Revue Belge de Numismatique et de Sigillographie* 145, 99–113.

Martin, Katharina (2013), *Demos. Boule. Gerousia. Personifikationen städtischer Institutionen auf kaiserzeitlichen Münzen aus Kleinasien*. Bonn: Rudolf Habelt.

Martin, Stéphane (2015), *Du statère au sesterce. Monnaie et romanisation dans la Gaule du Nord et de l'Est (IIIe s. a.C.—Ier s. p.C.)*. Bordeaux: Ausonius Éditions.

Martin, Thomas R. (1985), *Sovereignty and Coinage in Classical Greece*. Princeton: Princeton University Press.

Mattingly, H. (1962), *Roman Coins: From the Earliest Times to the Fall of the Western Empire* (Corrected edition). London: Methuen.

Maué, Hermann and Ludwig Veit, eds. (1982), *Münzen in Brauch und Aberglauben: Schmuck und Dekor, Votiv und Amulett, politische und religiöse Selbstdarstellung*. Mainz: von Zabern.

Maurer, Bill (2005), "Does Money Matter? Abstraction and Substitution in Alternative Financial Forms," in Daniel Miller (ed.), *Materiality*. Durham, NC: Duke University Press, 140–64.

Mayer, Emanuel (2010), "Propaganda, Staged Applause, or Local Politics? Public Monuments from Augustus to Septimius Severus," in Björn C. Ewald and Carlos F. Noreña (eds.), *The Emperor and Rome: Space, Representation, and Ritual*. Yale Classical Studies 35. Cambridge: Cambridge University Press, 111–34.

Meadows, Andrew (2014), "The Spread of Coins in the Hellenistic World," in Peter Bernholz and Roland Vaubel (eds.), *Explaining Monetary and Financial Innovation. A Historical Analysis*. Cham: Springer, 169–95.

Meadows, Andrew and Kirsty Shipton, eds. (2001), *Money and its Uses in the Ancient Greek world*. Oxford: Oxford University Press.

Meadows, Andrew and Jonathan Williams (2001), "Moneta and the Monuments: Coinage and Politics in Republican Rome," *Journal of Roman Studies* 91: 27–49.

Melmoth, William (1963), *Pliny Letters. With an English Translation by William Melmoth. Revised by W. M. L. Hutchinson, in two volumes*. Vol. 2. Cambridge, MA: Harvard University Press.

Melville-Jones, John R. (1993), *Testimonia numaria. Greek and Latin Texts Concerning Ancient Greek Coinage*. London: Spink.

Melville-Jones, John R. (2006), "Why Did the Ancient Greeks Strike Coins?" *Journal of the Numismatic Association of Australia* 17, 21–30.

Menger, Carl (1892), "On the Origins of Money," *Economic Journal* 2: 239–55.

Menu, Bernadette (2001), "La monnaie des Égyptiens de l'époque pharaonique (de l'Ancien Empire à la Ière domination perse)," in Alain Testart (ed.), *Aux origines de la monnaie*. Paris: Errance, 73–108.

Mermet, Christian (1993), "Le sanctuaire gallo-romain de Châteauneuf (Savoie)," *Gallia* 50: 95–138.

Meshorer, Ya'akov (2001), *A Treasury of Jewish Coins*. New York: Amphora.

Metcalf, William E. (1993), "Whose Liberalitas? Propaganda and Audience in the Early Roman Empire," *Rivista Italiana di Numismatica* 95: 337–46.

MGH AA = *Monumenta Germaniae Historica. Auctores Antiquissimi*. Multiple vols.

Michailidou, Anna (2010), "Measuring by Weight in the Late Bronze Age Aegean: The People behind the Measuring Tools," in Iain Morley and Colin Renfrew (eds.), *The Archaeology of Measurement. Comprehending Heaven, Earth and Time in Ancient Societies*. Cambridge: Cambridge University Press, 71–87.

Militký, Jiří (2015), *Oppidum Hradiště u Stradonic: Komentovaný katalog mincovních nálezu a dokladu mincovní výroby = Das Oppidum Hradiště bei Stradonice kommentierter Katalog der Münzfunde und Belege der Münzproduktion*. Prague: Abalon.

Millar, Fergus (1981), "The World of the Golden Ass," *Journal of Roman Studies* 71: 63–75.

Milne, Joseph G. (1922), "Two Notes on Greek Dies," *Numismatic Chronicle* 2, 43–8.

Milne, Joseph G. (1930), "Egyptian Lead Tokens," *Numismatic Chronicle* 10: 300–15.

Milne, Joseph G. (1971), *Catalogue of Alexandrian Coins*. Oxford: Oxford University Press.

Moens, Jan (2014), "The Problem of the Estimation of the Total Number of Dies Revisited," *Revue Belge de Numismatique et de Sigillographie* 160, 185–202.

Moesta, Hasso and Peter Robert Franke (1995), *Antike Metallurgie und Münzprägung. Ein Beitrag zur Technikgeschichte*. Basel: Birkhäuser Verlag.

Moorhead, Sam, Anna Booth, and Roger Bland (2010), *The Frome Hoard*. London: British Museum Press.

Mørkholm, Otto (1983), "The Life of Obverse Dies in the Hellenistic Period", in Christopher Nugent Lawrence Brooke (ed.), *Studies in Numismatic Method Presented to Philip Grierson*. Cambridge: Cambridge University Press, 11–21.

Morrisson, Cécile (1993), "Les usages monétaires du plus vil des métaux: le plomb," *Rivista Italiana di Numismatica* 95: 79–101.

Narain, Awadh K. (1973), "The Two Hindu Divinities on the Coins of Agathocles, from Ai-Khanum," *Journal of the Numismatic Society of India* 35: 73–6.

Nash, Daphne (1978), "Plus ça change . . . Currency in Central Gaul from Julius Caesar to Nero," in Robert A.G. Carson and Colin Kraay (eds.), *Scripta nummaria Romana. Essays presented to Humphrey Sutherland*. London: Spink and Son, 12–31.

Newton, Douglas P. (2006), "Found Coins as Indicators of Coins in Circulation: Testing Some Assumptions," *European Journal of Archaeology* 9(2–3): 211–26.

Nicolet, Claude (1971), "Les variations de prix et la 'théorie quantitative de la monnaie' à Rome, de Cicéron à Pline l'Ancien," *Annales. Économies, Sociétés, Civilisations* 26: 1203–27.

Nicolet, Claude (1984), "Pline, Paul et la théorie de la monnaie," *Athenaeum* 62 (1–2): 105–35.

Noreña, Carlos F. (2001), "The Communication of the Emperor's Virtues," *Journal of Roman Studies* 91: 146–68.
Noreña, Carlos F. (2011a), "Coins and Communication," in Michael Peachin (ed.), *The Oxford Handbook of Social Relations in the Roman World*. Oxford and New York: Oxford University Press, 248–68.
Noreña, Carlos F. (2011b), *Imperial Ideals in the Roman West. Representation, Circulation, Power*. Cambridge: Cambridge University Press.
Nouvel, Pierre (2013), "L'utilisation de la monnaie dans les sanctuaires gallo–romains," in Thierry Luginbühl, Cédric Cramatte, and Jana Hoznour (eds.), *Le sanctuaire gallo-romain du Chasseron. Découvertes anciennes et fouilles récentes*. Lausanne: Cahiers d'archéologie romande, 362–84.
Nouvel, Pierre and Matthieu Thivet (2011), "L'évolution architecturale du sanctuaire du Champ des Fougères à Mandeure," in Michel Reddé, Philippe Barral, François Favory, Jean-Paul Guillaumet, Martine Joly, Jean-Yves Marc, Pierre Nouvel, Laure Nunninger, and Christophe Petit (eds.), *Aspects de la romanisation dans l'est de la Gaule*. Glux-en-Glenne: Bibracte, 560–7.
Numismatic Literature. Some volumes available online at: http://numismatics.org/Numlit/Numlit (accessed April 14, 2016).
Michael, Nüsse (2013), *Archäologische, numismatische und archäometrische Untersuchungen zu den Fundmünzen vom Martberg bei Pommern im Moseltal (Lkr. Cochem–Zell)*. Ph.D. thesis, Goethe-Universität, Frankfurt am Main. Available online: urn:nbn:de:hebis:30:3–301294 (accessed July 11, 2016).
OGIS = *Orientis Graeci Inscriptiones Selectae*. Multiple vols.
Ollman, Bertell (1971), *Alienation: Marx's Conception of Man in Capitalist Society*. Cambridge: Cambridge University Press.
Osborne, Robin (1998), "Early Greek Colonization? The Nature of Greek Settlement in the West," in Nick Fisher and Hans van Wees (eds.), *Archaic Greece: New Approaches and New Evidence*. London: Duckworth, 251–69.
Osborne, Robin (2009), *Greece in the Making, 1200–469 BC*. London: Routledge.
Painter, Kenneth (2001), *The Insula of the Menander at Pompeii. Volume IV: The Silver Treasure*. Oxford: Clarendon Press.
Papadopoulos, John K. (2002), "Minting Identity: Coinage, Ideology and the Economics of Colonization in Akhaian Magna Graecia," *Cambridge Archaeological Journal* 12: 21–55.
Pare, Christopher (2013), "Weighing, Commodification and Money," in Harry Fokkens and Anthony F. Harding (eds.), *The Oxford Handbook of the European Bronze Age*. Oxford: Oxford University Press.
Paret, Oscar (1932), *Die Römer in Württemberg III. Die Siedlungen des römischen Württembergs*. Stuttgart: Kohlhammer.
Patterson, Clair C. (1972), "Silver Stocks and Losses in Ancient and Medieval Times," *The Economic History Review* 25(2): 205–33.
Peachin, Michael (1986), "The *Procurator Monetae*," *Numismatic Chronicle* 146: 94–106.
Peake, Rebecca and Valérie Delattre (2004), "L'apport des analyses 14C à l'étude de la nécropole de l'âge du Bronze de 'La Croix de la Mission' à Marolles-sur-Seine," *Revue archéologique du Centre de la France* 44: 5–25.
Perassi, Claudia (2011), "Monete amuleo e monete talismano. Fonti scritte, indizi, realia per l'età romana," *Quaderni Ticinesi. Numismatica e Antichità Classiche* 40: 223–74.

Perec, Georges (1973), "Approches de quoi?" *Cause commune* 5: 3–4.
Peter, Markus (1990), *Eine Werkstätte zur Herstellung von subaeraten Denaren in Augusta Raurica*. Studien zu Fundmünzen der Antike 7. Mainz: Gebr. Mann.
Peter, Markus (1996a), "Bemerkungen zur Kleingeldversorgung der westlichen Provinzen im 2. Jahrhundert," in Cathy E. King and David G. Wigg (eds.), *Coin Finds and Coin Use in the Roman World. The Thirteenth Oxford Symposium on Coinage and Monetary History March 25–27 (1993)*, Studien zu Fundmünzen der Antike 10. Berlin: Verlag Philipp von Zabern, 309–18.
Peter, Markus (1996b), *Untersuchungen zu den Fundmünzen aus Augst und Kaiseraugst*. Studien zu Fundmünzen der Antike 17. Berlin: Verlag Gebr. Mann.
Peter, Markus (2011), "Von Betrug bis Ersatzkleingeld—Falschmünzerei in römischer Zeit," in Marcus Reuter and Romina Schiavone (eds.), *Gefährliches Pflaster. Kriminalität im Römischen Reich*. Mainz: Philipp von Zabern, 106–19.
Pfisterer, Matthias (2007), "Limesfalsa und Eisenmünzen: Römisches Ersatzkleingeld am Donaulimes," in Michael Alram and Franziska Schmidt-Dick (eds.), *Numismata Carnuntina*. Forschungen und Material 2, 643–875.
Pflaum, Hans-Georg (1960–1), *Les carrières procuratoriennes èquestres sous le Haut-Empire romain*. Paris: Librairie orientaliste P. Geuthner.
Philp, Brian (1989), *The Roman House with Bacchic murals at Dover*. Kent Monograph Series. Research Report 5. Dover: Kent Archaeological Rescue Unit.
Picard, Olivier (1989), "Innovations monétaires dans la Grèce du IVe siècle," *Comptes rendus de l'Academie des Inscriptions et Belles–Lettre* 133(3): 673–87.
Piccottini, Gernot and Hermann Vetters (2003), *Führer durch die Ausgrabungen auf dem Magdalensberg*. 6th edition. Klagenfurt: Verlag des Landesmuseums Kärnten.
Pilon, Fabien (2004), "Unofficial Cast Coinage in 3rd c. Gaul: The Evidence from Châteaubleau," *Journal of Roman Archaeology* 17: 385–396.
Pilon, Fabien (2005), "Four Coin Production Techniques Used in the Three Officinae of Châteaubleau (ca 260–280 AD)," in Carmen Alfaro, Carmen Marcos, and Paloma Otero (eds.), *XIII Congreso Internacional de Numismática, Madrid, (2003), Actas, Proceedings, Actes*. Madrid: Ministerio de Cultura, 793–801.
Powell, Marvin A. (1996), "Money in Mesopotamia," *Journal of the Economic and Social History of the Orient* 39(3): 224–42.
Prices and Other Monetary Valuations in Roman History: Ancient Literary Evidence, database compiled by Walter Scheidel. Available online at: http://web.stanford.edu/scheidel/NumIntro.htm (accessed March 30, 2016).
Pritchard, David (2015), *Public Spending and Democracy in Classical Athens*. Austin: University of Texas Press.
Psoma, Selene (2009), "Tas sitarchias kai tous misthous ([Arist.], Oec. 1351b). Bronze currencies and cash-allowances in mainland Greece, Thrace and the Kingdom of Macedonia," *Revue Belge de Numismatique* 145: 3–38.
Putzeys, Toon (2007), "Contextual Analysis at Sagalassos. Developing a Methodology for Classical Archaeology," Ph.D. thesis, Katholieke Universiteit Leuven, Leuven.
Py, Michel (2006), *Les monnaies préaugustéennes de Lattes et la circulation monétaire protohistoriqueen Gaule méridionale*. 2 vols. Lattes: Édition de l'Association pour le Développement de l'Archéologie en Languedoc-Roussillon.
R.-Alföldi, Maria. (1958/9), "Epigraphische Beiträge zur römischen Münztechnik bis auf Konstantin den Grossen," Schweizerische Numismatische Rundschau 39, 35–48.
R.-Alföldi, Maria (1996), "Münze im Grab, Münze am Grab. Ein ausgefallenes Beispiel aus Rom," in Cathy E. King and David G. Wigg (eds.), *Coin Finds and Coin*

Use in the Roman World. The Thirteenth Oxford Symposium on Coinage and Monetary History March 25–27 (1993), Studien zu Fundmünzen der Antike 10. Berlin: Verlag Philipp von Zabern, 33–9.

Rageth, Jürg (1994), "Ein spätrömischer Kultplatz in einer Höhle bei Zillis GR," Zeitschrift für schweizerische Archäologie und Kunstgeschichte 51: 141–71.

Rahmstorf, Lorenz (2016), "From 'Value Ascription' to Coinage: A Sketch of Monetary Developments in Western Eurasia from the Stone to the Iron Age," in Colin Haselgrove and Stefan Krmnicek (eds.), *The Archaeology of Money. Proceedings of the Workshop 'Archaeology of Money', University of Tübingen, October (2013)*, Leicester Archaeology Monograph 24. Leicester: School of Archaeology and Ancient History, 19–42.

Ramage, Andrew and Paul Craddock (2000), *King Croesus' Gold. Excavations at Sardis and the History of Gold Refining*. Cambridge, MA: Harvard University Art Museums.

Ramos dos Santos, António (2008), "What Pays What? Cashless Payment in Ancient Mesopotamia (626–331 BC)," in Sushil Chaudhuri and Markus A. Denzel (eds.), *Cashless Payments and Transactions from the Antiquity to 1914*. Stuttgart: Franz Steiner Verlag.

Ranucci, Samuele (2010), "Il thesaurus di Campo della Fiera, Orvieto (Volsinii)," *Annali dell'Istituto Italiano di Numismatica* 55: 103–39.

Rathbone, Dominic (1996), "Monetization, not price-inflation in third-century A.D. Egypt," in Cathy E. King and David G. Wigg (eds.), *Coin Finds and Coin Use in the Roman World. The Thirteenth Oxford Symposium on Coinage and Monetary History March 25–27 (1993)*, Studien zu Fundmünzen der Antike 10. Berlin: Verlag Philipp von Zabern, 321–39.

Reece, Richard (2003), *Roman Coins and Archaeology. Collected Papers*. Wetteren: Moneta.

Rémy, Bernard (1999), "Religion populaire et culte impérial dans le sanctuaire indigène de Châteauneuf (Savoie)," *Revue Archéologique de Narbonnaise* 32: 31–8.

Renfrew, Colin (1985), *The Archaeology of Cult: The Sanctuary at Phylakopi*. London: Thames and Hudson.

Renfrew, Colin (1994), "The Archaeology of Religion," in Colin Renfrew and Ezra B.W. Zubrow (eds.), *The Ancient Mond. Elements of Cognitive Archaeology*. Cambridge: Cambridge University Press, 47–54.

Renfrew, Colin (2000), *Loot, legitimacy, and Ownership: The Ethical Crisis in Archaeology*. London: Duckworth.

Reusch, Wilhelm (1956), "Die kaiserliche Palastaula (Basilika). Archäologisch-historischer Beitrag," in Wilhelm Reusch (ed.), *Die Basilika in Trier: Festschrift zur Wiederherstellung 9. Dezember, 1956*. Trier: Paulinus, 11–39.

RIC II, etc. = Mattingly, Harold and Edward A. Syndenham et al. (1926–1994), *The Roman Imperial Coinage*. 9 vols. London: Spink & Son.

RIC^2 I = Sutherland, Carol Humphrey Vivian and Robert A.G. Carson (1984), *The Roman Imperial Coinage I: From 31 BC to AD 69* (Revised edition). London: Spink & Son.

RIC^2 II.1 = Carradice, Ian A. and Theodore V. Buttrey (2007), *The Roman Imperial Coinage II.1: From AD 69–96, Vespasian to Domitian*. London: Spink & Son.

Rich, John W. (1998), "Augustus's Parthian Honors, the Temple of Mars Ultor and the Arch in the Forum Romanum," *Papers of the British School at Rome* 53: 71–128.

Richter, Gisela M.A. (1959), "Calenian Pottery and Classical Greek Metalware," *American Journal of Archaeology* 63(3): 241–9.

Ritter, Stefan (2002), *Bildkontakte. Götter und Heroen in der Bildsprache griechischer Münzen des 4. Jahrhunderts v. Chr.* Berlin: Reimer Verlag.
Robertson, A.S. (1962), *Roman Imperial Coins in the Hunter Coin Cabinet University of Glasgow. Augustus to Nerva.* London: Oxford University Press.
Robinson, Edward Stanley Gotch (1930), "Sinope," *Numismatic Chronicle* 10, 1–15.
Roth, Jonathan (1999), *The Logistics of the Roman Army (264 BC–AD 235).* Leiden: Brill.
Roth, Martha Tobi (1997), *Law Collections from Mesopotamia and Asia Minor.* 2nd edn. Atlanta: Society of Biblical Literature.
Rowan, Clare (2010), "Slipping out of circulation: the after-life of coins in the Roman world," *Journal of the Numismatic Association of Australia* 20: 3–14.
Rowan, Clare (2011), *Under Divine Auspices: Divine Ideology and the Visualisation of Imperial Power in the Severan Period.* Cambridge: Cambridge University Press.
Rowan, Clare (2013a), "Coinage as Commodity and Bullion in the Western Mediterranean c. 550–100 BC," *Mediterranean Historical Review* 28: 105–27.
Rowan, Clare (2013b), "The Profits of War and Cultural Capital: Silver and Society in Republican Rome," *Historia* 61: 361–86.
Rowan, Clare (2014), "Iconography in Colonial Contexts. The Provincial Coinage of the Late Republic in Corinth and Dyme," in Nathan T. Elkins and Stefan Krmnicek (eds.), *"Art in the Round": New Approaches to Coin Iconography*. Tübinger Archäologische Forschungen 16. Rahden: Verlag Marie Leidorf, 147–58.
Roymans, Nico (1990), *Tribal Societies in Gaul: An Anthropological Perspective.* Amsterdam: Albert Egges van Giffen Instituut voor Prae-en Protohistorie.
Roymans, Nico and Joris Aarts (2005), "Coins, Soldiers and the Batavian Hercules Cult. Coin Deposition in the Sanctuary of Empel in the Lower Rhine Region," in Colin Haselgrove and David Wigg-Wolf (eds), *Iron Age Coinage and Ritual Practices.* Mainz: Philipp von Zabern, 337–60.
RPC I = Burnett, Andrew, Michel Amandry and Pere Pau Ripollès (2006), *Roman Provincial Coinage* I: *From the Death of Caesar to the Death of Vitellius* (Reprint of the 1998 corrected edition). London and Paris: The British Museum and the Bibliothèque Nationale de France.
RPC II = Burnett, Andrew, Michel Amandry and Ian Carradice (1999), *The Roman Provincial Coinage* II: *From Vespasian to Domitian (AD 69–96).* London and Paris: The British Museum and the Bibliothèque Nationale de France.
RPC III = Amandry, Michel and Andrew Burnett (2015), *Roman Provincial Coinage* III: *Nerva, Trajan, and Hadrian (AD 96–138).* London and Paris: The British Museum and the Bibliothèque Nationale de France.
RPC VII.1 = Spoerri Butcher, Marguerite (2006), *Roman Provincial Coinage* VII: *de Gordien Ier à Gordien III (238–244) après J.-C.). 1. Province d'Asie.* London and Paris: The British Museum and the Bibliothèque Nationale de France.
RPC IX = Hostein, Anthony and Jerome Mairat (2016), *Roman Provincial Coinage* IX: *From Trajan Decius to Uranius Antoninus (AD 249–254).* London and Paris: The British Museum and the Bibliothèque Nationale de France.
Rutter, N. Keith (1979), *Campanian Coinages: 475–380 B.C.* Edinburgh: Edinburgh University Press.
Rutter, N. Keith (1993), "The Myth of the Demareteion," *Chiron* 23, 171–88.
Rutter, N. Keith (2001), *Historia Numorum Italy.* London: The British Museum Press.
Sauer, Eberhard (2004), "Not Just Small Change: Coins in Mithraea," in Marleen Martens and Guy De Boe (eds.), *Roman Mithraism: The Evidence of the Small Finds. Papers of the international conference/Bijdragen van het internationaal*

congres, Tienen 7/8 November (2001) Brussels: Institute for the Archaeological Heritage, 327–53.

Sauer, Eberhard (2005), *Coins, Cult and Cultural Identity: Augustan Coins, Hot Springs and the Early Roman Baths at Bourbonne-les-Bains*. Leicester Archaeology Monographs 10. Leicester: School of Archaeology and Ancient History.

Sauer, Eberhard (2011), "Religious Rituals at Springs in the Late Antique and Early Medieval World," in Luke Lavan and Michael Mulryan (eds.), *The Archaeology of Late Antique "Paganism."* Brill: Leiden, 505–50.

Schäfer, Alfred (2013), "Gruben als rituelle Räume," in Alfred Schäfer and Marion Witteyer (eds.), *Rituelle Deponierungen in Heiligtümern der griechisch-römischen Welt*. Mainzer Archäologische Schriften 10. Mainz: Generaldirektion Kulturelles Erbe, 237–52.

Schaps, David (2008), "What was Money in Ancient Greece?" in William Harris (ed.), *The Monetary Systems of the Greeks and Romans*. Oxford: Oxford University Press, 38–48.

Schaps, David (2014), "War and Peace, Imitation and Innovation, Backwardness and Development: The Beginnings of Coinage in Ancient Greece," in Peter Bernholz and Roland Vaubel (eds.), *Explaining Monetary and Financial Innovation. A Historical Analysis*. Cham: Springer, 31–51.

Scheidel, Walter (2008), "The Divergent Evolution of Coinage in Eastern and Western Eurasia," in William V. Harris (ed.), *The Monetary Systems of the Greeks and Romans*. Oxford: Oxford University Press, 267–86.

Scheidel, Walter (2010), "Real Wages in Early Economies: Evidence for Living Standards from 1800 BCE to 1300 CE," *Journal of the Economic and Social History of the Orient* 53(3): 425–62.

Scheidel, Walter (2014), "Benford's Law and Numerical Stylization of Monetary Valuations in Ancient Literature," SSRN Scholarly Paper ID 2541608. Rochester, NY: Social Science Research Network. Available online at: http://papers.ssrn.com/abstract=2541608 (accessed May 1, 2016).

Scheidel, Walter, Ian Morris, and Richard P. Saller, eds. (2007), *The Cambridge Economic History of the Greco-Roman World*. Cambridge: Cambridge University Press.

Schindel, Nikolaus (2005), "Sasanian Coinage," in Ehsan Yarshater (ed.), *Encyclopaedia Iranica*, online edition. Available online at:www.iranicaonline.org/articles/sasanian-coinage (accessed June 3, 2016).

Seaford, Richard (2004), *Money and the Early Greek Mind: Homer, Philosophy, Tragedy*. Cambridge: Cambridge University Press.

Seaford, Richard (2008), "Money and Tragedy," in William V. Harris (ed.), *The Monetary Systems of the Greeks and Romans*. Oxford: Oxford University Press, 49–65.

SEG = *Supplementum Epigraphicum Graecum*. Multiple vols.

Sheedy, Kenneth, Paul Munroe, Floriana Salvemini, Vladimir Luzin, Ulf Garbe, and Scott Olsen (2015), "An Incuse Stater from the Series 'Sirinos/Pyxoes'," *Journal of the Numismatic Association of Australia* 26: 36–52.

Sherratt, Andrew (1993), "What would a Bronze-Age World System Look Like? Relations between Temperate Europe and the Mediterranean in Later Prehistory," *Journal of European Archaeology* 1(2): 1–57.

SIG = *Sylloge Inscriptionum Graecarum*. Multiple vols.

Simmel, Georg (1900 [2004]), *The Philosophy of Money*. London and New York: Routledge.

Smithin, John (2000), "What is Money? Introduction," in John Smithin (ed.), *What is Money*. London and New York: Routledge: 1–15.

Sosin, Josiah (2000), *Perpetual Endowment in the Hellenistic World: A Case Study in Economic Rationalism*. Durham, NC: Duke University (unpublished Ph.D. thesis).

Sosin, Josiah (2001), "Accounting and Endowments," *Tyche. Beiträge zur Alten Geschichte, Papyrologie und Epigraphik* 16: 161–75.

Spoerri Butcher, Marguerite (2006), *Roman Provincial Coinage VII.1*. London: The British Museum Press.

Stahl, Alan (2000), *Zecca: The Mint of Venice in the Middle Ages*. Baltimore: Johns Hopkins University Press.

Stahl, Alan M. (2013), "Roman Imperial Coins as An Inspiration for Renaissance Numismatic Imagery," in Ulrike Peter and Bernhard Weisser (eds.), *Translatio Nummorum. Römische Kaiser in der Renaissance*. Berlin: Verlag Franz Philipp Rutzen, 201–6.

Stannard, Clive (2005), "The Monetary Stock at Pompei at the Turn of the Second and First Centuries B.C.: Pseudo-Ebusus and Pseudo-Massalia," in Pietro Giovanni Guzzo and Maria Paola Guidobaldi (eds.), *Nuove ricerche archeologiche a Pompei ed Ercolano*. Naples: Electa, 120–43.

Stannard, Clive (2011), "Evaluating the Monetary Supply: Were Dies Reproduced Mechanically in Anquity?" in François de Callataÿ (ed.), *Quantifying Monetary Supplies in Greco-Roman Times*. Bari: Edipuglia, 59–79.

Stannard, Clive (2013), "Are Ebusan Coins at Pompeii, and the Pompeian Pseudo-mint, A Sign of Intensive Contacts with the Island of Ebusus?" in Alicia Arévalo, Darío Bernal, and Daniela Cottica (eds.), *Ebusus y Pompeya, ciudades marítimas: testimonies monetales de una relación*. Cádiz: Universidad de Cádiz, 125–55.

Stannard, Clive and Suzanne Frey-Kupper (2008), "'Pseudomints' and small change in Italy and Sicily in the late Republic," *American Journal of Numismatics* Second series, 20: 351–404.

Starr, Chester R. (1976), "A Sixth-century Athenian Tetradrachm Used to Seal a Clay Tablet from Persepolis," *The Numismatic Chronicle* 136: 219–22.

Steinbock, Bernd (2014), "Coin Types and Latin Panegyrics as a Means of Imperial Communication," in Nathan T. Elkins and Stefan Krmnicek (eds.), *"Art in the Round": New Approaches to Ancient Coin Iconography*. Tübinger Archäologische Forschungen 16. Rahden: Verlag Marie Leidorf, 51–67.

Stevens, Susan T. (1991), "Charon's Obol and Other Coins in Ancient Funerary Practice," *Phoenix* 45(3): 215–29.

Stewart, Peter (2008), *The Social History of Roman Art*. Cambridge: Cambridge University Press.

Stolper, Matthew W. (1985), *Entrepreneurs and Empire. The Murašû Archive, the Murašû Firm, and Persian Rule in Babylonia*. Istanbul: Nederlands historisch–archaeologisch instituut.

Straumann, Sven (2011), *Die Nordwestecke der Insula 50 von Augusta Raurica. Die Entwicklung eines multifunktional genutzten Handwerkerquartiers*. Augst: Augusta Raurica.

Stroobants, Fran and Jeroen Poblome (2015), "Buying and Selling in Late Roman Pisidia: A Hypothetical Framework of Coin Use in Sagalassos and its Countryside," *Revue Belge de Numismatique et de Sigillographie* 161: 73–104.

Sundqvist, Olof (2003), "Rituale," in Heinrich Beck, Dieter Geuenich, and Heiko Steuer (eds.), *Reallexikon der Germanischen Altertumskunde* 25. Berlin: de Gruyter, 32–47.

Surveys of Numismatic Research. The *Survey* for 2002–7 is available online at: http://inc–cin.org/survey.html (accessed April 14, 2016).
Sutherland, Carol Humphrey Vivian (1959), "The Intelligibility of Roman Imperial Coin Types," *Journal of Roman Studies* 49: 46–55.
Sutherland, Carol Humphrey Vivian (1976), *The Emperor and the Coinage. Julio–Claudian Studies*. London: Spink.
Sutherland, Carol Humphrey Vivian (1984), *The Roman Imperial Coinage I: From 31 BC to AD 69*. London: Spink.
Swan, Nancy Lee (1950), *Food and Money in Ancient China: The Earliest Economic History of China to A.D. 25* [Han Shu 24]. Princeton: Princeton University Press.
Sydenham, Edward A. (1920), *The Coinage of Nero*. London: Spink & Son.
Szaivert, Wolfgang and Reinhard Wolters (2005), *Löhne, Preise, Werte. Quellen zur römischen Geldwirtschaft*. Darmstadt: Wissenschaftliche Buchgesellschaft.
Szidat, Joachim (1981), "Zur Wirkung und Aufnahme der Münzpropaganda (Iul. Misop. 355d)," *Museum Helveticum* 38, 22–33.
Taborelli, Luigi (1982), "Vasi di vetro con bollo monetale (note sulla produzione, la tassazione e il commercio degli unguenti aromatici nella prima età imperiale)," *Opus* 1: 315–40.
Taborelli, Luigi (1992), "Vasi di vetro con bollo monetale. Addenda I," *Opus* 11: 93–104.
Teegen, Wolf-Rüdiger (2003), "Quellheiligtümer und Quellkult," in Heinrich Beck, Dieter Geuenich, and Heiko Steuer (eds.), *Reallexikon der Germanischen Altertumskunde* 24. Berlin: de Gruyter, 15–26.
Temin, Peter (2013), *The Roman Market Economy*. Princeton: Princeton University Press.
Thompson, Christine M. (2003), "Sealed Silver in Iron Age Cisjordan and the 'Invention' of Coinage," *Oxford Journal of Archaeology* 22(1): 67–107.
Thompson, Margaret (1979), "Paying the Mercenaries," in Leo Mildenberg, Arthur Houghton, Silvia Hurter, and Patricia Erhart–Mottahedeh (eds.), *Studies in Honor of Leo Mildenberg. Numismatics, Art History, Archaeology*, Wetteren: Editions NR, 241–7.
Thonemann, Peter (2015), *The Hellenistic World: Using Coins as Sources*. Guides to the Coinage of the Ancient World. Cambridge: Cambridge University Press.
Thüry, Günther (2006), "Bauopfer–Pilgeropfer–Passageopfer: drei Kategorien numismatischer Weihefunde," *MoneyTrend* 10: 134–7.
Toledo i Mur, Assumpció and Michel Pernot, eds. (2008), "Un atelier monétaire gaulois près de Poitiers, Les Rocheraux à Migné–Auxances (Vienne)," *Gallia* 65: 231–72.
Traimond, Bernard (1994), "La fausse monnaie au village. Les Landes aux XVIIIe et XIXe siècles," *Terrain* 23: 27–44.
Travaini, Lucia (2000), "Le monete a Fontana di Trevi: storia di un rito," *Rivista Italiana di Numismatica* 101: 251–9.
Treister, Michail J. (1996), *The Role of Metals in Ancient Greek History*. Leiden: Brill.
Trillmich, Walter (2003), "Überfremdung einheimischer Thematik durch römisch-imperiale Ikonographie in der Münzprägung hispanischer Städte," in Peter Noelke, Friederike Naumann–Steckner, and Beate Schneider (eds.), *Romanisation und Resistenz in Plastik, Architektur und Inschriften der Provinzen des Imperium Romanum*. Mainz: Philipp von Zabern, 619–33.
Trundle, Matthew (2010), "Coinage and the Transformation of Greek Warfare," in Garett G. Fagan and Matthew Trundle (eds.), *New Perspectives on Ancient Warfare*. Leiden: Brill, 227–52.

Trundle, Matthew (2013), "The Business of War Mercenaries," in Brian Campbell and Lawrence A. Tritle (eds.), *The Oxford Handbook of Warfare in the Classical World*. Oxford: Oxford University Press, 330–50.
van Alfen, Peter G. (2005), "Problems in Ancient Imitative and Counterfeit Coinage," in Zofia H. Archibald, John K. Davies, and Vincent Gabrielsen (eds.), *Making, Moving and Managing: The New World of Ancient Economies, 323–31 BC*. Oxford: Oxbow Books, 322–54.
van Alfen, Peter (2012), "The Coinage of Athens, Sixth to First Century BC," in William E. Metcalf (ed.), *The Oxford Handbook of Greek and Roman Coinage*. Oxford: Oxford University Press, 88–104.
van Heesch, Johan (2009), "Providing Markets with Small Change in the Early Roman Empire: Italy and Gaul," *Revue belge de Numismatique et Sigillographie* 155, 125–42.
van Heesch, Johan (2012), "Control Marks and Mint Administration in the Fourth Century AD," *Revue Belge de Numismatique et de Sigillographie* 158, 161–78.
Van Hoof, Catherine (1991), "Un aspect du rituel funéraire dans les tombes franques et mérovingiennes en Belgique: la présence des monnaies," *Analecta Archaeologica Lovaniensa* 30: 95–115.
Varner, Eric R. (2004), *Mutilation and Transformation: Damnatio Memoriae and Roman Imperial Portraiture*. Monumenta Graeca et Romana 10. Leiden: Brill.
Verboven, Koenraad (1997), "*Caritas nummorum*: Deflation in the Late Roman Republic?" *Münstersche Beiträge zur antiken Handelsgeschichte* 16(2): 40–78.
Verboven, Koenraad (2003), "54–44 BCE: Financial or Monetary Crisis?" in Elio Lo Cascio (ed.), *Credito e moneta nel mondo romano. Incontri Capresi di storia dell'economia antica. Convegno internazionale*, Capri (2000) Bari: Edipuglia, 49–68.
Verboven, Koenraad (2015), "The Knights who say NIE: Can Neo-institutional Economics Live Up to its Expectation in Ancient History Research?" in Paul Erdkamp and Koenraad Verboven (eds.), *Structure And Performance In The Roman Economy: Models, Methods and Case Studies*. Brussels: Latomus, 33–57.
Vermeule, Cornelius C. (1954), *Some Notes on Ancient Dies and Coining Methods*. London: Spink.
Vermeule, Cornelius C. (1975), "Numismatics in Antiquity. The Preservation and Display of Coins in Ancient Greece and Rome," *Schweizerische Numismatische Rundschau* 54: 5–31.
Versluys, Miguel John (2014), "Understanding Objects in Motion. An *Archaeological Dialogue* on Romanization," *Archaeological Dialogues* 21: 1–20.
Vindolanda Tablets Online. Available online at: http://vindolanda.csad.ox.ac.uk/ (accessed March 23, 2016).
von Kaenel, Hans-Markus (1986), *Münzprägung und Münzbildnis des Claudius*. Antike Münzen und Geschnittene Steine 9. Berlin: de Gruyter.
von Kaenel, Hans-Markus, Hansjörg Brem, and Jörg T. Elmer (1993), *Der Münzhort aus dem Gutshof in Neftenbach. Antoniniane und Denare von Septimius Severus bis Postumus*. Zürcher Denkmalpflege Archäologische Monographien 16. Zürich: Kommunikation Verlag.
von Kaenel, Hans-Markus and Fleur Kemmers, eds. (2009), *Coins in Context. I. New Perspectives for the Interpretation of Coin Finds: Colloquium Frankfurt a.M., October 25–27, (2007)*, Studien zu Fundmünzen der Antike 23. Mainz: Zabern.
von Reden, Sitta (2002), "Money in the Ancient Economy: A Survey of Recent Research," *Klio* 84: 141–74.

von Reden, Sitta (2010), *Money in Classical Antiquity*. Cambridge: Cambridge University Press.
Wallace, Robert W. (1987), "The Origin of Electrum Coinage," *American Journal of Archaeology* 91: 385–97.
Wallace-Hadrill, Andrew (1986), "Image and Authority in the Coinage of Augustus," *Journal of Roman Studies* 76: 66–87.
Wallace-Hadrill, Andrew (2008), *Rome's Cultural Revolution*. Cambridge: Cambridge University Press.
Wartenberg, Ute (2016), "Die Geburt des Münzgeldes. Die frühe Elektronprägung," *Mitteilungen der Österreichischen Numismatischen Gesellschaft* 56(1): 30–49.
Wigg-Wolf, David (2005), "Coins and Ritual in Late Iron Age and Early Roman Sanctuaries in the Territory of the Treveri," in Colin Haselgrove and David Wigg-Wolf (eds.), *Iron Age Coinage and Ritual Practices*. Mainz: Philip von Zabern.
Williams, Jonathan (2001), "Coin–inscriptions and the Origins of Writing in Pre-Roman Britain," *British Numismatic Journal* 71: 1–17.
Williams, Jonathan (2011), "Religion and Roman Coins," in Jörg Rüpke (ed.), *A Companion to Roman Religion*. Malden, MA: Wiley–Blackwell, 143–63.
Wiseman, Timothy P. (1971), *New Men in the Roman Senate*. Oxford: Oxford University Press.
Wolters, Reinhard (1999), *Nummi Signati. Untersuchungen zur römischen Münzprägung und Geldwirtschaft*. Vestigia 49. Munich: Verlag C.H. Beck.
Wolters, Reinhard (2003a), "Die Geschwindigkeit der Zeit und die Gefahr der Bilder: Münzbilder und Münzpropaganda in der römischen Kaiserzeit," in Gregor Weber and Martin Zimmermann (eds.), *Propaganda—Selbstdarstellung—Repräsentation im römischen Kaiserreich des 1. Jhs. n.Chr.* Wiesbaden: Franz Steiner Verlag. 175–204.
Wolters, Reinhard (2003b), "The Emperor and the Financial Deficits of the Aerarium in the Early Roman Empire," in Elio Lo Cascio (ed.), *Credito e moneta nel mondo romano. Atti degli Incontri capresi di storia dell'economia antica (Capri 12–14 ottobre 2000)*. Bari: Edipuglia, 147–60.
Wolters, Reinhard (2006), "Geldverkehr, Geldtransporte und Geldbuchungen in Römischer Republik und Kaiserzeit: Das Zeugnis der schriftlichen Quellen," *Revue belge de Numismatique et Sigillographie* 152, 23–49.
Wolters, Reinhard (2015), "Archäologie, Geschichte und Münzen," *Klio* 97: 229–44.
Woodward, Peter and Ann Woodward (2004), "Dedicating the Town. Urban Foundation Deposits in Roman Britain," *World Archaeology* 36(1): 68–86.
Woytek, Bernhard E. (2006), "Die Verwendung von Mehrfachstempeln in der Antiken Münzprägung und die "Elefantendenare" Iulius Caesars (RRC 443/1)", *Schweizerische Numismatische Rundschau* 85, 69–96
Woytek, Bernhard E. (2010), *Die Reichsprägung des Kaisers Traianus (98–117)*. Moneta Imperii Romani 14. Vienna: Verlag der Österreichischen Akademie der Wissenschaften.
Woytek, Bernhard E. (2012a), "The Denarius Coinage of the Roman Republic," in William E. Metcalf (ed.), *The Oxford Handbook of Greek and Roman Coinage*. Oxford: Oxford University Press, 315–34.
Woytek, Bernhard E. (2012b), "System and Product in Roman Mints from the Late Republic to the High Principate: Some Current Problems," *Revue belge de Numismatique et Sigillographie* 158, 85–122.
Woytek, Bernhard E. (2013), "Signatores in der römischen Münzstätte: CIL VI 44 und die numismatische Evidenz," *Chiron* 43, 243–84.

Woytek, Bernhard E. (2014), "Monetary Innovation in Ancient Rome: The Republic and its Legacy," in Peter Bernholz and Roland Vaubel (eds.), *Explaining Monetary and Financial Innovation. A Historical Analysis*. Cham: Springer, 197–226.

Wünsch, Richard (1900), "Der Abschied von Rom an der Fontana di Trevi," in *Strena Helbigiana*. Leipzig: Teubner, 341–6.

Xinwei, Peng (1994), *A Monetary History of China*. Bellingham, WA: Western Washington University.

Yang, Bin (2011), "The Rise and Fall of Cowrie Shells: The Asian Story," *Journal of World History* 22: 1–25.

Yavetz, Zvi (1970), "Fluctuations monétaires et condition de la plèbe à la fin de la République," in Claude Nicolet (ed.), *Recherches sur les structures sociales dans l'Antiquité classique*. Paris: Éditions du Centre National de la Recherche Scientifique, 133–57.

Zanker, Paul (1988), *The Power of Images in the Age of Augustus* (trans. A. Shapiro). Ann Arbor: University of Michigan Press.

Zanker, Paul (2000), "Bild–Räume und Betrachter im kaiserzeitlichen Rom," in Adolf H. Borbein, Tonio Hölscher, and Paul Zanker (eds.), *Archäologie. Eine Einführung*. Berlin: Reimer Verlag, 205–26.

Zanker, Paul (2010), *Roman Art* (trans. H. Heitmann-Gordon). Los Angeles: The J. Paul Getty Museum.

INDEX

Italic numbers are used for illustrations. **Bold** numbers are used for tables.

Aarts, Joris 139
abstraction, money as an 124–5
Aegina, Greece 6
aes grave (Rome) 3, 23, 103
aes rude (Rome) 102–3, 143
aes signatum (currency bars) 3, *4*
Agathocles, King of Bactria 143–4, *144*
agoras 96, 97
Alexander the Great
   antique coins of 100
   designs of coins 10–11, 144
   influence on prices 59, 60
   influence on Roman coinage 157
   mercenaries of 50, *50*, 52, 150
Alexandria, Egypt 29
alphabets used on coins 138
alternative currencies 160
amount of coins 52–6, **53**, *54*, *55*, 132–3
Anaxilas, Tyrant of Rhegium 7, 40–1
Andreau, Jean 135
animals on coins 32, 40–2, *40*, *42*, 105, 114, *145*
anthropological studies of money 126–7
Antioch, Turkey 17
Apamea, Syria 157
Apollo 41
Apuleius, *Golden Ass* 56
archaeological research 14, 65–7, 87–8, 127–8

aristocratic use of money 102–3
Aristophanes 96, 146
Aristotle 22, 32, 40–1, 145
   Politics 45, 141
Arrian of Nicomedia 64–5, 99, 146–7
art and representation 105–21
   agency and imperial coins 116
   coins and politics 106–7
   function of images 105–6, *106*
   imagery and audience 117–20, *117–18*
   monuments in miniature 120–1
   political communication 107–15, *108–9*, *113*, *115*
   See also designs of coins
as (Rome) 41, *41*
Athens, Greece
   early coinage 145–7, *145*
   military money 36
   minting equipment deposited at temple 156
   restriking of coins 23
   sources of silver 24–7
   tetradrachms (owls) 32, 105, *145*
Aubert, Jean-Jacques 89
audiences for coins 112, 117–20, *117–18*
Augst, Switzerland 92
Augustus, Roman Emperor 16, 99, 100, 111–12

Avenches, Switzerland 110
'Ayn Manâwir, Egypt 89

Bactria 8–9, 143–4, *144*
Baden (Aargau), Switzerland 74–5, *74*
ban liang (China) 148, *148*
banks 57, 95, 130
Barger-Compascuum, Netherlands 95
barter 52, 89, 125, 126, 129, 130
Bath, England 76
Bell, Harold W. 69
bent coins 76, 81
biographies of things 128
blanks or flans 27–8, 31
Bloch, Maurice 126–7
Bogaert, Raymond 97
Bohannan, Paul 126
Bolin, Sture 51
Bourbonne-les-Bains, France 76
Bronze Age currency 90–1, 94, 142
bronze coins 13, 44, 45, 56, 119, 137–8
buildings
    coins found in walls of 78, 79–81, 82
    depicted on coins 111–12, 118, 119, 120, 136
bullion 130
bulls on coins 41–2, *42*
burials, coins found in 15, 99, 100, 110
Burnett, Andrew 108
Butler, Howard C. 69
Buttrey, Theodore V. 132

Cales, Italy 101
Caligula, Roman Emperor 5, *5*, 109, *109*, 118
Cappadocia 51
Carrawburgh, England 75–6
Carter formula for coin quantification 37
Carthage, Tunisia 36, 160
Casa del Planetario, Spain 80
Cassius Dio 108, 115
cast coins 23–4, 91
cave sites, coin offerings at 71
Celtic World 11–13, *11*, 28, 91–2, 99
    See also Iron Age coins
ceramics, coins copied on 101
character, coins a metaphor for 146–7
Charon's obol 15, 86, 99
    See also burials, coins found in
Châteaubleau, France 92

Châteauneuf, France 99
Chilgrove Roman Villa, England 80
China 142–3, 147, 148–9, *148*, 152–3, 154, 158–9
Christianity, impact on coinage 157
Cicero 57, 152
circulation of coins 5, 12, 44, 48, 54, 119, 132, 134, 160
cities, coinage of 105–6
    See also Athens; Greek world; Roman world
clipping of coins 44
    See also mutilation of coins
coin trade, modern 139–40
collections of coins 100
Cologne, Germany 110
colonialism 152–6, *154*
commodities, images on coins 105–6
commoditization of ancient coins 139–40
commoditization of things 127–8
Condominas, Georges 89
congiarium (distribution of cash) 117, *117*, 118
Constantine the Great, Roman Emperor 157
Constantius II, Roman Emperor 33–4, *33*
Cook, John M. 69
copper-nickel alloy 144
Corinth, Greece 32
counterfeit coins 38–9, 92–3, 133
    See also imitation coins
countryside, use of money in 88, 97
Coventina's Well, England 75–6
cowrie shells 142–3
credit 56–7, 130, 151–2
Crummy, Nina 100
cultural contact and early coinage 142–4, *144*
currency bars 3, *4*
cutting of coins 94
    See also mutilation of coins
Cyzicus, Turkey 6, 32

Dalmatia 27
damnatio memoriae 150
databases of coins 14, 52–3, **53**
Davies, John K. 156–7
de Callataÿ, François 101
debasement of coinage 38, 151
defacement of coins 76, 81, 94, 98, 109, 149–50

INDEX

Delphi, Greece 38
demand and supply, law of 59
democracy
    and coinage 45–6, 60
    and imperialism 145–50, *145*, *148*, *150*
denarius (Rome) 3–4, 107, 108, *108*, 148
denominations, spectrum of 55
depletion silvering 38
designs of coins 7, 32–3, 100–1, 111–12, 117–19, 135–8
    See also art and representation
die-makers 34, 35
dies 28–9, 30–2, *31*, 132–3, 156
Dio Cassius 108, 115
distribution of coins 36–7
documentary evidence for everyday life 86–7
Domitian, Roman Emperor 114
Dover, England 80
dual nature of money 158
Duncan-Jones, Richard 133
Dunkirt Barn, Abbotts Ann, England 80
dupondius (Rome) 113–14, *113*

early money 1–2, 6, 9, 27, 68–9, *68*, 89, 142–3
economic models 57–61
Egypt 4, 57, 81, 86, 149, 160
electrum 27, 142, 153
Emerita, Spain 154–5
emperors, as audience for coin designs 112, 117
    See also portraits on coins
Entella, Sicily 151
Ephesus, Turkey 68–9, *68*, 142
Ephrem the Syrian 42, 158
Epictetus 64–5, 99, 146–7
epigraphic documents 87
ethnographical research 89
Eusebius 157
everyday money in the Roman world 85–103
    multiple money 88–91, *90*
    producing money 91–4, *93*
    social impact of money 101–3
    uses of money 94–101, *95–6*
expenditure, state 22, 46–7, 132

Felix, mint worker 35
ferryman, payments for 15, 86, 99
    See also burials, coins found in

Finley, Moses 56, 88
flans and blanks 27–8, 31
food products used as money 93–4
forged coins 38–9, 92–3, 133
    See also imitation coins
Fossé des Pandours, France 92
foundation deposits 68–9, *68*, *70*, *78*, *79*
fractioning of coins 94
France 12, *12–13*, 29, 76, 92–3, 99, 101, 143
funerary rituals 15, 99, 100, 110

Gaius (Caligula), Roman Emperor 5, *5*, 109, *109*, 118
Gallic Empire 17, *18*
game-boards 97
games, Roman 114–15
Gaul 91–2, 98–9
    See also France
Gela, Sicily 28–9
gems 101
Germany 14, 71–5, 80–1, 98, 110, 119, 150
glass, coins stamped on 101
gold 27, 55, *55*, 60, 70, 130, 134, 152
Gortyna, Crete 45
Graeber, David 155
graffiti 82, 86–7, *87*, 97, 99
Greek world
    coinage of 5–11, *6*, *8*, *10*, 32, 40–1, 105–6
    distribution of coinage 53–4, *54*
    early money 143, 147
    identity and colonialism 153–4, *154*
    military expenditure 3, 46–51, *47–8*, *50*
    mines 24–6, *25*
    minting in 34, 38, 44
    monetization of 55–6
    See also Athens
Güglingen, Germany 71

hacksilver 2, 89
hard cash 52–6, *53–5*
hares on coins 40, *40*
Harris, William V. 130
Hart, Keith 124, 158
Haselgrove, Colin 88
Hasmonean dynasty 157
Hellmann, Marie-Christine 101
Heracles 10, *10*

Hermeneumata Pseudodositheana 95, 97
Herodas 56
Herodotus 27, 142
Hispania 137, 138
Historia Augusta 86, 100
hoards
  contents of 5
  of militiary payments 48
  Piraeus hoard 27
  in religious and ritual contexts 68–72, *68*, *70*
  study of 14, 16
  and volume of coins 132, *133*, 135
Hobbs, Richard 96
Hogarth, David G. 68
Hollander, David B. 102, 131
Hopkins, Keith 48, 132, 133
houses, Roman coins found in walls of 80–1
Howgego, Christopher 22, 130, 131–2, 134

ideas of money 43–61, 64–5
  credit 56–7
  economic models 57–61
  hard cash 52–6, *53*–*5*
  mercenaries 49–51, *50*
  military expenditure 46–51, *47*–*8*, *50*
  profits from coins 51–2
  state control of money 43–5
identity and colonialism 152–6, *154*
  See also character, coins a metaphor for
identity of cities 7
imagery of coins. See art and representation; designs of coins
imitation coins 4, *11*, 137–8, 159–60
  See also counterfeit coins
income generated by coins 23
incuse technique 6, *8*, *9*, *10*, 153, *154*
India 9, 144, 160
indigenous communities 7–8
Indo-Greek coinage 143–4, *144*
inflation 59, 152
information, money as 123–8
interest 52
interpretation of money 123–40
  barter, money, coinage 128–31
  designs of coins 135–8
  making, using and losing money 131–5
  things money can't buy 139–40
  value of money 123–8

inventories of coins 14, 52–3, **53**
Iron Age coins 82–4, *83*, 91–2, 98
  See also Celtic World
Isidore of Seville 38
Isokrates 46
issues of coins 132–3
issues of the age 141–60
  cultural contact 142–4, *144*
  democracy and imperialism 145–50, *145*, *148*, *150*
  identity and colonialism 152–6, *154*
  other forms of money 158–60
  religion 156–8, *158*
  war and crisis 150–2
Italica, Spain 80
Italy 8, *8*, 32, 40, 75, 101, 134, 159
  See also Pompeii, Italy

jewelry 99–100, 101, 155
Jewish revolts 149, *150*
John Chrysostom 88–9, 100
Jones, Arnold H.M. 108
Judea 157
Julian the Apostate, Roman Emperor 41–2, *42*, 108, *109*, 157–8, *158*
Julius Caesar 16, 88, 152
Juvenal 86

Kalkriese, Germany 150
Karnak, Egypt 92, *93*
Kastabos, Turkey 69
Kay, Philip 61
Kemmers, Fleur 119
Knapp, Georg Friedrich 45
Kopytoff, Igor 128
Kraay, Colin 49
Krmnicek, Stefan 88
Kroll, John 2, 23

lamps, coins on 101
languages used on coins 138
Lattara, France 129
Lattes, France 12–13
laudatory texts and coins 112–15
Laurion mines, Greece 24–6, *25*
law of demand and supply 59
Le Rider, Georges 51–2
lead copies of coins 101
lead tokens 160
lending of money 97–8

INDEX

Lerouxel, François 57, 102–3
Levick, Barbara 112
lex Gabinia 107
liberalitas (imperial generosity) 118, *118*
Lion of Miletus 32
literary evidence 86
loans 102–3, 130, 152
local coinage 91, 93, 137, 138, 139
    See also provincial coinage
loss of coins 12–13, 134
Lucius Vibius Lentulus 116
Luley, Benjamin 13, 129
Lydia 6, 91, 142, 143
Lydney Park, England 75
Lyon, France 29

Magdalensberg, Austria 76–84, *78*, *83*
Mainz, Germany 119
maiorina (Rome) 41–2, *42*
Malkmus, William 28
Mandeure "Champ des Fougères,"
    France 99
Mani, prophet 24
Marcus Claudius Tacitus, Roman
    Emperor 72
market for ancient coins 139–40
marketplaces 96, 97
Mars Ultor 111–12
Marseille, France 129, 143
Martberg, Germany 98
Martial 114
martial imagery of coins 119
Marx, Karl 123–4
Massalia (Marseille), France 129, 143
Maurer, Bill 125
Mausoleum of Empress Helena, Rome 80
Maximian, Roman Emperor 115
Meadows, Andrew 107
melting down of coins 100
Melville-Jones, John 87
Menger, Carl 45
mercenaries 3, 49–51, 150, 151
Mesopotamia 86
Messina (Messana/Zancle), Sicily 7, 40–1,
    40, 106
metaphors of coins 146–7
Migné-Auxances, France 92
Miletus, Turkey 32
military expenditure
    Greek world 46–51, *47–8*, *50*

imagery of coins 119
production of coins for 22
Roman world 16, 36–7, 130
Millar, Fergus 56
mines 24–6, *25*, 27
minting equipment, temple deposits of 156
mints
    and design of coins 111, 116, 119
    Greek world 34, 44
    management of 33–6, *33*
    outsourced 37
    Roman world 16–17, 33–4, 44, 91–4
    techniques of 29–32, *30–1*
Minturnae, Italy 159
Mithradates VI Eupator, King of Pontus
    47–8, 50, 151–2
Mithraea, coin offerings at 70–1
Mnong Gar, Vietnam 89
modern use of Roman coins 93
modification of coins 39
molds for coins 28
monetary policies 58–9
monetary zones 131
monetization 12–13, 55, 58, 60, 88, 102,
    139
    See also volume of coins
money boxes 95
money supply 132–3
moneychangers 97
moneyers 34, *35*, 106–7, 116
moral and religious values, impact on use
    of coins 99
mules on coins 40, *40*
multiple money 89
mutilation of coins 76, 81, 94, 98, 109,
    149–50

Narni, Italy 75
Nero, Roman Emperor 29, 41, *41*, 64–5,
    99, 108, *117*, 146
Nerva, Roman Emperor 118
Neuenstadt am Kocher, Germany 71–2, *72*
New Institutional Economy 58
Niedernau, Germany, Roman spring 73–4
Nigeria 126
Nijmegen, Netherlands 37, 119
Noreña, Carlos 110–11
Noricum (Magdalensberg), Austria 76–84,
    78, *83*
notional money 131

Notitia dignitatum 34
NUMIS project 52–3, **53**
Numismatic Literature 87
numismatics 13–15, 37, 65–6, 87

obol of Charon 15, 86, 99
　See also burials, coins found in
offerings to the gods. See ritual and religion
offertory containers 15–16, 98
officials, mint 116
　See also moneyers
old or obsolete coinage 160
Oloron-Sainte-Marie, France 101
Oplontis, Italy 134
oracles 63–4
Oxyrhynchus, Egypt 160

pagan coinage 41–2, *42*, 108, *109*, 157–8, *158*
panegyric and coins 112–15
Parry, Jonathan 126–7
partes (shares) 130–1
Patterson, Clair 55, **55**
Paulus 39
Pausanias 63–4
pawning 97
payments for the ferryman 15, 86, 99
　See also burials, coins found in
payments in kind 89
Perec, Georges 85
Persia 157
personal adornments 99–100, 101, 155
personifications of imperial ideal on coins 110–11, 120
Peter, Markus 119
Petronius 64, 97
Pharae, Oracle at 63–4
Philip II, King of Macedon 150–1
Phrygia 157
Piraeus hoard, Greece 27
pits, coins found in 78–9, *78*
plated coins 27, 39, 133
Plautus, *Asinaria* 55–6, *57*
Pliny the Younger 73
Plommer, William H. 69
poetry and coins 112–15
politics and coins 106–15, *106*, *108–9*, *113*, *115*
Polybius 130, 148
Pompeii, Italy

distribution of coinage 96, *96*, 134
graffiti about money 86–7, 97
imitation coins in 137–8, 159
storage of coins in 94, 135
Portable Antiquities Scheme 14, 52–3, **53**
portraits on coins 9–11, 16, 150, 155–6, 157
postholes, coins found in 79
posthumous condemnation of emperors 150
pottery, coins copied on 101
price increases 59, 152
private coinage 23, 34, 39, 158–9
Proculus, jurist 52
procurator monetae 116
production and minting techniques 29–32, *30–1*
profits from coins 23, 51–2
propaganda, coins as instruments of 110–15, 136
provincial coinage 44, 106, 111–12, 137–8, 139
　See also local coinage
pseudo-Aristotle, *Economics* 46–7
pseudo-coins 137–8, 159–60
pseudo-Platonic, *Eryxias* 22
Ptolemy II Philadelphus, King of Egypt 55
public buildings, images on coins 111–12, 118, *119*, *120*, 136
purses 95, **95**
Py, Michel 12

quadrantes (Rome) 118–19
quantification of coins 37–8
quantitative theory of money 59

raw materials 24–7, *25*
rebellions and money 149
Reece, Richard 87
Regalianus, usurper of the Roman Empire 17
religions, impact on coinage 157
Renfew, Colin 67, 140
representations on coins. See art and representation
restriking of coins 23, 27, 149
Rhegion, Italy 40
rhinoceroses on coins 114
Rhodes, Greece 106
ritual and religion 63–84

deposits in water 72–6, 74
ideas of money 63–6
ideas of ritual 66–8
Magdalensberg case study 76–84, 78, 83
money of the gods 68–72, 68, 70
uses of coins 13, 15–16, 156–8
See also burials, coins found in; loss of coins; sanctuaries
Roman world
  bullion, use of 130
  coinage of 13–19, 18, 18, 41–2, 106–8
  coins, use of 131–5
  cutting of coins 94
  distribution of money 36
  early forms of money 88–91
  identity and colonialism 154–5
  imperialism and money 147–8, 149
  military expenditure 16, 36–7, 130
  minting in 33–4, 44, 91–4
  monetization of 52–5, 53, 55
  other forms of money 131–2
  private coinage 23, 39, 159
  propaganda, coins as instruments of 110–15
  social impact of money 101–3
  uses of money 94–101
  warfare in 151
Rome, Italy
  army, auxiliaries of 48
  burials, coins found in 110
  coins found in 80
  early money 3–4, 143
  Imperial mint 35–6, 91
  rebuilding of the Capitol 70
  temple of Mars Ultor 111–12
rural use of coins 88, 97

Sagalassos, Turkey 96, 97
sanctuaries 98–9
Sanctuary of Hemithea, Kastabos 69
Sardis, Turkey 69–70, 70, 81
Scheidel, Walter 86
Seaford, Richard 147
seals 2, 101
Selinunte, Sicily 32
Septimius Severus, Roman Emperor 115, *115*
sestertius (Rome) 117, *117*, 118
Sestos, Turkey 23, 51

shares 130–1
shekels 149
Sicily 28–9, 32, 40–1, 151
Sigmaringen, Germany 74
silver 2, 24–7, 89
silver coinage
  debasement of 151
  ritual deposits of 69–70, 76, 82
  in the Roman provinces 133–4
  special-purpose money 129–30
  spread of 6–7, 143–4
  volume of 55, 55
  See also Athens, Greece; *denarius* (Rome); *tetradrachms*
Simmel, Georg 123
Sinope, Turkey 29
slaves 24, 26, 35
social impact of money 101–3
Social War (91–88 BCE) 149
Socrates of Constantinople 42, 108, 157–8
soldiers, imagery of coins supplied to 119
solidus (Rome) 33–4, *33*
Sozomen 158
Spain 27, 80, 137, 138, 154–5
Sparta 4, 26, 51, 148, 152
special-purpose money 129
springs 73–4
Stannard, Clive 138
state control of money 43–5
state expenditure 22, 46–7, 132
staters (Corinth) 32
Strabo 88, 152
Suetonius 41, 99, 100, 108, 114
Sumelocenna (Rottenburg), Germany 73–4
Surveys of Numismatic Research 87
Sybaris, Italy 8, *8*
Syracuse, Sicily 32, 101
Szaivert, Wolfgang 87

Taborelli, Luigi 101
Tacitus, historian 70
Tacitus, Roman Emperor 72
Tarento, Italy 32
technologies 21–42
  blanks or flans 27–8
  counterfeit coins 38–9
  dies 28–9
  mint management 33–6
  production and minting techniques 29–32

quantification of coins 37–8
raw materials 24–7
success of coins 22–3
transport of coins 36–7
understanding of coins 40–2
Temple of Artemis, Ephesus 68–9, *68*, 142
Temple of Artemis, Sardis 69–70, *70*, 81
temples 156
termination deposits 78
tessera (token) 30, *30*
testing of coins 97
tetradrachms
   of Alexander the Great 10, *10*
   of Athens 32, 145, *145*
   circulation of 44
   imitations of 4, *11*
   mercenary payments 48, 51
   of Messana 40, *40*
   of Mithradates Eupator 47, *47*
   restriking of 27
   Roman production of 37
   of Syracuse 32
text on coins 138
Theophrastus 56
thesauri (offertory containers) 15–16, 98
Thompson, Margaret 50
Tiberius, Roman Emperor 113–14, *113*
Tigranes the Great, King of Armenia 50–1
tiles, coins stamped on 101
Tiv people of Nigeria 126
token currency of Egypt 160
Tolsum, Netherlands 98
torques (neck rings) 155
Trajan, Roman Emperor 29, 64–5, 116
transfers of money 131
transport of coins 36–7
tresviri monetales (moneyers) 34, 35, 116

Trevi Fountain, Rome 72–3
tri-metallic systems 55, 134
Trier, Germany 75, 80–1
triumphs 36
trust in money 45

unofficial coinage 92–3
using money 94–101, *95–6*, 131–5

Valerius Maximus 113
value of money 22, 87, 123–8
van Alfen, Peter 38
Velleius Paterculus 113
veteran settlements 154–5
Vietnam 89
Villa of L. Crassius Tertius, Oplontis, Italy 134
Villeneuve-Saint-Germain, France 92
Vindolanda tablets, England 86
Vindonissa, Switzerland 74–5, *74*
volume of coins 52–6, *53*, *54*, *55*, 132–3
von Reden, Sitta 102

walls, coins found in 78, 79–81, 82
warfare 3, 16, 22, 150–2
washing of money 39
water, ritual deposits in 72–6, *74*, 78, *79*
wealth, storage of 135
weighing of money 2, 90–1, *90*
Wigg-Wolf, David 98
Williams, Jonathan 107
Wolters, Reinhard 87
women, imagery of coins 17–19, **18**

Yavetz, Zvi 102

Zancle (Messina), Sicily 7, 40–1, *40*, 106
Zillis, Switzerland 71